SKILL FORMATION

This book is the first of its kind to provide an up-to-date review of theories and research on skill formation in psychology, economics, political science, and sociology. It addresses issues of skill learning and measurement, institutional and policy differences among countries, and the issue of skill formation across the life course and disparities among socioeconomic groups. Today, marked changes in skill requirements in modern societies seem to be common sense, yet major questions about the processes of skill formation remain puzzlingly unresolved. Among them are, first, basic questions about what we mean when we talk about skills, qualifications, and competencies. Second, the book deals with questions concerning the institutions in which skills are being trained and learned, such as "Are market economies and firms systematically underinvesting in skills?" Finally, the book advances our knowledge on issues of provision, access, and returns to training.

Karl Ulrich Mayer has been professor of sociology at Yale University since 2003 and currently serves as chair of the department. He is also co-director of the Center for Research on Inequalities and the Life Course. Before that, he was director at the Max Planck Institute for Human Development in Berlin, Germany, and, from 1979 to 1983 at the German National Survey Research Center. He is the principal investigator of the German Life History Study. From 1993 to 1999, he was member and vice-chair of the German National Science Council (Wissenschaftsrat).

Heike Solga has been director of the research unit Skill Formation and Labor Market at the Social Science Research Center Berlin (WZB) since 2007 and member of the board of directors of the Institute for Sociological Research Göttingen (Germany) since 2006. She was professor of sociology at the Institute for Sociology at the Georgia Augusta University Göttingen (2005–2007) and at the University of Leipzig (2004–2005). Before that, she was head of the independent research group Lack of Training: Employment and Life Chances of the Less Educated at the Max Planck Institute for Human Development from 2000 to 2005.

Skill Formation

Interdisciplinary and Cross-National Perspectives

Edited by

KARL ULRICH MAYER
Yale University

HEIKE SOLGA
Social Science Research Center Berlin (WZB/Germany)

CAMBRIDGE
UNIVERSITY PRESS

CAMBRIDGE UNIVERSITY PRESS
Cambridge, New York, Melbourne, Madrid, Cape Town, Singapore, São Paulo, Delhi

Cambridge University Press
32 Avenue of the Americas, New York, NY 10013-2473, USA

www.cambridge.org
Information on this title: www.cambridge.org/9780521867528

First published 2008

Printed in the United States of America

A catalog record for this publication is available from the British Library.

Library of Congress Cataloging in Publication Data

Mayer, Karl Ulrich.
Skill formation : interdisciplinary and cross-national perspectives / Karl Ulrich Mayer,
Heike Solga.
    p.   cm.
Includes bibliographical references and index.
ISBN 978-0-521-86752-8 (hardback)
1. Occupational training.   2. Skilled labor.   3. Vocational education.   4. Employees –
Training of.   I. Solga, Heike.   II. Title.
HD5715.M39   2008
658.3′124 – dc22   2007027339

ISBN   978-0-521-86752-8 hardback

Contents

Contributors

Frank Achtenhagen, Professor of Vocational Education at the University of Göttingen, Germany

Lena Arends, Researcher at the Institute for Sociological Research (SOFI), Göttingen, Germany

Martin Baethge, President of the Institute for Sociological Research (SOFI), Göttingen, Germany

Pepper D. Culpepper, Associate Professor of Public Policy at Harvard University, Boston, Massachusetts, US

Christian Dustmann, Professor of Economics at University College, London; and Director of the Centre for Research and Analysis on Migration (CReAM), UK

Hans Gruber, Professor of Education at the University of Regensburg, Germany

Christian Harteis, Senior Researcher of Education at the University of Regensburg, Germany

Steffen Hillmert, Professor of Sociology at the University of Tübingen, Germany

Marita Jacob, Assistant Professor of Sociology at the University of Mannheim, Germany

Jean-Marie Jungblut, Senior Researcher at the Mannheim Center for European Social Research (MZES), Mannheim, Germany

Karl Ulrich Mayer, Professor of Sociology and Co-Director of the Center for Research on Inequalities and the Life Course (CIQLE) at Yale University,

New Haven, Connecticut, US; Director Emeritus of the Max Planck Institute of Human Development, Berlin, Germany

Walter Müller, Professor Emeritus at the Mannheim Center for European Social Research (MZES), Mannheim, Germany

Philip J. O'Connell, Research Professor at the Economic and Social Research Institute (ESRI), Dublin, Ireland

Monika Rehrl, Researcher of Education at the University of Regensburg, Germany

Heike Solga, Director of the Research Unit "Skill Formation and Labor Markets" at the Social Science Research Center (WZB), Berlin, Germany; and Co-Director of the Institute for Sociological Research (SOFI), Göttingen, Germany

Uta Schoenberg, Assistant Professor of Economics at the University of Rochester, UK

Kathleen Thelen, Professor of Political Science at Northwestern University, Evanston, Illinois, US; and External Scientific Member of the Max Planck Institute for the Study of Societies, Cologne, Germany

SKILL FORMATION

1 Skill Formation

Interdisciplinary and Cross-National Perspectives

Karl Ulrich Mayer and Heike Solga

TRENDS AND CHALLENGES

Changes in the demand for skills and qualifications in the workplace have been a constant feature of economies since the onset of industrialization. Shifts of manpower among the sectors of agriculture, manufacturing and services, changes in technology, increasing specialization, and growth in firm size and expansion of managerial control have also brought about changes in the vocational and professional skills required. In the twentieth century, broad social changes, such as the growing labor force participation of women and the ever-increasing level of educational enrollments, have been triggered by these varying demands for labor and have also strongly contributed to them. For a long time, the adaptation of vocational and professional training to these changes has essentially taken the form of extension (i.e., by increasing levels of participation at ever more advanced levels of general schooling) in early training periods for occupations both inside and outside the workplace and in further training. Mostly, such training concentrated in the late teens and then extended into the early if not mid-twenties. However, there was little change in that people made their longer skill investments for just one occupation and expected that these would serve them through most, if not even all, of their working lives.

In recent decades, the pressures for more and better skills have greatly intensified both in regard to the extent and kind of skill acquisition, especially in the so-called advanced societies in the West and their new Southeast Asian rivals (Bamber & Lansbury, 1998). Automation of production and services, as well as the outsourcing of manufacturing into low-wage developing countries, have left fewer skilled manual jobs and few unskilled jobs in advanced societies. Noyelle (1986: 106) stated, "The tendency is to automate low-skilled jobs and retain those jobs with relatively high skills." As a consequence, skills

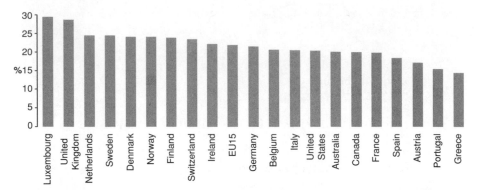

Figure 1.1. Share of ICT-related occupations[a] in the total economy, 2004[b]. [a]Broad definition based on methodology described in OECD (2004) and van Welsum and Vickery
(2005). The shares for non-European countries are not directly comparable with shares
for European countries as the classifications were not harmonized. [b]Austria, Canada
2003 instead of 2004. *Source:* Organisation for Economic Co-operation and Development (OECD) (2004). Information Technology Outlook 2004, 8b. Share of ICT-related
occupations in the total economy. Paris: OECD. Available at: http://www.oecd.org/
dataoecd/37/13/34963969.xls.

have become the entry ticket to any kind of self-maintaining and productive life. Although the new information technology brought about a new
breed of expert jobs and occupations in the 1960s and 1970s, information
technology and computer skills have now become mandatory in all sectors
and on almost all levels of the job hierarchy. In many countries, the share
of (directly) information-communication-technology-related occupations
already accounts for one-fourth to one-third of all jobs (cf. Figure 1.1). Skills
have become a highly valued commodity in the new "knowledge society" and
a strategic asset in the economic competition among nations.

This transformation of work has profound implications for the processes
of skill acquisition in schools, in institutions of vocational training, and at
the workplace. They relate to the substance of skills required, the timing
of these processes across the life course, and the optimal interplay of the
institutions involved in skill formation. The postulated consequences for the
kind of competences and skills are assumed to include not only a shift away
from more narrow job-specific skills toward broader, more analytic general
skills, but also a move from hierarchically fixed activities to autonomous
work in processual and cooperative work settings. For advanced societies, this
implies an increase in the level of average skill requirements (coupled with the
constant risk of polarization of skills), as well as a much more rapid turnover
in the content and outcomes of training than in the past. It is also claimed

that in addition to task-solving skills, social and emotional competences (so-called soft skills) have become more important as cooperative work groups, services, and management tasks proliferate (e.g., Murnane & Levy, 1996; Gallie et al., 1998; Giloth, 1998; Thurow, 1999).

Alterations in the *timing of skill formation* involve readjusting the relationship between schooling, initial training, and continuing education. Despite the transformations of the past few decades, schooling and initial vocational and professional training have retained their primary significance for occupational careers. To keep pace with the developments in the world of work (without implying even longer periods of education and training, but rather streamlining the process), the contents and temporal organization of schooling and training are under pressures to change. Initial and further education become more demanding, and skill formation starts even in preschool years (cf. Heckman, 2006). All too frequently, vocational training and skill enhancement are still concentrated early in the occupational career, and further training is based on an ad hoc and short-term logic of opportunities rather than on a systematic, lifelong learning approach. Moreover, further vocational training rarely serves a compensatory function; rather, it tends to widen skill gaps between groups, as the well educated at their demanding workplaces are well placed to invest in further skill acquisition. Finally, the aging working population, increasing life expectancy, and depleted pension funds mean that the 55- to-70-year-olds will have to remain in the labor market for a longer time and in larger numbers than in the past. The relationship between career paths, skill development, and skill maintenance across working life will thus become a key issue for employers and their (older) employees.

The institutional implications of these changes in the world of economy and work involve a paradigm shift away from jobs for life toward the flexible updating of occupational skills throughout the life course, as well as a move away from rigidly structured university and training courses toward flexible, modular systems based on cumulative credits and intermediate certificates. Such a modular training system could offer an opportunity to overcome the (artificial) segregation of various places of learning and instruction – schools, the workplace, and the community. Educational institutions require reforms and new financing solutions to counteract the existing discrimination and bias in public funding of education and to ensure that education as a civic right finally becomes a reality.

The urgent questions to be answered by the policy makers in advanced societies therefore are: How will it be possible to promote individual educational growth and motivation and to also improve the fit between developed skills and available jobs? How can the distinctiveness of learning and instructional settings – from schools to firms to communities – be combined to provide relevant opportunities to learn and develop skills needed for life and work? Which changes in educational provision and labor market reforms could effectively permit a more flexible use of the available human resources while taking into account legitimate expectations for access to further training?

One does not need to go far to find the empirical evidence for the urgency of reform addressing these questions. Almost all national governments have commissioned white papers and have introduced policy reforms in the area of skill provision. The Organisation for Economic Co-operation and Development (OECD) has greatly extended its attention to skill deficits and has taken several initiatives in the area of measurement and comparative assessment of skills and competencies. According to the Lisbon declaration of the European Council (in 2000), European countries want to become "the most competitive and dynamic knowledge-based economy in the world"[1] – accompanied by the Copenhagen Declaration, which aims to enhance European cooperation in vocational education and training (VET). Among the European Union goals are a unitary framework of qualifications and competencies, common quality criteria and principles, and improvements in citizens' access to lifelong learning (cf. Lisbon-to-Copenhagen-to-Maastrich Consortium Partners, 2004).

The academic literature has marshalled a great deal of arguments and evidence (some of which are partly controversial) to lend plausibility to this picture of changing demands and shortage of skills. Research on changes in occupational structures has consistently shown that long-term processes are characterized by trends of occupational upgrading and skill polarization (cf. Wright & Dwyer, 2003; Spitz, 2004). Economists have documented the skill bonus (i.e., the demand for higher skills as one of the reasons for increasing disparities in returns to education) (cf. Heckman et al., 2003, 2006; Beaudry & Green, 2005). The consequences of the computerization of workplaces on skill requirements have been forcefully argued by a group of Massachusetts Institute of Technology economists (cf. Katz & Krueger, 1998; Levy & Murnane, 2003a, 2003b).

OBJECTIVES OF THIS BOOK

Although the case for marked changes in the demand side of skill requirements has been made relatively convincingly, major questions about the processes of skill formation remain puzzlingly unresolved. A *first set of open questions* concerns the *institutions* where skills are being trained and learned. Advanced societies face similar competitive pressures on their economy and similar demands for highly skilled labor but have developed historically quite different institutional settings for providing skills. Thus, under which conditions of policy making and in which kinds of ensembles of various collective actors are training systems put in place, maintained, and developed? How important is the involvement of the state, trade unions, and employers' associations in shaping and regulating training systems? Are nations stuck with traditional institutions (e.g., Germany) or a lack of institutions (e.g., Britain, the United States)? What are the consequences of varying national systems and their path dependencies for the qualifications they are able to provide, and how well are they able to adapt to changing requirements?

A *second set of questions* raises the issue of *provision, access, and returns to training*, including questions on skill acquisition across the life course and the socioeconomic disparities that give rise to skill inequalities. These are some of the questions on skill formation in this area: How are qualifications, competencies, and skills transmitted, lost, and preserved? Are educational, vocational, and professional attainments just credentials that open access to more demanding and more rewarding jobs, or are they actually conditional for performance at the job? How useful is it to train for specific occupations if occupations are not for life? How meritocratic are skill formation regimes in advanced societies in terms of equality in educational opportunities? Do inequalities in education and training and their impacts on income and chances for promotion increase or flatten out across the working life? Finally, are market economies systematically underinvesting in skills, or under what conditions are firms prepared to invest in training?

The *third set of open questions* is connected to the "nature of the beast": *What do we mean when we talk about skills, qualifications, and competencies?* Of what kind and how many are there, and how can they best be measured? How do the aptitudes required at the workplace stand in relation to what we learn in schools? What are the best places to learn the qualifications one needs at work – the general educational system, vocational tracks and vocational schools, the workplace itself, or a combination of schools and the workplace, as in the German dual system of apprenticeships? Is the best way to train for occupational tasks to teach general competences and skills, or should one concentrate on highly specific vocational and professional profiles?

Given the salience of the topic, it is surprising how many of these questions seem to be settled more by strong convictions than by sound theory and basic research. The ongoing policy and academic debates are characterized by a high level of redundancy in describing the situation (e.g., increasing skill requirements, collapse of the German dual system) and buzzwords (e.g., "lifelong learning"), coupled with a limited empirical research base and even more limited theoretical foundations. We do believe that one major reason for this can be found in the way our knowledge about skill formation is currently organized. Academic approaches do not only tend to be segmented and isolated, but, consequently, are also characterized by the sometimes rather narrow perspectives of particular disciplines. They also hardly take much notice of each other. In addition, within academic disciplines, vocational training often plays the role of a greatly neglected child. It has received much less attention than general schooling and advanced professional training.

For this book, we wanted to bring together, therefore, specialists with expertise from various academic disciplines and from various countries. We asked scholars from educational psychology and vocational education science (*Berufspädagogik*), political science, economics, and sociology to contribute chapters. We asked them to specify, on the one hand, what the specific contributions of their disciplines are for the analysis of skill formation processes and, on the other hand, to present exemplary, preferably comparative research.

Besides these objectives, another major goal of the book is to inform about the *different definitions of "skills"* in these disciplines – aiming at supporting a better understanding across these disciplines and facilitating interdisciplinary research on skill formation processes in the future.

Political scientists came to the topic of skills through their interest in understanding the political and institutional foundations of national political-economic systems associated with divergent political and distributive outcomes. Therefore, political science has no definition of skills or competences, but only of skill production regimes or training institutions. This definition is derived from the main institutional goal *to train*, regardless of whether educational institutions actually train the skills they claim or are obliged to train.

Economists define skills as an individual's *human capital*. In empirical research, this is mostly *indirectly* measured by educational degrees achieved or years of schooling. They are looking at training as a major process of *human capital formation* primarily under two micro-level perspectives. First, economists look at training as a personal investment into human capital. The yields to such investments are examined as differential returns to education. In a second perspective, they look at training from the point of the view of the employer and of the economy as a whole. They ask, on the one hand, under which conditions firms *do* invest in training and, on the other hand, whether their behavioral logics lead to an overall underinvestment in training that might have to be offset by public subsidies.

Sociologists, like political scientists, are concerned with institutional frameworks of skill acquisition, as well as their variation across time and among societies. Crucial institutions for sociologists include not only the educational system with the streams and curricula it provides for skill acquisition, but also the institutions that structure and regulate the labor market and influence the conditions of skill use. Differing from political science, sociological inquiry is not primarily concerned with the political processes establishing and maintaining skill formation regimes, but with the consequences different regimes have on individuals' life courses. In sociology, skills are recognized as institutionally defined and often credentialed bundles of work-related *qualifications*, frequently cast in the form of occupations and professions. Analyzing the processes of the acquisition of qualifications and their use refer to (1) the access to skills and the "returns" they provide and (2) the institutions that set the conditions, in particular, in terms of opportunities, costs, and benefits of skill acquisition. In many respects, sociology in this area shares the interests and approaches of economists. But sociologists, more than economists, focus on the social inequalities that are transmitted by differential access and "returns" to education and training. Thus, they also consider a plurality of outcome dimensions (e.g., employment opportunities, class, status, income). Besides these substantive interests of sociology, its focus on *qualifications* – and not assuming that they are purely indicators of "skills and abilities," as economists do – has a major advantage for empirical research: qualifications can be assessed relatively reliably and at low costs in population surveys, and information on individual's qualifications can be taken from the administrative registers of institutions that provide education and training.

Finally, *psychology* considers skill formation as individual learning processes. This explains why most psychological research in the field of skill formation takes a microperspective, focusing on how individuals process information during learning, how they perceive stimuli, how they acquire, store, retrieve, and apply knowledge, and how they solve problems within their professional field. Accordingly, this discipline brings to the table a long-standing expertise in highly general and universal theories about learning. It should, therefore, be best equipped to answer questions about the relative advantages of training generalized competences or specialized skills and about the transfers from generalized competences to the solving of specific tasks. It should also help resolve the issue of whether vocational (and professional) training is best organized in classrooms, work settings, or mixed environments.

These differences in the disciplinary definitions of skills are one of the main sources for the difficulties or even the lack of interdisciplinary research on skill formation. Nonetheless, these differences in definitions should not be regarded as an insurmountable obstacle preventing researchers from taking notice of relevant research on skill formation in other disciplines and from participating in answering the cross-disciplinary questions mentioned previously. Because of this consideration and our complaint that the disciplines in the field of skill formation are segmented, the ordering of the chapters in the book does not follow a disciplinary approach. Instead, we use the cross-disciplinary framework of our previous questions, situating the chapters and their contributions within this framework.

Part I: Cross-National Diversity in Skill Formation Regimes: Origins, Changes, and Institutional Variation in Individuals' Labor Market Placements

Chapter 2 by Culpepper and Thelen considers contributions from the political science literature to understand the causes and consequences of cross-national diversity in training regimes across the most developed democracies. The recent surge of interest by political scientists in skills has developed as an offshoot of debates over distinctive "Varieties of Capitalism" (Hall & Soskice, 2001). Here, national skill formation models are linked to recent claims about how vocational education and training systems fit into broader national models of the political economy, which are argued to have important implications for a range of economic, social, and political outcomes. In these debates, those skill formation systems (or skill regimes) that have attracted the most attention are those, like the German one, that appear capable of reconciling high wages with high productivity via high skills and high value-added production. In their chapter, therefore, the authors pay particular attention to Germany, while situating that case in the context of a broader comparative literature on the origins, operation, and future of distinctive skill regimes. Culpepper and Thelen address three main issues in their chapter. First, they present an overview of the various typologies that have been devised to characterize cross-national differences in training systems and of arguments on the implications of these different, nationally specific models of skill formation. Second, they explore the origins of cross-national differences in training and skill formation systems, and ask how firm-based training and high-quality apprenticeships have survived in some countries while they faded away in others. To explicate their arguments, they explore briefly the origins and development of the German system, drawing out comparisons to Britain, the United States, Japan, and Denmark. Finally, the authors connect their findings to contemporary debates on the continued viability of distinct skill regimes and focus, in particular, on the question of the robustness of the German model against the backdrop of contemporary changes in national economies and world markets. Here, Culpepper and Thelen analyze the current strains on Germany's apprenticeship system and reflect on the extent to which this system can adapt to a new set of challenges, including the incorporation of eastern Germany and the rise of the service sector, as well as technological and other changes that have rendered training more costly by increasing the importance of broad-based theoretical training. One of the chapter's major contributions to the book is demonstrating how highly contingent the provision of skills is and that formerly efficient institutional solutions might actually impede adaptations to new sets of skill demands.

The variety of national institutional configurations of skill provision – discussed by Culpepper and Thelen – is often connected to the assumption that these configurations (or skill formation regimes) constrain what kinds of skills are available on the labor market. A contrasting view, however, emerges out of Hillmert's empirical comparison in Chapter 3 of skill formation in Britain and West Germany. Taking long-term historical trends into account, the two countries represent different types of skill formation regimes. Hillmert shows that these regimes can both adapt, although in different ways, to similar new skill demands. Based on longitudinal data from the British Household Panel Study and the German Life History Study, the chapter compares school-to-work transitions in Britain and West Germany. It pays particular attention to the differences in the institutional structures in which qualifications are formed and allocated in the two labor markets and their specific pathways to adapt to new skill requirement – becoming visible especially during the 1990s. Among the institutional differences considered by Hillmert are a relatively low degree of standardization and more on-the-job training in Britain, in contrast to the dominance of the dual system and vocational specificity in Germany. Varying involvement of collective actors has also led to differences in the level of trust associated with the provision and acceptance of skills. The chapter assesses the effects of formal qualifications on the quality of first jobs and the stability of early careers. The results of the empirical analyses show that differences in skill investment, labor market entry, and life course patterns can be observed. For instance, in Britain, criteria of timing, in addition to the hierarchical grading of educational tracks, have played a larger role for allocating entry positions; in Germany, substantive occupational skills and the level of qualifications have been important. However, comparison of these two cases clearly reveals that there have also been functionally equivalent solutions to similar problems, as well as more specific problems and different economic strategies. Looking more closely at the German case from a life course perspective, Hillmert illustrates the fact that young adults increasingly experience multiple episodes of education and training and, as a consequence, shift jobs. This side of skill formation trajectory is largely invisible in aggregate indicators. Moreover, for both training and labor market mobility, Hillmert is able to demonstrate how social class closure takes effect early and then cumulatively through later stages of the life course.

Part II: The Economics and Sociology of Skill Formation: Access, Investments, and Returns to Education

In Chapter 4, the economists Dustmann and Schoenberg evaluate why the German apprenticeship system works. Competitiveness and performance of national economies are inherently linked to the productivity of its workforce. Many countries consider training and education increasingly important for productivity and have therefore made attempts to improve their educational and training institutions. As a result, economists have investigated successful components of national educational institutions and how they might be adopted by other countries. In this context, the so-called German dual system or *German apprenticeship system* has received the most attention. It combines on-the-job training in private firms with formal, state-provided education at vocational schools. Whether apprenticeship-type training schemes can be successful in other national contexts is not evident, however. One important question is *who finances the scheme.* There is evidence that a considerable part of the skills workers acquire during their apprenticeship period are general rather than specific and that the employing firm pays partly for its acquisition. Simple models of human capital investment show that firms have no incentive to invest in general skills because workers can quit and use these skills with other employers. One reason why firms may nevertheless find it advantageous to train workers is wage compression (i.e., wages increase less with training than workers' productivity). In their chapter, Dustmann and Schoenberg discuss three reasons for wage compression: the complementarity between firm-specific and general human capital, asymmetric learning, and the influence of trade unions. They present empirical implications of each of these theoretical explanations and then provide some empirical evidence for Germany. The second important question for individuals' skill formation is who pockets the returns to enrolling in such training schemes. If returns are too low, potential trainees may not be willing to enroll in training schemes that pay lower wages than they could obtain as unskilled workers. The authors present results on returns to German apprenticeship training. Based on these results, they conclude their paper with some discussion on difficulties of implementing a similar firm-based training scheme in other economies, and on whether institutional changes and economic developments in Germany may lead to a breakdown of Germany's apprenticeship model.

The starting point of Chapter 5 by O'Connell and Jungblut is also the human capital approach. The authors critically review this dominant theoretical framework. In contrast to the majority of economic research on educational investments, the authors focus *on continuing job-related training at work*. Some of the individual's productivity is created by full-time primary and secondary education, as well as initial training. However, a significant part is built up later, while workers participate in the workforce. The main questions addressed by O'Connell and Jungblut are: Who is receiving training at the workplace and who is not? Who benefits from this further training? Following human capital theory, in competitive labor markets individual workers decide to undertake further training, and employers decide to invest in training based on their estimates of future returns (e.g., employment prospects, wages, productivity gains). O'Connell and Jungblut take a critical look at this approach. Their review of the international research literature reveals that in many countries much training at work is general and transferable in nature but is, nonetheless, paid for by employers. This is contrary to the expectations of human capital theory. The authors argue that the conflicting findings are rooted in one of human capital theory's key assumptions, namely, that labor markets are competitive. Sociologists understand that this is a crude assumption that oversimplifies the nature of the employment relationship. They augment economic analyses by adding a more sophisticated understanding of employment relations and institutional factors – within the workplace and in the wider society – also taking account of employment regulation and collective organization.

Sociology's main interest in skill formation is to understand which consequences qualifications have for working life and other life course outcomes. One of the core issues of sociological inquiry is the unequal access of individuals and social groups (e.g., constituted by gender, class, or ethnicity) to different kinds and levels of qualifications and the implications this has for society's social structure and stratification. Beyond such a more narrowly defined stratification perspective, sociology investigates many other implications of skill formation processes and outcomes such as those for social attitudes and civic and political engagement, social behavior such as union formation or fertility, social cohesion, and social conflicts. Chapter 6 by Müller and Jacob gives a review of the state of sociological research on these issues of skill formation. It elaborates the basic social processes underlying participation by various actors in skill formation and skill use over the life course. Although the basic mechanisms are often assumed to be similar across countries, the chapter investigates how varying institutional settings (with respect to the education/training institutions, labor market regulations, and welfare state arrangements) impact the specific forms and strategies of skill formation and skill use in labor markets. In particular, it focuses on how countries differ in initial versus continuing education and the role of general versus occupation- and firm-specific skills for a variety of labor market outcomes (e.g., school leavers' labor market integration, work participation over the life course, unemployment risks, returns to education in terms of income and status).

In Chapter 7, Solga investigates the employment opportunities of low-skilled persons from sociological and microeconomic perspectives. The employment opportunities of low-skilled youth are currently a hot topic in sociological and economic labor market research. This has to do with the policy agenda to combat low-educated youths' exclusion from the labor market – an agenda in many Western societies. In her chapter, she focuses on the unemployment risk of low-skilled young adults as a *consequence* of individual's participation in skill formation processes. She argues that a comprehensive explanation of the higher unemployment risk of low-skilled persons can only be achieved by taking account of the processes of "becoming low educated" – instead of only considering the consequences of "being low educated" – and of the institutional conditions shaping the processes of "becoming low educated." In doing so, she develops a multidimensional framework of education and educational groups in which education is considered to be not only skills and qualifications, but also a social phenomenon that is connected to social meanings and social relations or group memberships. She defines four social mechanisms that help explain the rise of educational disadvantage. Two of her mechanisms – displacement and discredit – are based on microeconomic theories; here, "low education" is considered to be an individual characteristic in terms of (relative) skill certification and attribution. The other two mechanisms – impoverished network resources and stigmatization – are of a sociological nature and incorporate processes of becoming low skilled by defining "low education" as a group membership in terms of resources and social identity. The cross-sectional country comparison on the relative unemployment risk of youth with less than upper secondary education shows differences in the relative weight of the relevance of the four mechanisms in the countries considered. The results of her analyses corroborate the idea of "social embeddedness" (cf. Granovetter, 1985) of the consequences of low education, in particular, and skill formation processes, in general. One major advantage of this economic-sociological approach is that in contrast to the common "single-cause" economic explanation of displacement, it explains low-skilled persons' different risks of labor market exclusion by recognizing the heterogeneity of the low-skilled group in terms of school experiences and educational biographies (i.e., risk of stigmatization) as well as social background and network resources (i.e., risk of impoverished networks).

Part III: Individuals' Acquisition of Skills and Competencies: Learning Environments and Measurements of Skills

In Chapter 8, Gruber, Harteis, and Rehrl clarify the specific use of the term "competence" in their disciplinary tradition. In educational psychology, the use of the concept of "competence" is closely related to the use of the concepts of "performance" or even more narrowly of "expertise." Gruber and his coauthors are highly critical of the popular and – in public debates and educational research – overstretched concept of "key qualifications" claiming general competences that can be used in many different situations (e.g., communication skills). In contrast to the notion of key qualifications, *professional competence* is usually closely related with professional performance and, thus, domain specific in nature. The use of such a concept of "professional competence" implies that a discussion about learning is pointless if it contains no notion of what is being learnt and what kind of behavior it enables. Moreover, Gruber and his coauthors state that theories of competence have only recently been developed that extend the perspective by addressing the sociocultural development of professional practice at specific workplaces. The authors present such conceptions of expertise and professional development. These conceptions emphasize that expertise not only includes individual cognitive capacities, but also other components (e.g., successful participation in a community of experts and its shared knowledge and actions). The authors clearly suggest that an exclusively individual-centered concept of skills at the workplace might be seriously misleading. In this line of reasoning, the main goal of Gruber, Harteis, and Rehrl is to address the differences between formal learning, as in schools, and learning in situated context, as in work settings. It is their major contention that a better understanding of the role of formal and situated learning during skill formation can only be obtained if the interplay between both forms, rather than the mere contrast between them, is analyzed. In professional learning, both formal learning and situated learning are obviously taking place. During skill formation or expertise development, individual acquisition of domain-specific knowledge and problem solving, on the one hand, and social embedding within communities of practice, on the other hand, complement each another. Recent empirical research acknowledges the importance of such integration. Thus, psychology leads to the following recommendation of "optimal" learning or individual skill formation process: good training has to include both formal and situated learning irrespective of where it takes place, in schools, during apprenticeships, or at the workplace.

Such a general theory of the formal and situated aspects of learning, however, still leaves open not only the question of how skill acquisition systematically changes between tasks and between groups, but also the question of *how best to define and measure skills relevant for the labor market.* In recent years, both the OECD and national governments have begun initiatives to conduct cross-nationally comparative assessments of adult skills in analogy to the international assessment of reading, math, and other competences among fourth-graders or 15-year-olds (Progress in International Reading Literacy Study [PIRLS], Programme for International Student Assessment [PISA]). In Chapter 9, Baethge, Achtenhagen, and Arends address the second issue of measuring skills and skill acquisition in different training systems. In their chapter, they present insights from their research on preparing such a skill assessment for Germany in comparison to selected European countries. In contrast to school assessments, the complexity and diversity of VET systems make it difficult to assess and quantify their relative success or failure. Moreover, compared to PISA and other school-based student assessments, a skill assessment in VET has to be concerned about domain-specific (occupation-specific) skills and not only about generic skills. That is one reason why economists use educational degrees achieved or years of schooling as a measure of "human capital," although according to the theory they would need direct measures of skills and competences, irrespective of where they have been acquired. Furthermore, given the different places of learning in VET systems across countries, to measure the individual's progress in skill formation and, based on that, to assess the success of a VET system is confronted with problems of defining and identifying the relevant cohorts and a sampling procedure applicable across countries. For assessing the success of vocational education's skill formation, the sample construction has to allow comparing different VET systems both vertically and horizontally. Vertical comparison is related to the VET level, which can be defined by types of secondary and tertiary education, duration, or age, whereas horizontal comparison refers to VET curricula or assessment. With the background of a feasibility study for an international large-scale assessment of vocational and occupational education and training (VET-PISA) and the current preparation of such an assessment study (planned for the year 2008), Baethge and his coauthors address several of the important issues on how best to define and measure skills acquired in diverse VET systems. Among them are the following: Why is there a political interest in comparing the success of VET systems across countries (interestingly, much less within countries)? What does this mean for the definition of the scientific and political criteria of success of VET systems? What are possible designs of a "VET-PISA"? What are their advantages and disadvantages? What are the challenges of an appropriate sample construction? The authors conclude that for an appropriate design for a VET-PISA one needs a comprehensive and well-defined model of competences that is focused on general and domain-specific knowledge and attitudes, measuring the impact of institutional and individual conditions on the quality of processes of VET.

OPEN ISSUES

The chapters in this book considerably advance our knowledge on several open issues. Regarding the meaning of skills, we learn about the mixed formal-situated nature of skill learning (Chapter 8) and the practical problems of measuring and comparing adult skills cross-nationally (Chapter 9). Concerning training institutions, we provide insights on the collective actor preconditions of national training systems (Chapter 2) and the adaptability of labor markets in mobilizing skills (Chapter 3). In the area of inequality in access to skill formation, there exists profound knowledge on life course mechanisms of skill formation (Chapter 6) and processes of becoming low skilled, as well as the social embeddedness of their consequences in labor markets (Chapter 7). Finally, economics and sociology contribute insights on microeconomic mechanisms of skill investment and financing and their variation across countries (Chapters 4–6).

In many of these areas, this should be seen, nonetheless, as a first step into what might be portrayed as an agenda for an interdisciplinary and comparative research on skill formation. Why?

1. The rapidly changing landscape of occupational structures and skill distributions is inadequately mapped because sectoral shifts, occupational codes, and educational credentials represent increasingly less actual qualifications or skill requirements. Moreover, still unanswered is our question on how aptitudes acquired and required at the workplace are related to what is learned at schools and in vocational education. Although a number of national and international

initiatives aim at measuring skills by proxy variables or scales similar to school performance, many of these attempts are directed too quickly at developing (shorthand) survey variables. Much more extensive basic research is needed to develop instruments for observing skill formation (cf. Chapter 9) and skill requirements in specific work settings over longer periods of time. Such research would need to focus on the multidimensional nature of skills and the interrelationships between skills as personal capacities and skills as collective abilities of groups of workers.

2. Although knowledge has far advanced in regard to measurements, changes and cross-national differences in school achievements, such as reading, math, and science competencies, and also in regard to the changes of cognitive competencies over the life span, knowledge about transmission, preservation, and change of skills and competencies over the life course is almost totally absent. This concerns, on the one hand, the interrelationships between measured school achievements, grades and later occupational performance, and the predictability of the latter by the former, and, on the other hand, the changes of specific skills over the working life. This deficit is most glaring regarding older workers where assumptions of public policy ("anti-age discrimination"), gerontological-psychological claims, and practices by employer diverge widely. "Lifelong learning" is a shallow slogan, and little is known about the optimal combination and lifetime patterning of vocational and professional learning.

3. Although our understanding of the historical emergence and past trajectories of institutional training regimes has grown markedly, we still lack adequate comparative analyses of ongoing collective decision making within market, étatist, and corporatist models of training institutions and to what extent such decision-making processes are actually stimulated by changes in economic and societal skill requirements. More important, we lack in-depth studies of how path-dependent outcomes of these institutional trajectories affect the capacity of national economies to effectively respond to global competitive challenges. But, likewise, we have too few case studies of how identical production processes (e.g., of multinational firms) are being organized under the varying conditions of *local* skill provision (Buss, 2003, 2006; Wittke, 2003). The attempts to institutionalize a common set of vocational and professional credentials within the European Union in analogy to the Bologna process for higher education provides fertile ground for research for the solution of practical problems (e.g., of mutual skill recognition).

4. One of the most dramatic developments over the most recent decades has been the emergence of an "underclass" of low-skilled persons with marginal employment opportunities. This is partly due to the vanishing un- and semiskilled jobs in manufacturing, as well as automation in services. In many countries, this has evolved primarily as a problem of disenfranchised young males, and thus exacerbates the problems of social and economic exclusion of ethnically or racially disadvantaged groups. Here, the dominance of economic explanations obscures innovative policies drawing on insights from multiple disciplines. Besides sociology (cf. Chapter 7), the interplay among economic, sociological, *and* psychological factors in the processes of becoming low skilled, as well as their consequences in labor markets and other life domains, is still underinvestigated.

5. The impact of migration on skill formation is another underdeveloped, if not ignored, area of skill research that should be of particular importance in political science, sociology, and economics given globalization and transmigration processes. Thus, questions on the supply of a skilled labor force can be less adequately addressed in a national framework of skill regimes, on the one hand, and individual's investments in skill acquisition take place increasingly in different skill regimes, on the other hand. Migration and globalization, therefore, give raise to new challenges for skill research on provision, access, and return to vocational education and training.

In these areas, interdisciplinary and comparative theory building and research will be indispensable. It is hoped that with this book we are able to contribute to such an enterprise.

Note

1. See http://www.europarl.europa.eu/summits/lis1_en.htm.

References

Bamber, G. J., & Lansbury, R. D. (1998). *International and Comparative Employment Relations: A Study of Industrialised Market Economies.* London: Sage.

Beaudry, P., & Green, D. A. (2005). Changes in US wages, 1976–2000: Ongoing skill bias or major technological change? *Journal of Labor Economics*, 23(3), 609–648.

Buss, K.-P. (2003). *How to Get Skills for High-Tech Manufacturing: New Strategies in the Supply of Vocational Qualifications in the U.S. – The Case of Semiconductors.* Paper presented at SASE 2003, Aix-en-Provence, France, June 26–28. Available at: http://www.sase.org/index.php?option=com_wrapper&Itemid=53.

Buss, K.-P. (2006). A new mode of qualification supply: The realization of a high road strategy in the U.S. semiconductor industry. In K.-S. Rehberg (Ed.), *Soziale*

Ungleichheit – Kulturelle Unterschiede. Verhandlungen des 32. Kongresses der Deutschen Gesellschaft für Soziologie in München 2004. Frankfurt: Campus (CD-ROM).

Gallie, D., White, M., Cheng, Y., & Tomlinson, M. (Eds.). (1998). *Restructuring the Employment Relationship.* Oxford, UK: Clarendon Press.

Giloth, R. P. (Ed.). (1998). *Jobs & Economic Development: Strategies and Practice.* London: Sage.

Granovetter, M. (1985). Economic action and social structure: The problem of embeddedness. *The American Journal of Sociology*, 91(3), 481–510.

Hall, P. A., & Soskice, D. (Eds.). (2001). *Varieties of Capitalism: The Institutional Foundations of Comparative Advantage.* New York: Oxford University Press.

Heckman, J. J. (2006). Skill formation and the economics of investing in disadvantaged children. *Science*, 30(312), 1900–1902.

Heckman, J. J., Krueger, A. B., & Friedan, B. M. (2003). *Inequality in America. What Role Does Human Capital Play?* Boston: MIT Press.

Heckman, J. J., Sixtrud, J., & Ursner, B. (2006). The effects of cognitive and non-cognitive abilities on labor market outcomes and social behavior. *Journal of Labor Economics*, 24, 411–482.

Katz, L. F., & Krueger, A. B. (1998). Computing inequality: Have computers changed the labor market? *Quarterly Journal of Economics*, 113(4), 1169–1213.

Levy, F., & Murnane, R. (2003a). *The New Division of Labor.* Princeton, NJ: Princeton University Press.

Levy, F., & Murnane, R. (2003b). The skill content of recent technological change: An empirical exploration. *Quarterly Journal of Economics*, 118(4), 1279–1333.

Lisbon-to-Copenhagen-to-Maastrich Consortium Partners. (2004). *Achieving the Lisbon Goal: The Contribution of VET – Final Report to the European Commission.* Available at: http://ec.europa.eu/education/policies/2010/studies/maastricht_en.pdf.

Murnane, R., & Levy, F. (1996). *Teaching the New Basic Skills.* New York: Free Press.

Noyelle, T. (1986). *Beyond Industrial Dualism: Market and Segmentation in the New Development.* Boulder, CO: Westview.

Organisation for Economic Co-operation and Development (OECD). (2004). ICT skills and employment. In *OECD Information Technology Outlook 2004* (pp. 217–382). Paris: Author.

Spitz, A. (2004). *Are Skill Requirements in the Workplace Rising? Stylized Facts and Evidence on Skill-Based Technical Change.* Discussion Paper 04–33. Mannheim, Germany: Zentrum für Europäische Wirtschaftsforschung.

Thurow, L. C. (1999). *Building Wealth. The New Rules for Individuals, Companies, and Nations in a Knowledge-Based Economy.* New York: HarperCollins.

van Welsum, D., & Vickery, G. (2005, April 22). *New Perspectives on ICT Skills and Employment.* Paris: OECD. Available at: www.oecd.org/dataoecd/26/35/34769393.pdf.

Wittke, V. (2003). *Innovationsmodelle und Nationale Kapitalismen: Zur Frage der PfadabhängigkeitIindustrieller Restrukturierung am Beispiel der Mikroelektronik.* Habilitation thesis, University of Göttingen, Göttingen, Germany.

Wright, E. O., & Dwyer, R. (2003). The patterns of job expansions in the USA: A comparison of the 1960s and 1990s. *Socio-Economic Review*, 1, 289–325.

PART ONE

CROSS-NATIONAL DIVERSITY IN SKILL FORMATION REGIMES

Origins, Changes, and Institutional Variation

2 Institutions and Collective Actors in the Provision of Training

Historical and Cross-National Comparisons

Pepper D. Culpepper and Kathleen Thelen

This chapter considers contributions from the political science literature to understanding the causes and consequences of cross-national diversity in training regimes across the most developed democracies.[1] The recent surge of interest by political scientists in skills has developed as an offshoot of debates over distinctive varieties of capitalism. Although economists are mostly interested in the efficiency effects of different skill formation systems, and sociologists, often, in the effects of educational opportunities on social stratification, political scientists came to the topic of skills through an interest in understanding the political and institutional foundations of national political-economic systems associated with divergent political and distributive outcomes. In these debates, the skill systems that have attracted the most attention are those, such as the German one, that appear capable of reconciling high wages with high productivity via high skills and high value-added production (Streeck, 1991). In this chapter, therefore, we focus particular attention on Germany, while situating this case in the context of a broader comparative literature on the origins, operation, and future of distinctive skill regimes.

The chapter is divided into three main sections. The first section briefly considers a range of arguments by political scientists on the implications of different, nationally specific models of skill formation. It presents an overview of the various typologies that have been devised to characterize cross-national differences in training systems, and it links these to recent claims about how vocational education and training systems fit into broader national political-economic models. Different production regimes, characterized by distinctive institutional constellations in which training institutions are a central component, are argued to have important implications for a range of economic, social, and political outcomes.

The second section explores the origins of cross-national differences in training and skill formation systems. Here, we ask how plant-based training and strong apprenticeship survived in some countries while it faded away in others. To explicate the argument, we briefly explore the origins and development of the German system, drawing out comparisons to Britain, the United States, Japan, and Denmark. The historical analysis underscores the importance of employer coordination – facilitated, frequently, by the state and anchored politically in cross-class coalitions – as a crucial factor in the survival of strong firm-based apprenticeship training, especially those varieties of apprenticeship that are governed through national frameworks.

The third section of the chapter turns to contemporary debates on the continued viability of distinct skill regimes and focuses, in particular, on the question of the robustness of the German model against the backdrop of contemporary changes in national economies and world markets. The German system relies on a high degree of voluntary participation by employers, although it is supported by institutions that encourage this participation and sustain continued employer coordination on training. This section, therefore, analyzes the current strains on Germany's historically evolved system for skill formation and speculates about the extent to which this system can be adapted to a new set of challenges, including not only the incorporation of eastern Germany and the rise of the service sector, but also technological and other changes that have rendered training more costly by increasing the importance of broad-based theoretical training.

VARIETIES OF TRAINING SYSTEMS

Vocational training institutions occupy a central role in the contemporary literature on the political economies of the advanced democracies. Current research suggests that skills are associated with a variety of important social and political outcomes. Economists have mostly focused on the efficiency effects of various training regimes (see Chapters 4 and 5), but political scientists and sociologists are at least as interested in the impact of skills on social in/exclusion, inequality, gender differences, and social policy regimes (e.g., Mares, 2000; Brown et al., 2001; Iversen & Soskice, 2001; Lauder, 2001).

Within comparative politics and political science more generally, the politics of training and education, historically, have not attracted a great deal of attention. Early forays into the comparative analysis of political-economic institutions (and specifically those institutions that mediate relations between labor and capital) were prompted by the upsurge in labor conflict in the late 1960s in several European countries. An emergent scholarship linked cross-national differences in conflict and cooperation to different types of political exchange among organized business, labor, and the state (Schmitter, 1974; Goldthorpe, 1984; Katzenstein, 1985). Although education and training were not initially seen as central to the core distinctions (at the time, between "corporatist," "pluralist," and "statist" polities), subsequent analyses soon began to show that the success or failure of national economic and political strategies had complex political roots that also involved financial systems and the organization of production more generally (Zysman, 1983; Piore & Sabel, 1984; Hall, 1986).[2] By about 1990, social scientists began to converge on the understanding that if there were distinctive national modes of production that depended on certain skill profiles, then skill systems must be incorporated into institutional analysis of the political economy (Soskice, 1991; Streeck, 1991).

Thus, most of the political science literature does not treat training regimes in isolation, but rather draws attention to how skill formation systems fit into broader political-economic models that support different types of employer strategies in the market. Vocational education and training systems play a central role in defining and sustaining the logic of distinctive "varieties of capitalism" (Streeck, 1991; Boyer, 1997; Hall & Soskice, 2001). Wolfgang Streeck's (1991) early work on what he called "diversified quality production" showed how specific institutional arrangements associated with strong labor unions could "force and facilitate" employers to move up-market and into areas in which their strategies could focus on the kind of high-quality, high-skill, high value-added production that was necessary to support high wages. Hall and Soskice's (2001) recent version of the "varieties of capitalism" argument puts more of the emphasis on employers. Their framework distinguishes between "liberal market economies" (e.g., the United States, the United Kingdom [UK]), where employers coordinate mostly through market mechanisms, and "coordinated market economies" (including Germany, Japan, and Sweden, among others), where various nonmarket institutions (coordinated collective bargaining, patient capital achieved through concentrated shareholdings, strong plant-based mechanisms for union management cooperation) support "strategic" interaction among employers (i.e., allow employers to achieve joint gains through coordination). Despite differences in emphasis on the exact causal mechanisms that drive and support the observed cross-national differences (Streeck [1991] emphasized labor power, whereas Hall and Soskice [2001] emphasized employer rationality), there is an extremely high degree of consensus on the kinds of institutions (including training institutions) that matter and how they support distinctive employer strategies in the market.

The Hall and Soskice (2001) framework pays particular attention to the link between institutional structures and individual-level incentives, both for firms to train (or not) and for young people to acquire skills (and of what sort). Coordinated market economies such as Germany are associated with institutions providing incentives for companies to train, but also, and equally important, for workers to acquire particular, *specific* skills (specific either to the firm or the industry).[3] The institutions associated with liberal market economies (LMEs), in contrast, discourage strong employer investment in skill formation; in these LMEs, workers therefore have an incentive to acquire *general* skills that are broadly portable across the various industries and firms in which they might seek employment.

The "varieties of capitalism" framework also emphasizes the mutual interactions of vocational training with other, "complementary" political-economic institutions (Aoki, 1994; Soskice, 1994; Ashton & Green, 1996; Estevez-Abe et al., 2001; Culpepper, 2003; Iversen, 2005). Thus, for example, short-term financing arrangements and weak employment protections in liberal market economies – and the associated tendency for firms to respond to economic downturns by laying off workers – encourage young people to acquire skills that are generally marketable rather than firm specific or even industry specific. Companies may upgrade this education with some company training, but they would typically attempt to add only nontransferable (firm-specific) skills whose full benefit only they could recoup (Hall & Soskice, 2001). The U.S. training regime does not favor strong firm-based investment in private sector vocational training. However, it appears to support very well the production of a plentiful supply of "high-end" skills (e.g., engineering, programming) that thrive in a context that rewards strong general (especially university) education and where demand for training on the part of young people is driven by intense competition among firms and associated high labor market mobility.

In the coordinated market economies, in contrast, firms are more likely to invest in training workers because other institutions exist that introduce labor market imperfections that reduce labor turnover or compress wages, and/or that reduce poaching and free riding – all of these being factors that make it "safe" and profitable for firms to invest in human capital development (see especially Acemoglu & Pischke, 1998, 1999; Thelen, 2004: 13–20). In Japan, for instance, long job tenure and seniority wages allow employers and employees to share the gains from their joint investment in skills. In Germany, industry-level bargaining compresses the wages of skilled and unskilled workers. This allows firms to earn rents from training and encourages them, as indicated previously, to move into high value-quality market niches. However, wage compression should also dampen the demand for training among youth, especially training that involves high investments of their own time and money, because these workers will not be able to capture the full rents on their training investment, which helps explain observed skill shortages at the very high end of the labor market in some "coordinated" market economies (Smith, 2000).

In sum, then, the political economy literature on skills is embedded in broader analyses of distinctive production regimes that support different types of strategies on the part of firms in the market. Although the categories and labels sometimes differ (Streeck [1991] talked of liberal vs. nonliberal capitalism, Hall and Soskice [2001] of liberal vs. coordinated market economies, and Albert [1993] of Anglo-Saxon vs. Rhineland capitalism), there is actually substantial agreement on the substance even between political scientists who come out of different intellectual traditions (e.g., more sociological vs. more economistic perspectives).

For political scientists, the most interesting cases of training are those that rely in some way on political mechanisms to solve coordination problems in the market. Germany occupies an especially prominent place in the literature because it is a prime example of a "nonliberal," or "coordinated," market economy, where firms have organized around production strategies based on diversified quality production and in which firms themselves are deeply involved (and invested) in firm-based training and a strong apprenticeship system. The next two sections, respectively, look backward and forward — back to the historical origins of strong plant-based training in Germany and elsewhere, and forward to the durability of the German system in the face of changing domestic and international markets.

ORIGINS OF CROSS-NATIONAL DIFFERENCES IN TRAINING REGIMES

One of the overall lessons to emerge from the literature is that the structure and operation of skilled labor markets can be significantly influenced by the interaction of vocational training regimes with other, adjacent political-economic institutions. Such arguments that situate the economic logic of training in a broader political-institutional context provide the basis for arguments about the historical origins of cross-national differences in training. Training regimes developed in tandem with the development of other key labor market institutions and organizations, in particular, employer associations, unions, collective bargaining institutions, and, in some cases, artisanal associations. The interactions among these institutional arenas had a profound effect on the kinds of production and training regimes that would develop cross-nationally.

This section explores briefly the political conditions that, historically, supported the emergence and maintenance of strong plant-based apprenticeship training.[4] It focuses on Germany as a premier example of such a system and asks what factors allowed apprenticeship to survive in Germany, even as it was fading in liberal market economies such as Britain and the United States. Further comparisons to Denmark and Japan provide additional insights into the conditions that support strong company investment in training. Briefly, our argument is a political-coalitional one and points above all to the role of employers (specifically, employers in skill-intensive sectors), whose strategies with respect to training were heavily influenced by state policy and often realized in the context of cross-class alliances with labor.

One broad and consequential divergence among these countries goes back to the early industrial period and concerns the extent to which skills came to be contested across the class divide (i.e., between emerging unions and employers). This is a question that is also, it turns out, bound up in the fate of the traditional artisanate and its connections or conflicts with emergent industrial interests and organized labor. We begin by sketching the argument for Germany and then bring in comparisons to the other four cases mentioned (United States, UK, Denmark, and Japan) to underscore the similarities and differences among them in the coalitional alignments that supported (or opposed) the survival and expansion of firm-based training in emerging industry.

In Germany, industrialization occurred under authoritarian auspices, and the traditional artisanal sector survived as an important corporate actor in apprenticeship training. Indeed, the imperial state actively supported the organization of German artisans and delegated to them (as corporate actors) important parapublic responsibilities in the area of apprenticeship and training. The oversight and monitoring provided by the handicraft chambers helped prevent apprenticeship in Germany from degenerating (as it did in Britain) into cheap child labor.

Beyond this, artisanal control over apprenticeship encouraged coalitional alignments that were congenial to the extension and adaptation of this type of in-plant training to emerging industrial sectors. On the labor side, the handicraft sector's monopoly position with respect to apprenticeship meant that unions developed in a context in which strategies based on controlling craft labor markets were not a viable option – which in turn meant that skill formation in industry would not be contested across the class divide. Instead, conflicts over skills in Germany in the early industrial period (and into the 1920s) featured conflicts between the artisanal sector and the "modern" industrial sector. This competition proved constructive rather than destructive to the preservation of firm-sponsored training in industry as skill-intensive firms (often in explicit or implicit alliance with labor) embraced strategies that were premised on emulating and gaining control over the institutions governing skill formation that had traditionally been monopolized by artisans.

In liberal market economies such as the United States and Britain, in contrast, industrialization occurred in a context in which traditional artisanal organizations had either been destroyed (Britain) or never developed (United States). In both countries, the advance of industry had the effect of blurring the line between masters and journeymen, whereas market conditions (skill scarcity) and a relatively liberal political environment encouraged skilled workers as a whole to band together to defend their interests by attempting to control the market in their crafts. This constellation produced a situation in which skill formation came to be heavily contested across the class divide as early unions (organized by skilled workers, often along craft lines) sought to use apprenticeship to maintain the value of their scarce skills and as employers sought to defeat union attempts to control training to get the upper hand in labor conflicts.

Employers fought furiously against the imposition of union controls, and the ongoing struggles between unions and employers over skills and apprenticeship undermined firm-based training over time. Underinvestment on the part of firms in training produced recurrent skill shortages that often shored up the power of skilled unions in the short run. But the resulting fierce competition among firms for scarce skilled labor, over the longer run, mostly pushed employers toward strategies that minimized their dependence on skill (see also Finegold & Soskice, 1988). In short, where conditions in the early industry period provoked conflict between skilled unions and employers over apprenticeship, the result was typically deadly for the survival of strong in-plant training.

The case of Denmark highlights the importance of employer organization and strategies (even over union organization) because the coalitional alignments more closely resemble Germany than the UK, despite the emergence of craft unions. As in Germany, relatively strong artisanal associations survived the onset of industrialization in Denmark, even in the wake of legislation that formally abolished the guilds. These associations (again, similar to Germany) were specifically assigned a significant parapublic role in administering and organizing training, in this case through an elaborate network of technical schools that were originally founded by artisans, but which by the late nineteenth century were increasingly financed and sponsored by the state. Through their craft chambers, organized artisans in Denmark (much as in Germany) oversaw and monitored firm-based apprentice training (Kristensen, 1997: 22–23; Kristensen & Sabel, 1997).

As in the UK, and different than Germany, unions of Danish journeymen organized themselves into craft unions rather than industrial unions. What prevented the decline of apprenticeship, however, is that unlike in Britain, skills were not contested across the class divide. On the contrary, the master craftsmen in Denmark who administered the training system and who employed skilled workers relied on craft unions to monitor and police coordination among themselves to avoid cut-throat competition that would have redounded to the detriment of all (Kristensen & Sabel, 1997). Joint regulation of wages with craft unions prevented individual firms from gaining advantage in product markets through strategies based on wage competition and lower quality, whereas joint regulation of apprenticeship (institutionalized in the Apprenticeship Law of 1889, which was supported both by associations of independent artisans and by craft unions) supported skill formation and encouraged high-end strategies that enhanced the reputation of all Danish producers in international markets. Thus, as in Germany, the survival of an independent and vibrant artisanal class in Denmark was crucial to the persistence of plant-based apprenticeship training, and the important point is that the coalitional alignment in emerging industry brought employers together with skilled unions rather than pitting them against each other over skills.

The Japanese case provides another angle on the issue of employer interest and investment in skills because this is a case that resembles Germany in terms of strong firm-based training, but the system is organized around a completely different model (firm-based training and without a national corporatist framework). As in Germany, Japanese industrialization occurred under authoritarian auspices, and here, too, the traditional artisanal sector was a key actor in apprenticeship training. Unlike in Germany, however, state policy did not shore up traditional artisanal associations, and although skill formation was contested between artisans and the modern industrial sector, the site on which such conflicts were played out was at the firm, not the national, level. Emerging industry covered its skill needs by hiring or subcontracting to traditional artisans who would preside over skill formation for younger workers (see, e.g., Taira, 1978; Gordon, 1985). However, this solution created problems of high turnover, to which skill-intensive firms responded with a cross-class coalition with local (company) unions to stabilize internal labor markets. The essential difference to Germany lies mostly in the level at which this cross-class coalition emerged and was consolidated. In Japan, labor management alliances in large industrial firms institutionalized internal labor markets and in the process also stabilized company unionism. In Germany, where organized labor formed along industrial lines, more encompassing organization (also on the employer side) facilitated a national-level solution in support of a system based on a higher degree of skill standardization across firms and industries.

Summarizing the overall argument in its most skeletal version, the history surveyed here suggests that the *absence* of class conflict over skills was *necessary* for the survival of strong plant-based training, and the *presence* of such conflict was *sufficient* to undermine it. In the United States and Britain, the alliance in the early industrial period of unions and independent artisans on the one hand (or the absorption and dominance of the latter into the former), against skill-intensive employers on the other hand, was destructive of apprenticeship because it meant that conflicts over skills were played out across the class divide. In contrast, political alignments in Germany and Japan pitted skill-intensive industries (and, later, their unions) against artisans but in support of strong in-plant apprentice training, while in Denmark artisans collaborated rather than fought with craft unions to the same ends.

One of the lessons that emerges from the historical material is that although organized employers are the crucial actors with respect to the survival of strong plant-based training, the state plays a critical role in facilitating coordination among them, and also influences mightily the kinds of coalitional alignments that favor different skill regimes. Historically, unions have played a secondary role in the origins of different systems, and as we have seen, the survival of strong in-plant training is consistent with a variety of organizational forms for unions – from company unionism (Japan) to craft unionism (Denmark) to industrial unionism (Germany). The key and common denominator across all three was the absence of interclass conflict over in-plant training and indeed the forging of cross-class alliances in support of it.

CONTEMPORARY STRAINS IN THE GERMAN MODEL

Current debates in the political science literature – on varieties of capitalism in general and on skills in particular – focus increasingly on the impact of changing market dynamics on the continued viability of the institutional arrangements associated with "coordinated" market economies (including training institutions). At stake is the extent to which globalization pressures, associated among other things with increased competition in international markets and higher levels of capital mobility, will drive convergence in institutions and practices cross-nationally through competitive deregulation. In this section, we explore this issue by evaluating contemporary trends in the

German system against the backdrop of new strains and tensions associated with globalization, secular trends such as the decline of manufacturing, and the impact of unification.

As in the past, employer interests, cross-class coalitions, and the state continue to play a crucial role in supporting strong in-plant training today. Those most invested in the German system of apprenticeship are large, western German employers whose ability to compete in export markets depends on the capacity of their workforce to support constant, incremental innovation (Culpepper, 2003). These large employers dominate many of the major employer organizations in Germany, and these associations are consequently strong supporters of the existing skill provision regime. Cross-class alliances are also strong in the large firm sector, as evidenced by the proliferation of company-based employment pacts negotiated between workers' councils and large firms (Rehder, 2003). However, several fissures have emerged among employers over the relevance and cost of the training system, as they have over the issue of wage bargaining (Silvia, 1997; Thelen & van Wijnbergen, 2003; Thelen & Kume, 2006). These fissures have been compounded in eastern Germany, where economic and political restructuring have led to the development of a dual apprenticeship system that runs in practice quite differently than the western German system. In this section, we trace the contours of each of these contemporary challenges to the dual system.

Firm Size and the Cost of Apprenticeship

As shown in the previous section, one of the things that distinguishes Germany from the liberal market economies such as the United States is a high degree of employer involvement and investment in training. However, this discussion also underscored an important difference to Japan, namely, that in Germany training occurs within the context of a uniform national framework and, importantly, one in which a wide range of firms participates. In Japan, large firms are the key "carriers" of a more company-oriented system of training, and significant numbers of small and medium-size enterprises are part of a more encompassing German system. This is a direct legacy of the historical differences just sketched out, and the German system continues to rely heavily on the participation of small and medium-size enterprises. As shown in Figure 2.1, nearly 50% of all German trainees continue to acquire their skills in firms with less than 50 workers, and Germany's largest firms (500+ employees) train about the same percentage of apprentices as the country's smallest firms (1–9 employees), each accounting for approximately 20% of the apprentice "classes" of the last several years.[5]

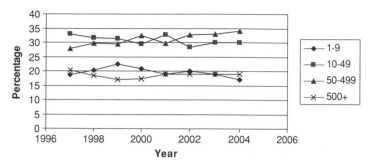

Figure 2.1. Proportion of apprentices, by firm size.

From the late 1980s to the mid-1990s, the rising costs of the apprenticeship system made apprenticeship training particularly onerous for small and medium-size firms (Wagner, 1999). Table 2.1 uses two common measures of company engagement in training to show the sharp drop in small firm training in the early 1990s. The first set of columns depicts the proportion of firms within a size category that train at least one apprentice; the second set charts the apprentice ratio, which measures the proportion of apprentices to overall employment. As Table 2.1 demonstrates, firms in all size categories decreased the amount of training they did between 1990 and 1996, and the drop was most pronounced in the smallest firms. However, after 1996, the number of apprenticeship places in western Germany stabilized again, and apprentice ratios even rebounded somewhat across companies of all sizes (although not back to 1990 levels). Therefore, as we discuss in the next section of this chapter, the main story in German training since the mid-1990s has less to do with the size of firms and much more to do with the fact that new jobs are increasingly in the service sector.

How do we evaluate the significance of the drop in small firm training during the first half of the 1990s? In this context, it is important to understand that the training that takes place in small firms, although meeting the minimal qualifications required in the German system, is typically much less technologically sophisticated than the training that takes place in large firms. Large German firms spend much more in training their apprentices than do small firms, and the training received at large firms goes far beyond the minimal requirements imposed by the chambers (Wagner, 1999). Calculations by the Federal Institute for Vocational Training suggest that the average annual costs per apprentice of firms with more than 500 employees exceed those by firms with 1 to 9 employees by *fifteen times*: the smallest firms spend only 542 euros per year, whereas the largest spend 8,176 euros per year

Table 2.1. Evolution of training behavior, by size category, 1990–2003

Size of firm	Proportion of companies training (Western states only)					Apprentice ratio (Western states only)				
	1990	1996	1999	2003	% Change 1990–03	1990	1996	1999	2003	% Change 1990–03
1–9	21.4	16.9	17.5	17.9	−16.4%	11.1	8.0	8.4	8.6	−22.5%
10–49	51.7	46.9	47.8	47.0	−9.1%	8.5	6.6	7.1	7.0	−17.6%
50–499	73.6	67.1	70.2	69.3	−5.8%	6.0	4.5	5.3	5.4	−10.0%
500+	94.3	93.2	92.6	91.6	−2.9%	5.2	4.1	4.8	5.0	−3.8%
Total	28.3	23.7	24.5	24.6	−13.1%	7.1	5.5	6.1	6.2	−12.7%

Source: BMBF (2005a).

Table 2.2. Net average annual training costs per
apprentice, by firm size

Employees	1–9	10–49	50–499	500+
Cost (euros)	542	1,423	3,402	8,176

Source: Beicht and Walden (2004: 102).

(Table 2.2; Beicht & Walden, 2004: 102). One reason that firms of different sizes
and with different production structures are able to participate in the system
is that there is a relatively high degree of flexibility in how the in-plant component of training can be organized. Large firms, which are looking to retain
most of their apprentices after training – in whom they have after all invested
so much – are more likely to have separate training facilities and to keep
apprentices out of the production process for a significant proportion of their
training terms. Small firms, in contrast, are more likely to arrange for training
to be accomplished on the job and when there are pauses in production.

The political problem of sustaining training in western Germany is therefore different for small firms than for large firms. Large firms in western
Germany make the large net investments in the combination of general and
specific skills that the dual system provides and that have contributed to the
country's status as the world's leading export nation. Large firms are therefore
highly invested in maintaining the goose that lays the golden eggs, as long as
the goose continues to lay quality eggs. The (much more numerous) small
and medium-size firms that participate in the training system are more sensitive than the large firms to changes in the costs of training; they have thus
been more directly affected by recent technological and market changes that
push in the direction of broader and more theoretical skills. In other words,
they think the costs of the goose have got well out of hand, given that regular
eggs would suit many of them just fine. At the national and industry level, the
social partners (with state support) have been quite aggressive in upgrading
(and in many cases combining) skill profiles to keep pace with market and
technological developments.[6] But these developments come bundled with
higher training expenditures, which overall small and medium-size firms are
less able to absorb. The problem may be particularly intense for those small
and medium-size firms that serve as suppliers to large firms because the latter
insist on high quality but have often increasingly taken to forcing the costs
of adjustment onto their suppliers (Casper & Hancké, 1999).

Mediating between the interests of firms of different sizes and with different production profiles is a political balancing act, and it is one that will
continue to bedevil employers' associations that try to represent groups of all

sizes. Yet, the rebound of training for German small firms since 1996 suggests that this may not be the most pressing political issue for German employers. Instead, the bigger problem lies in the failure of the dual system to persuade service sector firms to use apprenticeship as heavily as do manufacturing firms.

The Rising Service Sector

As we noted previously, western German industrial employers – especially large, manufacturing employers – continue to support the existing structure of apprenticeship training in Germany. In addition to the stabilization of the ratio of apprentices to employees since 1996, a further important indicator of the investment of such firms in the apprenticeship system is the rate at which companies hire their apprentices after their training period: the retention rate. These rates are a good measure of the extent to which firms are investing heavily in apprenticeship training because (other things equal) the more they invest in an apprentice, the more they want to retain that apprentice. According to the Institut für Arbeitsmark (IAB)-Betriebspanel, in 1995, 60% of apprentices in western Germany were hired by their training company after successful completion of their apprenticeship (Pfeiffer, 1997: 15), whereas, in 2002, 58% of apprentices were hired (Bundesministerium für Bildung und Forschung [BMBF], 2004: 152). This is a negligible difference, and it suggests that further confidence is warranted in asserting that the training behavior of companies, at least in western Germany,[7] has not changed dramatically since the mid-1990s.

Moreover, it is clear that German employers' associations demonstrate a collective commitment to preserving this system. In a context in which tripartite bargaining of any sort is rare (and where it occurs, rarely successful; e.g., the *Bündnis für Arbeit*), it is surely noteworthy that in the area of training, employers' associations are committed to working with both organized labor and the state to engage in necessary adaptations of the vocational training system. We saw this in 1984 in the metalworking industry, where, in the middle of what to them was the most bitter industrial conflict of the postwar period (over working time reduction), employers and unions successfully – and completely consensually – negotiated a complete overhaul of the metalworking trades (Streeck et al., 1987: 3–4). We saw this again more recently, in 2004, when employers' associations rallied their membership to voluntarily create 21,700 additional apprenticeship slots, an increase of 4.4% (European Industrial Relations Observatory [EIRO], 2005).[8] The relative success of this National Pact (*Nationaler Pakt für Ausbildung und Fachkräfteanwuchs*) was enough to cause the government, which preferred a voluntary solution, to set

Table 2.3. Sectoral differences in use of apprentices, 1995–2002 (western Germany)

	Percent change in no. of apprentices, 1995–2002	Apprenticeship ratio, 1995	Apprenticeship ratio, 2002
Metal, electric	−2.8	11.3	12.3
Other industrial	−9.6	6.8	7.7
Tech, scientific	−22.4	1.9	1.5
Primary services	18.5	4.4	5.1
Secondary services	−1.1	4.0	3.6

Source: Werner (2004: 59).

aside its threat of an alternative state-imposed training levy. German employers, particularly the large German manufacturing concerns that dominate the employers' associations, are clearly not walking away from the German training system on which, as we noted in the opening section of this chapter, their competitive strategies continue to rely.

However, the growth of the service sector is creating a large and expanding group of employers whose skill needs have not, thus far, made them big users of the dual system of apprenticeship training (Troltsch, 2004; Werner, 2004). The reasons for this are complex. Certainly, important German service sectors (e.g., banking) have continued to use apprenticeship in recent years as a way to attract a skilled labor force (Finegold & Wagner, 2002). Studies suggest that service sector firms can become big investors in the dual system but that their investment depends on receiving help and advice from associations and, especially, from other companies (Culpepper, 2002). For many service sectors, though, the system that has served industry so well is apparently less attractive. If the model of industrial training was a competent and broad skill base that would enable workers to participate meaningfully in the development of processes of incremental innovation, many elements of the service sector depend less on the broad technological training that is a requisite for diversified quality production.

Indeed, if we consider the evolution of training behavior among different economic sectors since the mid-1990s, it becomes clear that firms in the industrial sector augmented their apprentice ratio, even though employment in some of these sectors is shrinking. As documented in Table 2.3, firms in the metal and electronics sector increased their proportion of apprentices between 1995 and 2002, although their overall number of apprentices fell; the same is true of other industrial sectors. At the same time, the real growth in jobs, and in apprenticeships, was occurring in the primary services sector,

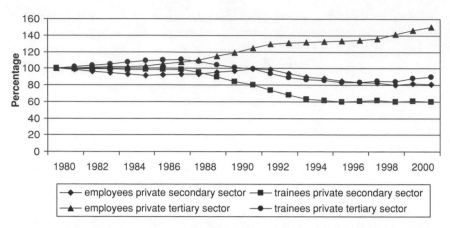

Figure 2.2. Development of apprenticeship and employment in the private secondary (manufacturing) and tertiary (services) sectors, 1980–2001 (base year 1980; western Germany only).

and apprentice ratios increased moderately in these sectors of the economy. However, these service sector jobs are replacing jobs in the industrial sectors, which tend to have higher apprentice ratios.

If we look over a slightly longer time period, it becomes clear that the disjuncture between growing service sector jobs and service sector apprenticeships dates only to 1988. In the early part of the 1980s, both jobs and apprenticeships grew in the service sector, as shown in Figure 2.2. Since then, however, service sector jobs have increased dramatically, whereas apprenticeships in the service sector have, until recent years, been on the decline. Because virtually all employment growth (to the extent that there is any in Germany) is coming from increases in employment in the service sector, the German training system – to remain stable – has to "take hold" in the service sectors to a degree that has not yet begun to materialize. We can attribute much of the difficulty of the current apprenticeship system to the fact that service sector firms have clearly not bought into the appeal of apprenticeship since 1990.[9]

In light of this gap, we are struck by the wide gulf between the challenge of the service sector for the future of German training and the political discourse surrounding apprenticeship in Germany. The short-term problem of "lacking apprenticeship places" underpinned the government's proposal for a training levy in 2004. Such a measure implies that some firms are shirking, while others are being burdened by the shirkers. This is probably a deceptive rendering of what is actually occurring. In reality, western German firms (again, especially large firms) in the manufacturing sector continue to train apprentices at relatively high levels, as a proportion of their employment. Yet, their share in the overall employment of the German economy is declining, and it is on this ineluctable fact that much of the future uncertainty of the traditional apprenticeship system must rest. The character of political discourse on the issue of training veers between extremes of saying companies are avoiding their responsibility for hiring apprentices and then plowing large sums of money into soaking up the excess youth on the labor market. New strategies for convincing service sector firms that it might be in their economic self-interest to begin using the dual apprenticeship system are not apparent in this political discourse.

Eastern Germany

The political incorporation of eastern Germany after 1990 has also set the stage for playing out the new training politics because it highlights the shifting interaction of employer organizational capacities with the level and character of state intervention in the apprenticeship system. Employers' associations in the east, faced with the twin challenges of retaining old members and attracting new ones in a difficult economic context, responded by establishing parallel associations that opted out of wage bargaining arrangements. Because wage bargaining is the central feature of German employer coordination, these new associations were likely to have less coordinating capacity (and certainly less capacity to compel their members) than traditional employers' associations. Although these organizations were capable of facilitating the information circulation required for large employers – who were in any case likely to retain apprenticeship training structures – their organizational fragility was especially marked in their relations with small and medium-size firms (Culpepper, 2003: 102–107). It was these firms who were least likely to invest in training and whose absence from the training landscape in eastern Germany is present to this day.

Fifteen years after unification, the disjuncture in the practice of apprenticeship training between eastern and western Germany remains stark. One-fourth of all apprenticeship places in eastern Germany are located outside firms. Many of the remaining in-firm places are partially subsidized by state governments. As Table 2.4 demonstrates, this is in stark contrast with practice in western Germany. The practice of out-of-firm training is marginal in western Germany. If the fundamental characteristic of the German training system is one in which employers voluntarily offer apprenticeship places in large numbers, eastern Germany is not operating according to this logic.

Table 2.4. Proportion of apprenticeship
places that are out of firm

	Western Germany	Eastern Germany
2000	4.1%	26.9%
2001	4.0%	28.2%
2002	4.8%	30.5%
2003	4.8%	32.0%
2004	4.4%	27.7%
2005	3.6%	25.3%

Source: BMBF (2006).

Table 2.4 shows stability in both areas – eastern German practice is not seeping into western Germany, but neither is eastern German practice progressively moving closer to the western German standard.

When companies are not paying to train their own apprentices – as they are clearly not in the case of out-of-firm apprentices in eastern Germany – someone has to pay for them. In Table 2.5, we have combined expenditures of the federal government and the *Bundesagentur für Arbeit* or apprenticeship training. Most striking is the absolute growth of this expenditure: between 1995 and 2003, expenditure from these two sources (but excluding state-level expenditure) more than doubled, going from 1.2 billion euros in 1995 to 2.8 billion euros in 2003.[10] As Table 2.5 shows, much of the spending comes through two programs run by the federal employment agency. In 1999, the employment agency financed 42% of the out-of-firm places, with the rest financed through federal discretionary policies; by 2003, these figures had reversed, with the employment agency sponsoring 60% of the out-of-firm places. Eastern German out-of-firm training is well on its way to becoming an established part of general German employment policies, rather than a discretionary measure created each year by the federal government.

The disequilibrated state of the eastern German apprenticeship market is, to be sure, partly a result of the general state of the eastern German economy. Yet, it also results from the deliberate choice of policy makers not to articulate public policy closely with the private information of employer associations (Culpepper, 2003). Governments of both the right and the left, for different reasons, have preferred to emphasize that training is the responsibility of the private economy rather than develop policies aimed at persuading small and medium-size firms in eastern Germany to use apprenticeship to develop

Table 2.5. Federal spending on apprentices in constant million euros (base year 2000)

Prices in millions of (constant 2000) Euros	1995	1996	1997	1998	1999	2000	2001	2002	2003
Subsidy of out-of-firm training sites	67	66	60	63	76	64	44	38	nd
Special program for additional apprenticeship places for the new (eastern) federal states	45	118	133	88	104	122	101	96	87*
Construction and removal of training sites	133	69	72	144	64	nd	nd	nd	nd
Apprenticeship assistance aid	379	465	530	523	639	716	727	1,072	1,141
Apprenticeships of young people with disabilities	564	678	735	770	752	783	827	1,113	1,163
European recovery program (ERP) for apprenticeship	0	0	99	95	63	38	19	0	0
Urgent program for reduction of youth unemployment	0	0	0	0	480	436	449	394	369
Total	**1,188**	**1,396**	**1,629**	**1,683**	**2,178**	**2,159**	**2,167**	**2,713**	**2,760**

nd, no data.

*Projected.

Source: Own calculations, based on published data in the *Berufsbildungsbericht*, BMBF 1999, 2004. This table includes federal government subsidy programs and money allocated by the federal employment agency.

future skilled labor. Rather than promoting policies that draw new firms into training, as employers (and unions) advocated, the federal government created out-of-firm places in eastern Germany, which responds to the structural imbalance of the apprenticeship market in eastern Germany, but which assumes it will eventually take care of itself.[11]

As we argue in the previous section, public intervention has often had important implications for the emergence of institutional innovations in the area of training. Although it is far too early to make definitive assessments, there is some evidence to suggest that the eastern German experience has engendered a shift in the locus of organized employer intervention in the German training system, from the national level to the regional (state) level. If we examine the state-level funding of apprenticeship in Germany in Table 2.6, two things stand out: (1) not surprisingly, eastern states are much more involved than western states in subsidizing training; and, more surprisingly, (2) eastern and western states vary among themselves, substantially, in the degree to which they attempt to intervene in the apprenticeship training system. Eastern states subsidize eight times more apprenticeship places and devote five times more money to these policies (controlling for size of apprentice population) than do the western states.

In eastern Germany, it is not only the degree, but also the character of regional intervention that varies among states. Culpepper (2003) argued that the most effective state-level policies for eastern Germany are those that bring together new training companies with existing training companies. Such partnerships, if they are structured to have a long duration, provide opportunities for new firms to learn experientially about the advantages of investing in apprenticeship training and to learn from company trainers who themselves believe strongly in the value added by dual system training. Others who have studied the eastern German training system in detail have come to similar conclusions (Lutz & Grünert, 1999). With respect to training through a *Verbund* or other sort of structured alliance, the policy practices of the five eastern German states depicted in Table 2.6 vary widely. Brandenburg devoted 57% of its subsidized training places to *Verbund*-training in 2003 and 2004, and Saxony devoted 40% of its places to such training; in the same year, Berlin devoted 28%, Saxony-Anhalt devoted 26%, and Mecklenburg-West Pomerania devoted only 25% of its subsidized places to *Verbund*-training.[12] It is analytically interesting to observe that 15 years after unification, eastern states still have dramatically different practices in terms of how they choose to subsidize apprenticeship. There has been no convergence on a single best way of coping with the problem, and it is quite possible that experimentation among states and social actors will lead to further divergence among the states.

Table 2.6. State training subsidies, eastern and western Germany

	Proportion of total places subsidized	Cost of state subsidies (million euros)	Cost/total apprentices (euros)
EG states average	**12.0%**	**14.8**	**246.0**
Saxony-Anhalt	8.2%	11,2	189.7
Berlin	6.8%	12.3	207.8
Brandenburg	9.9%	11.6	220.5
Thüringen	25.2%	13.6	246.9
Saxony	13.2%	23.8	250.9
Mecklenburg-West-Pomerania	8.7%	16.6	360.2
WG states average	**1.5%**	**3.2**	**47.1**
Baden-Wuerttemberg	0.2%	0.8	3.9
Bayern	0.7%	2.3	8.5
Nordrhein Westfalen	0.6%	4.5	13.5
Rhineland Pfalz	0.9%	1.1	13.6
Niedersachsen	0.6%	4.7	31.1
Bremen	2.4%	0.6	38.3
Hessen	3.1%	8.2	74.8
Hamburg	1.2%	2.5	76.0
Saarland	1.2%	2.0	94.4
Schleswig Holstein	4.4%	6.0	117.2

Expenditure data for Baden-Wuerttemberg, Bayern, and Berlin are from 2003.

Source: Own calculations, based on data provided by individual state statistical services.

This would represent a significant change in the governance arrangements of German training.

CONCLUSIONS AND PROSPECTS

This chapter reviews and analyzes the contributions of political science to the study of skills. Recent contributions to the skills literature (including our own work) have emphasized that employers and their associations play an extremely important role in the politics of training. Yet, it is also clear that skill demands often divide employers among themselves, and in such cases, the alliances they strike with state actors and with representatives of organized labor often determine whose institutional preferences prevail at any given moment in time. The organization of our chapter follows the logic of employer interests and the politics of training in three "passes" and with particular focus on the German case: (1) in contemporary cross-national perspective (how do skill regimes such as the German one fit into distinctive national political-economic models?); (2) in historical and comparative perspective (what kinds of employer interests and coalitional alignments supported the survival of strong apprenticeship in Germany in the first place?); and (3) in prospect for the immediate future of training in Germany (what are the forces – political and economic – that account for the observed elements of stability and erosion in the German model?).

Historically, the difference between national skill provision systems that incorporate significant in-firm training elements emerged from cross-class compromises – achieved in different ways, consolidated at different levels. Where political conflicts over skills pitted employers against emergent unions who tried to use apprenticeship as a way to gain control over the price and use of scarce skills – as in Britain and the United States – employers won, unions lost, and apprenticeship became marginal to national systems of skill provision. In contrast, in the "coordinated market economies" whose history we have studied (Germany, Denmark, Japan), firm-based training has coexisted with a variety of types of unions, but in all of these cases states have played an important role in fostering cross-class coalitions and, especially, in helping employers coordinate their activities in this area.

The national governance arrangements that emerged to govern firm-based skill provision in the three systems we studied differed in important ways among themselves. The two striking characteristics of the German dual system of apprenticeship were (1) its establishment of governance at the national level (as opposed to the plant level in Japan); and (2) its supervision through employer organizations (the chambers) rather than the state, as in Denmark. As we show in the previous section, the contemporary strains facing the dual system of apprenticeship training in Germany are serious, and they may eventually call one or both of these specificities into question. Although the system continues to work well for the large manufacturing firms in western Germany that are its staunchest supporters, the dual system faces challenges from three different directions. First, the demands of technological change have led to an expansion of the general educational requirements in dual system qualifications. This is one of a number of factors that has raised the cost of the system for firms and that has disproportionately dissuaded especially the small and medium-size firms, who are more cost sensitive on average than the large firms. Second, there is little evidence that firms in the service sector – who will provide an increasing number of the jobs of the future – find the dual system as attractive as firms in the manufacturing sectors, even in western Germany. If this continues to be the case, then the number of workers trained through the apprenticeship system will inevitably shrink as the relative size of the service sector expands. Finally, companies in eastern Germany have not been attracted by the dual system in sufficient number to provide anywhere near the amount of apprenticeship places sought by younger eastern Germans. As a result, federal and local governments have subsidized training in the east at a scale unknown in the west. Despite the potential demographic change of a shrinking number of apprenticeship-age workers in eastern Germany, there are no immediate signs that the eastern German system could run on the same voluntary terms as its western counterpart.

Indeed, the image that emerges from our analysis is that of a dual system that continues to meet the demands of Germany's largest and technologically most advanced manufacturing exporters, but that is less well placed to adapt to the conflicting set of demands now being put on the system by a broader set of employers, particularly companies in eastern Germany and in the service sector. The recent developments in the area of training bear a striking similarity to those in the area of industrial relations, where the apparent stability of German institutions of coordination belies the variety of experiments taking place at the firm level, many of which deviate from the norms of sectoral coordination. The core firms continue to play by the rules and indeed to support the rules in the dual system, but there are ever fewer firms in the core. Because those that are in the core are the large manufacturing firms who dominate the employers' associations, we do not find credible the prospect of a radical change from the current training system. Yet, we do believe that the system is being subtly reconfigured in important ways, not only through explicit state policy, but also through the behavior of firms and youth themselves. Moreover, we expect that the politics of training over the coming years will center increasingly on how the costs of vocational training in Germany are to be shared among employers, governments, and individuals.

The historical episodes we have reviewed suggest that when employers are divided, governments can play an important role in determining which set of employer preferences prevails. Our analysis of the current situation in Germany reinforces this expectation. The federal government and the federal employment agency have already stepped into the breach in the eastern German labor market. Their structural role in the system gives them a strong incentive and voice in influencing the directions of reforms in eastern German labor markets. However, the most likely direction of state intervention in the governance of the system seems to come from the federal states themselves. Those state governments are far less concerned than the federal government with preserving the national governance arrangements of the dual system, and much more concerned with creating the conditions under which many employers are interested in hiring apprentices. The disparities we show in the structure of state subsidy programs are the most visible instantiation of this prospect.[13] State-level experiments in reallocating the costs of dual system training would allow for groups of employers and unions to try to build various new arrangements to attract smaller firms and/or those working in the service sector. It is too early to say whether such experiments will succeed, although they are already under way, especially in the east.

If, as we hypothesize, the renegotiation of the political compromises underlying the dual system was to occur at the state (rather than the national) level, would this favor any given sort of compromise over others? Obviously, it militates against a large-scale directive intervention by the national government, although given German federalism and the preferences of most social actors, the failure of such an outcome is overdetermined. It is worth pointing out that the discourse of the national training levy, in which the federal government threatens to compel nontraining firms to contribute to a training fund (as in France), has little support in the actual coalitions we find on the ground in training politics. It has thus far proved a symbolic weapon used to extract promises from employers' organizations rather than a real instrument by which the state monitors the system. Given that neither the federal government nor employers have any interest in encouraging federal takeover of the system, this is an unlikely vector of change.[14]

More likely, in our view, is a dual system in which costs are shifted in explicit or subtle ways to the states or federal government – for example, through direct subsidies for more collectivized training provision for small and service sector employers, or by shifts in the balance between the in-plant and school-based components of training more generally. The dual system cost compromise involves not only firms and the government, but also individuals whose contribution in the traditional structure of the dual system has been to forego higher wages by accepting their apprenticeship wage in exchange for high-quality training and, often, preferential access to internal labor markets. If the earlier phases of training involve collective training centers for small firms, or if the balance shifts toward a wider range of educational institutions becoming more important in training, it is likely that individuals will also be asked to pay more of the costs of this general skills training.

Renegotiating social compromises is delicate and incremental work, especially in a polity with as many veto points as we see in Germany. It is not yet clear, at least to us, where this renegotiation will lead. However, the conflicts among German employers about the balance of the system indicate that this conversation has already begun.

Notes

1. We thank Steffen Duemig and Nicole Richardt for excellent research assistance, and Uli Mayer, Heike Solga, and Karin Wagner for comments on this chapter.
2. For an extended discussion of the relationship between earlier models of the political economy and the current literature on the varieties of capitalism, see Thelen (2002).
3. This categorization can be criticized for collapsing firm-specific skills and occupational skills into the same broad category, "specific." Wolfgang Streeck's work, discussed previously, distinguishes the two and lays out the distinct logics, and elsewhere Thelen has explored the historical sources and important differences in the dynamics and operation of regimes based on firm-specific skills versus those based on occupational skills (Thelen, 2004, 2006). Coordinated market economies also differ among themselves and change over time, with respect to their relative emphasis on specific versus general skills. See Culpepper (2007) for a discussion of the different trajectories pursued in Austria and Switzerland over the postwar period.
4. The argument that is presented here is spelled out in detail, with historical evidence, in Thelen (2004). We also draw on a summary version of the historical argument, including comparison to the Danish case that appears in Thelen (2007).
5. Of course, a much higher percentage of large firms offer training as compared to smaller firms. Although 90.4% of all firms with 500 or more employees offer apprentice places, only 16.8% of the smallest firms (1–9 employees) offer training places (BMBF, 2005a). However, in absolute terms, there are of course far more small firms than large firms involved in training – in 1995, more than 200,000 very small firms (1–9) offered training places versus 4,241 large (500+) firms (Wagner, 1999).
6. One sees this, for example, in significant reorganizations of skill profiles for particular industries (reforms in metalworking in the 1980s), as well as in the recent major initiatives on the part of the National Vocational Training Institute to update training ordinances on a relatively broad scale (e.g., BMBF, 2000: 8ff, 2001: 145ff). The BMBF reports that recent years have seen the "biggest modernization push since 1969 when the Vocational Training Law was passed" (BMBF 2005b: 2). More than half of all new training contracts are now in occupations that have been modernized in recent years (ibid). In fact, overall average training periods, as a result of these kinds of changes, have steadily increased over the past decades, rising from just less than 34 months in 1980 to just less than 37 months by 2003 (Bundesinstitut für Berufsbildung [BIBB], 2005: Figure 7.1).
7. The retention rate in eastern Germany was 44% in 2002, well below the western German norm and indicative that companies may not be investing heavily in training there.
8. This was accomplished against the threat from the government to impose a training levy, but it was no secret that the government much preferred a voluntary solution. The same thing (threat of training levy followed by a concerted, voluntary, and highly successful effort on the part of employers' associations to increase training slots) had also occurred in the 1970s (Baethge, 1999; Thelen, 2004: 266).

9. School-based alternatives to the dual system have consequently acquired a more prominent place in the universe of German vocational training. The Berufsfach-schulen, which offer school-based vocational training and are regulated at the state level rather than by the federal vocational training law, saw their enrollment grow by roughly 2.5 times between 1988 and 2003 (www.bibb.de/de/wlk8246.htm# literatur).

10. These values are based on constant (year 2000) euros. Tables 2.5 and 2.6 were assembled with the help of Steffen Duemig, whose research assistance we gratefully acknowledge.

11. Demographic movements may ultimately validate this governmental choice. After 1990, the birth rate in eastern Germany plummeted. As of 2005, these numerically smaller age cohorts have begun to enter the apprenticeship market (Brandenburg, 2004: 81). Between 1990 and 2003, the younger than 1 age cohort in Germany decreased by more than 20%. This is a dramatic shift, one which may have an impact on the youth labor market and on other parts of the German political economy (cf. Brosi, 2004).

12. Thuringia actually subsidized 88% of all its subsidized places through *Verbund*-aid, but this aid represented much less money per actual training relationship subsidized than in Saxony or Brandenburg.

13. The rising importance of training at the Berufsfachschulen, whose vocational certificates are not controlled through the federal vocational training law but instead at the state level, are another such indicator.

14. It is also worth noting that this sort of discourse tends to frame skills as a battle across the class divide, with employers accused by unions of failing in their responsibilities to provide training places. The historical evidence we have presented suggests that such a configuration of the political landscape may not lead to a protection of in-firm training. Countries that have imposed a levy (e.g., France, Australia) have failed to persuade employers to buy into a system that is not voluntary (Culpepper, 2003).

References

Acemoglu, D., & Pischke, J. (1998). Why do firms train? Theory and evidence. *Quarterly Journal of Economics*, 113(1), 79–119.

Acemoglu, D., & Pischke, J. (1999). Beyond Becker: Training in imperfect labour markets. *Economic Journal*, 109, F112–F142.

Albert, M. (1993). *Capitalism versus Capitalism*. New York: Four Walls Eight Windows.

Aoki, M. (1994). The Japanese firm as a system of attributes: A survey and research agenda. In M. Aoki & R. Dore (Eds.), *The Japanese Firm: Sources of Competitive Strength* (pp. 11–40). Oxford, UK: Clarendon Press.

Ashton, D., & Green, F. (1996). *Education, Training, and the Global Economy*. Cheltenham, UK: Edward Elgar.

Baethge, M. (1999). Glanz und Elend des deutschen Korporatismus in der Berufsausbildung. *Die Mitbestimmung Online*, 4, 15.

Beicht, U., & Walden, G. (2004). Kosten der Ausbildung. In U. Beicht, G. Walden, & H. Herget (Eds.), *Kosten und Nutzen der betrieblichen Berufsausbildung in Deutschland* (pp. 21–168). Bonn, Germany: Bertelsmann Verlag.

Boyer, R. (1997). French statism at the crossroads. In C. Crouch & W. Streeck (Eds.), *Political Economy of Modern Capitalism: Mapping Convergence & Diversity* (pp. 71–101). London: Sage.

Brandenburg, B. (2004). Zur Lage auf dem Lehrstellenmarkt in Ost- und Westdeutschland. *Wirtschaft im Wandel*, 3, 78–84.

Brosi, W. (2004). Ausbildungsbeteiligung der Jugendlichen und ein Versuch einer kurz- und mittelfristigen Vorausschätzung. In *Der Ausbildungsmarkt und seine Einflussfaktoren* (pp. 115–128). Results of Expert Workshop, Bundesinstitut für Berufsbildung, Bonn, Germany, July 1–2.

Brown, P., Green, A., & Lauder, H. (2001). *High Skills: Globalization, Competitiveness, and Skill Formation*. Oxford, UK: Oxford University Press.

Bundesinstitut für Berufsbildung (BIBB). (2005). *Schaubilder zur Berufsbildung: Strukturen und Entwicklungen*. Bonn, Germany: Author.

Bundesministerium für Bildung und Forschung (BMBF). (1999). *Berufsbildungsbericht*. Bonn: Author.

Bundesministerium für Bildung und Forschung (BMBF). (2000). *Berufsbildungsbericht*. Berlin: Author.

Bundesministerium für Bildung und Forschung (BMBF). (2001). *Berufsbildungsbericht*. Berlin: Author.

Bundesministerium für Bildung und Forschung (BMBF). (2004). *Berufsbildungsbericht*. Berlin: Author.

Bundesministerium für Bildung und Forschung (BMBF). (2005a). *Berufsbildungsbericht*. Berlin: Author.

Bundesministerium für Bildung und Forschung (BMBF). (2005b). *Reform der Berufsbildung*. Available at: www.bmbf.de/de/1644.php.

Bundesministerium für Bildung und Forschung (BMBF). (2006). *Berufsbildungsbericht*. Berlin: Author.

Casper, S., & Hancké, B. (1999). Global quality norms within national production regimes: ISO 9000 standards in the French and German car industries. *Organization Studies*, 20(6), 961–985.

Culpepper, P. D. (2002). Associations and non-market coordination in banking: France and Eastern Germany compared. *European Journal of Industrial Relations*, 8(2), 217–235.

Culpepper, P. D. (2003). *Creating Cooperation: How States Develop Human Capital in Europe*. Ithaca, NY: Cornell University Press.

Culpepper, P. D. (2007). Small states and skill specificity: Austria, Switzerland, and inter-employer cleavages in coordinated capitalism. *Comparative Political Studies*, 40(6), 611–637.

Estevez-Abe, M., Iversen, T., & Soskice, D. (2001). Social protection and the formation of skills: A reinterpretation of the welfare state. In A. Hall & D. Soskice (Eds.), *Varieties of Capitalism: The Institutional Foundations of Comparative Advantage* (pp. 145–183). New York: Oxford University Press.

European Industrial Relations Observatory (EIRO). (2005). *Gesamtmetall Proposes Reforms of Education System*. Available at: www.eiro.eurofound.eu.int/2005/05/feature/de0505105f.html.

Finegold, D., & Soskice, D. (1988). The failure of training in Britain: Analysis and prescription. *Oxford Review of Economic Policy*, 4(3):21–53.

Finegold, D., & Wagner, K. (2002). Institutional determinants of firms' training decisions: The case of German bank apprenticeships. *Industrial and Labor Relations Review*, 55(4), July, 667–85.

Goldthorpe, J. H. (Ed.). (1984). *Order and Conflict in Contemporary Capitalism*. New York: Oxford University Press.

Gordon, A. (1985). *The Evolution of Labor Relations in Japan: Heavy Industry, 1853–1955*. Cambridge, MA: Harvard University Press.

Hall, P. A. (1986). *Governing the Economy: The Politics of State Intervention in Britain and France*. New York: Oxford University Press.

Hall, P. A., & Soskice, D. (Eds.). (2001). *Varieties of Capitalism: The Institutional Foundations of Comparative Advantage*. New York: Oxford University Press.

Iversen, T. (2005). *Capitalism, Democracy and Welfare*. New York: Cambridge University Press.

Iversen, T., & Soskice, D. (2001). An asset theory of social policy preferences. *American Political Science Review*, 95(4), 875–893.

Katzenstein, P. J. (1985). *Small States in World Markets*. Ithaca, NY: Cornell University Press.

Kristensen, P. H. (1997). National systems of governance and managerial prerogatives in the evolution of work systems: England, German and Denmark compared. In R. Whitley & P. H. Kristensen (Eds.), *Governance at Work: The Social Regulation of Economic Relations* (pp. 3–48). Oxford, UK: Oxford University Press.

Kristensen, P. H., & Sabel, C. F. (1997). The small-holder economy in Denmark: The exception as variation. In C. F. Sabel & J. Zeitlin (Eds.), *World of Possibilities: Flexibility and Mass Production in Western Industrialization* (pp. 344–380). New York: Cambridge University Press.

Lauder, H. (2001). *Innovation, Skill Diffusion, and Social Exclusion*. Oxford, UK: Oxford University Press.

Lutz, B., & Grünert, H. (1999). *Evaluierung der Vorhaben zur Förderung der beruflichen Erstausbildung*. Magdeburg, Germany: Ministerium fur Arbeit, Frauen, Gesundheit und Soziales des Landes Sachsen-Anhalt.

Mares, I. (2000). Strategic alliances and social policy reform: Unemployment insurance in comparative perspective. *Politics & Society*, 28(2), 223–244.

Pfeiffer, B. (1997). Das Ausbildungsangebot der westdeutschen Betriebe 1995 – Ergebnisse des IAB-Betriebspanel. *BWP*, 26(2), 10–16.

Piore, M., & Sabel, C. F. (1984). *The Second Industrial Divide: Possibilities for Prosperity*. New York: Basic Books.

Rehder, B. (2003). *Betriebliche Bündnisse für Arbeit in Deutschland: Mitbestimmung und Flächentarif im Wandel*. Frankfurt/Main: Campus.

Schmitter, P. (1974). Still the century of corporatism? *The Review of Politics*, 36(1), 85–131.

Silvia, S. (1997). German unification and emerging divisions with German employers' associations: Cause or catalyst? *Comparative Politics*, 29, 2.

Smith, M. (2000). Warning over IT skills gap. *Financial Times*, March 7, 3.

Soskice, D. (1991). The institutional infrastructure for international competitiveness: A comparative analysis of the UK and Germany. In A. B. Atkinson & R. Brunetta (Eds.), *The Economics of the New Europe* (pp. 45–66). London: Macmillan.

Soskice, D. (1994). Reconciling markets and institutions: The German apprenticeship system. In L. M. Lynch (Ed.), *Training and the Private Sector: International Comparisons* (pp. 25–60). Chicago: The University of Chicago Press.

Streeck, W. (1991). On the institutional conditions of diversified quality production. In E. Matzner & W. Streeck (Eds.), *Beyond Keynesianism* (pp. 21–61). Aldershot, UK: Edward Elgar.

Streeck, W., Hilbert, J., van Kevalaer, K.-H., Maier, F., & Weber, H. (1987). *The Role of the Social Partners in Vocational Training and Further Training in the Federal Republic of Germany.* Berlin: CEDEFOP.

Taira, K. (1978). Factory labour and the Industrial Revolution in Japan. In P. Mathias (Ed.), *The Cambridge Economic History of Europe: Volume VII, Part 2* (pp. 166–214). New York: Cambridge University Press.

Thelen, K. (2002). The political economy of business and labor in the developed democracies. In I. Katznelson & H. V. Milner (Eds.), *Political Science: The State of the Discipline* (pp. 371–397). New York: W.W. Norton & Company.

Thelen, K. (2004). *How Institutions Evolve: The Political Economy of Skills in Germany, Britain, the United States and Japan.* New York: Cambridge University Press.

Thelen, K. (2006). *The Future of German Vocational Training, in Light of Its Past.* Manuscript, Northwestern University, Evanston, IL.

Thelen, K. (2007). Skill formation and training. In G. Jones & J. Zeitlin (Eds.), *The Oxford Handbook of Business History* (pp. 558–580). Oxford, UK: Oxford University Press.

Thelen, K., & van Wijnbergen, C. (2003). The paradox of globalization: Labor relations in Germany and beyond. *Comparative Political Studies, 36*(8), 859–880.

Thelen, K., & Kume, I. (2006). Coordination as a political problem in coordinated market economies. *Governance, 19*(1), 11–42.

Troltsch, K. (2004). *Berufsbildung und Strukturwandel – Zum Einfluss wirtschaftsstruktureller Veränderungen auf das betriebliche Ausbildungsstellenangebot seit 1980.* Ergebnisse des Experten-Workshops, Bundesinstitut für Berufsbildung, Bonn, Germany, July 1–2.

Wagner, K. (1999). The German apprenticeship system under strain. In P. D. Culpepper & D. Finegold (Eds.), *The German Skills Machine: Sustaining Comparative Advantage in a Global Economy* (pp. 37–76). New York: Berghahn Books.

Werner, D. (2004). Ausbildung zwischen Strukturwandel und Investitionskalkül. In *Der Ausbildungsmarkt und seine Einflussfaktoren* (pp. 53–66). Results of Expert Workshop, Bundesinstitut für Berufsbildung, Bonn, Germany, July 1–2.

Zysman, J. (1983). *Governments, Markets, and Growth: Financial Systems and the Politics of Industrial Change.* Ithaca, NY: Cornell University Press.

When Traditions Change and
      Virtues Become Obstacles

Skill Formation in Britain and Germany

Steffen Hillmert

INTRODUCTION

In recent years, there has been an increasing interest in cross-national comparisons of education and training systems. But how similar or different are national skill systems? To what extent, how, and why do they change? The public and scientific discourse about the modern "knowledge society" seems to imply that they will follow uniform trends rather than take specific pathways. Still, the attractiveness of particular national "models" may change over time, with varying success and different demands put on them. This leads to the following general questions:

1. Is there one best way of organizing vocational training systems?
2. How stable are national skill systems over time?
3. If systems are different, do relative advantages and disadvantages change over time?
4. To what extent can the systems be deliberately changed?

This chapter analyzes the questions of the reproduction and transformation of skill systems from a sociological perspective by focusing on two particular cases. As a study on contemporary changes in skill systems, it emerges from an historical *comparison of the skill formation systems in Germany and Britain* since World War II, with a special emphasis on developments during the 1990s. As advanced and economically competitive societies, Germany and Britain face, in principle, comparable economic challenges. When looking at these two cases more closely, however, one finds functionally equivalent solutions to similar problems as well as more specific problems and different economic strategies. The aim of this chapter is to demonstrate how and why the two skill systems – often labeled as representatives of "high skill regimes" and "low skill regimes," respectively – differ.

As it turns out, Germany and Britain have taken specific pathways in attempts to adapt to specific challenges regarding adequate skill provision. Different trends in the skill systems of Germany and Britain become visible, especially during the 1990s. The recent trends can be characterized as radical and incremental change, respectively, and they cannot be adequately described as a mere process of one country catching up in terms of its average qualification level. Rather, there is evidence for *long-term consequences* in the specific, historically evolved logic of skill formation in the two countries. It will be argued that this *path dependency* can best be understood by looking at "microlevel" differences (i.e., differences in the individual rationales of skill investment as well as different transition and life course patterns).

This chapter is structured as follows. The next section outlines the conceptual framework of an international comparison of skill systems that emphasizes microlevel links between the vocational training system and other institutions. Following these distinctions, the next section presents an historical account of training systems and school-to-work transitions in Britain and the former West Germany after World War II, and until the late 1980s. Although any clear-cut historical periodization is to some extent arbitrary, results from analyses of this phase may be used to explain the developments in the following decade. Comparing the two countries, it becomes clear that fundamental differences in the institutions guiding the process of labor market entry evolved in the postwar period. The subsequent section provides evidence that these differences have also been crucial for the recent developments in the 1990s. The final section provides concluding observations.

LINKS OF THE TRAINING SYSTEM: A FRAMEWORK FOR COMPARISONS

As major institutions (still) act on the level of the nation-state, there exists an increasing sensitivity in both research and public debates about international institutional differences. This applies, in particular, to the consequences for education, training, and the labor market. The criteria that are used to evaluate the performance of training systems vary, but the most common (see also Ryan & Büchtemann, 1997) are measures of *output* (high proportion of young people in at least upper secondary education, high standards of training, broad coverage) and measures of *efficiency* (fast transitions to employment, low levels of youth unemployment, effective allocation as measured by terminations of training contracts and later job stability). Direct measures of *impact* (particularly on economic performance) are less common.

Still, a different task is to *explain* the structure and the developments of training systems, and they cannot be evaluated without a deeper understanding of the political functioning of the economies in which they are embedded and that this chapter emphasizes. To characterize the complex institutional configurations, use can be made of ideal-type aggregate typologies that have gained some prominence, not least in the form of welfare state regimes that differ in the degree of "decommodifaction" of labor by welfare provision (Esping-Andersen, 1990). Such typologies allow allocating various countries to a limited number of types in a simple way and hence to reduce analytical complexity considerably. More directly related to the field of labor market–oriented skill formation are distinctions between various forms of capitalism as they have been proposed by comparative political economy (Albert, 1992; Hall & Soskice, 2001). Political economies differ in the degrees and the forms of internal coherence, for example, between the financial sector, firm cooperation, and production strategies due to typical features of social interaction, such as the degree of trust in social relations. In particular, the Anglo-Saxon model of "liberal market economies" and the continental (or Rhineland) model of flexibly "coordinated market economies" are distinguished, assuming a systemic nature of institutional configurations where particular types of institutions are necessarily associated with each other. As a consequence, it is often assumed that these configurations are relatively stable. This assumption can first be contested with respect to empirical variability. Second, it can be argued in theoretical terms that the creation and sustaining of institutions need to be supported by the activities of social actors. As a consequence, institutional changes are themselves a prominent topic for sociological explanation (see, e.g., Streeck & Thelen, 2005).

To explain specific developments in training systems, one needs to look more closely at the (institutional) links with their major social contexts, allowing also for conflicts and dysfunctional relationships. Studies in political economy have often concentrated on the role of corporate actors in sustaining and changing these links. A complementary strategy, which is also pursued in this chapter, is to look at typical individual-level situations involved in the process and the consequences of skill formation. This, of course, raises the question of how to actually relate the qualification process on the individual level to relevant institutions. There is a wide gap between the explanation of macrostructures and the trajectory of individual behavior (see also Mayer, 1997), and it can be assumed that many individual transitions are structured by a complex variety of historically changing institutions – not necessarily showing consistent effects. It should also be noted that institutions may also serve more "latent" functions. Training institutions, for example, may not

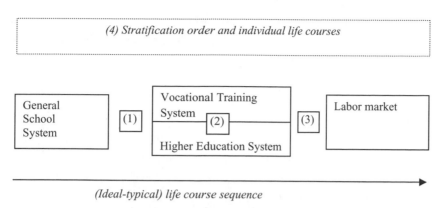

Figure 3.1. Skill production systems and selected links with other subsystems within a society.

only provide skills and qualifications, but also keep young people out of a difficult labor market.

The following paragraphs intend to keep the conceptual framework rather simple, but to make some of the more direct relationships more explicit in order to account for the typical configurations and specific developments of national skill systems. They look at links between the system of skill formation and other subsystems as they are reflected by both institutional regulations and specific market conditions. Both have implications for individual-level experiences and decisions (Figure 3.1). The following paragraphs provide further descriptions of these links.

General Schooling and Further Education and Training

In the formal structure of educational systems (labor market related), further education and training normally succeed general school education. One of the main relationships between these systems is that a preselection for various tracks of training already occurs within the general school system. Direct institutional links are set by entry requirements and regulations regarding access to further training programs from general education. In some instances, this also holds true for transitions in the reverse direction or forms of parallel education and training ("second chance education").

In the first instance, school qualifications are entitlements for further education that individuals may use or may not use. However, in combination with the quantitative output at different levels of the general school system, they define the pool of possible competitors for specific levels of further education. Empirically, there is often an inherent tendency to make use of such entitlements, so that a collective upgrading in general school education may exert a "supply-side pressure" on specific (higher) forms of further education.

Vocational Training and Higher Education

Various forms of training vary in their accessibility, structure, content, and consequences. For reasons of simplicity, this chapter distinguishes just two broad forms of postcompulsory education: vocational training (be it primarily firm- or school-based training) and higher education.

On the microlevel, vocational training and higher education are alternative or even competing pathways for the generation and employment of skills (by employers) and for the educational decisions made by individuals. Such choices will be at least partly based on relative returns to different training options in the labor market, be it due to their signaling capacity (Spence, 1973) or the amount of actual general or firm-specific human capital that they carry (cf. Mincer, 1974).

Although this relationship already points to links with the labor market, there are also more or less institutionalized links between various parts of the training system itself. Variation in this regard concerns the degree to which courses and degrees in one path of the further training system provide access to an alternative path, hence defining the "permeability" of the system of skill production.

Training and the Labor Market

Any modern economy faces the problems of providing sufficient qualifications and allocating workers efficiently. Therefore, national systems of education and training tend to be linked to the labor market. However, the degree of coordination between educational and employment systems may vary considerably between societies (Hillmert, 2001). Not only the intrafirm, but also the societal division of labor determines which qualifications are regarded as essential for particular jobs (cf. Windolf & Wood, 1988). Because training profiles often correspond to career paths, the structures of qualification systems remain relevant beyond the immediate point of entry into the labor market.

The links between the subsystems of employment and training are, on the one hand, affected by the degree to which information on the aggregate demand of necessary qualifications is successfully transmitted from the employment to the training system. In this regard, features of the institutional structure of the training system are important, such as whether training is provided directly by employers, who tend to have immediate information on their skill needs. In some cases, vocational training may even include an employment contract. Relevant information for individual choices made before entering training programs is also transmitted by the situation of preceding cohorts (e.g., by how many and which kinds of jobs they were offered on completion of training).

On the other hand, when looking at the skill output from the employers' point of view, the quantity and the quality of attained skills, as well as an efficient allocation, are of major importance. The balance between aggregate skill supply and demand is a necessary but insufficient condition for a close match at the level of the individual. One major allocative mechanism is that formal qualifications carry a high amount of information for potential employers and can hence serve as screening devices in recruitment procedures. These screening capacities are likely to be influenced by how educational systems are regulated and formally structured. Educational systems can be classified, for example, along the dimensions of *stratification* and *standardization* as proposed by Allmendinger (1989). However, as to the question of allocation, once again, the labor market relevance of vocational training is even more important, inclusive of whether vocational training is provided at the workplace or in schools.

For individuals, of course, among the most important consequences of their qualifications are their consequences in the labor market. Segmentation theories and the theory of closed positions (Doeringer & Piore, 1971; Sørensen & Kalleberg, 1981) have made it clear that the labor market may be internally differentiated with a particular structure, which is not least defined by formal entry requirements into specific occupations and positions (most notably, the public service). Hence, the concept of competition in the labor market cannot be reduced to competition about wages as a function of human capital. There may also be considerable competition regarding positions and opportunities, and the type of aspired job will determine the level of required qualifications. In most cases, the level of entry positions is especially important with regard to the prospect of further careers.

Social Stratification Order and Life Courses

In a sociological perspective, society plays a major mediating role in any of these linking processes. Labor market outcomes and other effects of qualifications cannot be understood in economic terms alone; they always have social implications in terms of social inequality. The assumption here is not that economic outcomes per se, but rather socially evaluated outcomes, form the basic foundations for regulations and individual decisions. For example, what counts as "essential skills" that need to be taught is open to social definition. The same holds true for acceptable durations of transition periods, importance of income levels, job positioning, and promotion chances that transform economic consequences into central aspects of the stratification order. It is important to note this aspect when examining the impact that perceived consequences of formal qualifications might have on individual decisions taken regarding investment in particular forms of qualification.

Consequently, social stratification also has a direct influence in transmitting differences in qualification over the generations. Among the most prominent examples is the high degree to which early selection within the school system is influenced by social origin. According to the theory of Breen and Goldthorpe (1997), for example, the main rationale of schooling decisions by parents is to preserve their original social status, attainable only on successfully completing particular educational tracks.

Studying such microlevel links is essential because there is normally no simple way to observe the development of aggregate skill supply and demand in a society independently of one another. Rather, they are constrained by each other. Assuming a systemic nature of the institutions that are involved, international differences may be conceptualized in the form of life course regimes (Lessenich, 1995; Mayer, 2001). It is also important to study such effects over time: consequences of qualification may evolve over a longer period, and training decisions are often long-term decisions. Hence, one may look at particular transitions people make between different parts of the education and training system and labor market, as well as longitudinal measures of stability (e.g., job durations). However, only in an ideal-typical sense, the general school system, vocational training, and employment form a clear sequence that all individuals follow. In reality, one also finds reverse orders, multiple and parallel episodes of both training and work.

A perspective that primarily looks at the situation of individual actors seems, in the first instance, not to focus on institutional change, but tends to emphasize adaptive processes within a given institutional structure. It is unlikely that individual actors are able to change institutional structures. However, imbalances that show up at this level are often the starting point for institutional adaptation and change put forward by collective actors and implemented by state regulation.

The following sections present examples for such links between institutions and life courses. To enter into greater detail, this chapter presents an historical comparison of two countries rather than a multicountry comparison (a type of research prevalent in many macroeconomic studies).

TRAINING SYSTEMS AND THEIR CONSEQUENCES IN BRITAIN AND WEST GERMANY UNTIL THE 1980S

Education and Training

The system of education and training is probably the most important determinant for the process of transition to the labor market. Despite some common, long-term historical traditions (in particular, apprenticeships for artisans), for most of the period after World War II, the national systems of general and vocational education in Germany and Britain have shown important differences[1] (see also Hillmert, 2001, 2002). In a long-term historical comparison of skill systems (Thelen, 2004), it becomes clear that changes can be both sudden and incremental, and that the circumstances of the generation of these systems need to be distinguished from their present way of functioning. The following summary describes major differences after World War II through the 1980s.

BRITAIN

For our focus period, the British system of education and training can be characterized by a relatively clear distinction between general education and vocational training. Important developments in general education after World War II include successful attempts to standardize, and subsequently, also to centralize general education by raising the minimum school-leaving age, by introducing general school qualifications, and, finally, by instituting a national curriculum and standardized testing at various stages of the schooling career. Since the 1960s, most of the schools have become comprehensive schools, but the differentiation among various levels of (postcompulsory) school qualifications has, in many respects, taken the function of different school tracks and become important means of selection by employers. In addition, a small but influential sector of high-status private schools has retained social relevance. Academic training in Britain has been rather general and has had a relatively high reputation, but there has also been a clear hierarchy with regard to specific academic institutions.

Vocational training has been heterogeneous and often basic. Traditional forms such as apprenticeships have been limited to the manufacturing sector and have declined dramatically in number since the 1960s. Forms of school-based training have increased, and secondary school qualifications have gained growing importance as selection criteria in the labor market, especially in the service sector (Windolf, 1984). For decades, governments have attempted to upgrade the collective level of training. In the case of the *Youth Training Scheme* or *Youth Training* programs, which were introduced progressively since 1983, this has been closely associated with measures to thwart high rates of youth unemployment. As part of market-oriented reforms during the 1980s, efforts have been made to introduce standards for practical and transferable vocational skills, particularly in the form of *[General] National Vocational Qualifications* (NVQ/GNVQ), an integrated five-tiered classification system of general and vocational qualifications.

For young people, an alternative to any kind of formalized vocational training has, however, always been prominent: leaving school relatively early and entering employment immediately. In fact, the majority of young people finishing school has entered the labor market without any formal vocational training, some acquiring qualifications on a part-time basis parallel with employment (Kerckhoff, 1990). The normative standard has often been a fast transition to the labor market at any cost (cf. Bynner & Roberts, 1991). Given the low skill strategies of many British employers (and formerly, also trade union influence focused on pay, rather than qualification issues), they could expect to earn reasonable wages despite having received no or only restricted on-the-job training. The consequence of this has been that, despite overall educational expansion, there has been a considerable proportion of persons who have acquired only general school qualifications, if any (cf. Figure 3.2).

When asking about the underlying institutional configurations, one finds that Britain can serve as an example of a "deregulated liberal market economy," which has relied more on individual bargaining than on coordination. British enterprises have acted under conditions of high-profit orientation, a lack of mutual trust, and a relatively short-time perspective. Therefore, they have often been reluctant to invest in long-term training. Moreover, in a highly flexible labor market, there has been no particular requirement for training as a screening period for long-term personnel. If one looks at the role corporate actors have played in the regulation of training after World War II, one of the main results is that the trade unions in Britain aimed at retaining control over skill formation in the workplace. Therefore, training has been regarded as an issue of conflict in industrial relations, with the employers looking for low skill strategies where possible, preferring on-the-job training and continuing education, and relying on academically trained personnel for higher positions. Trade unions had an interest in keeping vocational

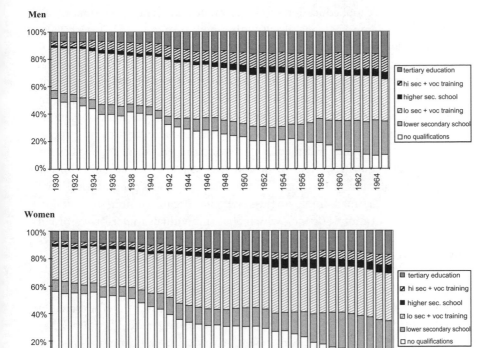

Figure 3.2. Highest qualification of the British birth cohorts 1930–1965. *Source:* British Household Panel Survey 1995 (birth cohorts combined in 5-year moving averages).

boundaries but – even in collective institutions such as the Industrial Training Boards during the 1960s and 1970s (Dingeldey, 1996) – showed little interest in a standardized, general supply of training. Not least as a result of such market failures, the United Kingdom (UK) has traditionally been regarded as having a skill deficit or a "low skills equilibrium" (Finegold & Soskice, 1988).

WEST GERMANY

Compared with the UK, there appears to have been more continuity in the German educational system after World War II. Qualification paths have been well established, and this has allowed for individual planning with a longer time perspective than under the conditions of the more dynamic, market-oriented system in Britain.

Secondary school education has largely followed hierarchical tracks, and the early selection has gone along with a high degree of social selectivity. Higher education has often been directed to specific occupational fields – especially in technical studies – and relatively standardized. There has also been a hierarchy between the traditional universities and the lower-level institutions of tertiary education (*Fachhochschulen*), which were introduced in the 1970s. Although participation in tertiary education has increased, vocational training has remained the standard experience for most young people. It has been commonly accepted as necessary and has formed the basis for further skill acquisition. Apart from the *dual system*, which accounts for the largest part of training, there have also been school-based forms of vocational training. The German employment system has organized human capital in the form of vocations (*Berufe*), which allow individuals to perform a broad range of related, rather complex tasks and incorporate the concept of a career with prospects on the basis of initial vocational training.

After World War II, Germany also experienced a major educational expansion that actually started before major structural changes were introduced in the educational systems. As Figure 3.3 indicates, educational expansion across birth cohorts (regarding vocational and higher qualifications) has been especially marked for women who have attained a near equal share of participation in the dual system and whose numbers dominate school-based vocational training.

Using the terms of comparative political economy, Germany comes close to the ideal-typical model of a "flexibly coordinated market economy." This is generally characterized by corporatist decision making and long-term trust relationships that allow control over free-riding behavior associated with training provision. Centralized wage bargaining in Germany has reduced the possibility of employers offering high wages in order to recruit qualified personnel who were trained elsewhere – thereby saving the costs of internal training. In turn, reducing the probability of "poaching" trained workers has increased the incentive for employers to provide training (Streeck, 1989). The corporatist nature of decision making in German industrial relations and strong associations of both employers and workers have facilitated trust for investments in general skills and have allowed for a longer time perspective in the actors' decision making. This has been further enhanced by close interfirm ties, a system of long-term finance, and a successful transfer of technology from technical universities. Vocational training has been regulated by legislation relatively late (especially the *Berufsbildungsgesetz* of 1969), but employers have a long tradition of a commitment to a high level of transferable skills, coordinated by intermediate institutions (e.g., chambers of commerce). The

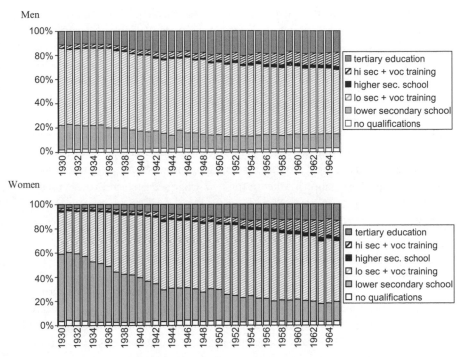

Figure 3.3. Highest qualification of the West German birth cohorts 1930–1965. *Source:* German Microcensus 2000.

responsibility for training and certification has been shared among different institutions; instructors have been required to meet the standards; and formal qualifications are, therefore, widely recognized by employers. For the majority of young people finishing school, training in the dual system has been the standard route toward employment at an intermediate level, including occupations in the service sector. In addition, it is not only the informative ("signaling") capacity of vocational credentials that offers a close connection to the labor market. Although not combined with an employment contract, apprenticeships can already be regarded as entry positions that grant employers a long screening period for future personnel.

School-to-Work Transitions and Early Careers

This brief overview (for details, see Hillmert, 2001) may provide a basis for an interpretation of individual-level consequences. In Britain, criteria such as timing (referring especially to individual age) rather than (occupation-)specific formal qualifications have ruled labor market integration, although educational expansion and an increasingly difficult labor market have weakened their importance since the 1960s; the level of general educational credentials has always had importance for job allocation. Not least due to the influence of unions, occupational boundaries in many British industries were previously quite rigid. Over the past three decades, they have increasingly become weaker, so that the role of specific qualifications is also likely to have further decreased. Legal requirements were traditionally low, and the youth labor market, in particular, was further deregulated during the 1980s (Ashton et al., 1990), so that internal labor markets have coexisted with a large "secondary" labor market in the low-wage sectors (cf. Brown, 1990).

In contrast to this, Germany can be regarded as a model for a combination of a widespread skilled occupational labor market with (higher-level) internal and lower-level labor markets (Blossfeld & Mayer, 1988). Regarding both education and labor market policies, institutional change appears to have been much greater in Britain than in Germany, especially since the early 1980s. In Germany, both the level of education and substantive occupational skills have been major criteria of job allocation. In general, the standardized and (horizontally and vertically) differentiated education and training system in Germany, as well as more cooperative industrial relations, have allowed for a higher degree of coordination between skill production and employment than in Britain.

Major differences in the transition behavior of individuals in both countries can already be inferred from descriptive summaries (Hillmert, 2002). Young Germans have spent longer periods in education and training. The vocational training system has played a considerable role in smoothly integrating young people into the employment system, although waiting times and military service for men have led to extended transition periods, larger numbers returning to education, and relatively late entries into the labor market. There has always been a larger dispersion of ages at labor market entry, but this has been quite stable across birth cohorts. In Britain, entry into the labor market was, initially, highly standardized with respect to age, but since the 1970s there appears to have been a significant change with the age differentials rising considerably. This is, on the one hand, due to an expansion and differentiation of higher-level education and training and, on the other hand, to increasing difficulties for young people to find stable employment (Coffield, 1995; Roberts, 1995).

Another aspect concerns access to particular entry positions. As previous studies of status attainment processes have shown, the association between formal qualifications and social positioning appears to be closer in Germany than in the UK (Brauns et al., 1997; Müller & Shavit, 1998). Analyses by Hillmert (2002) have confirmed a stratification of (entry) job positions by formal qualifications for both countries over a longer period of time. In both the UK and Germany, formal qualifications have obviously been an essential condition for entry into skilled work at various levels, but in Germany, these differences have been much more significant. For example, labor market entrants with intermediate vocational qualifications (i.e., apprenticeship or equivalent) have had a significantly lower chance of entering higher service positions compared to people with higher (academic) degrees, even if the public sector with well-defined qualification requirements has become less relevant as the provider of (higher) entry positions in Germany. The relative difference between Germany and Britain is, however, even larger when comparing qualifications at lower levels. So, for people with vocational training, it has been much easier to gain access to routine nonmanual and skilled manual work than for people without any formal credentials (or only with general school qualifications). In general, formal qualifications have been more important predictors of successful transitions to adequate jobs in Germany than in Britain. Additional analyses suggest that this reflects not only differences in the allocative capacity of formal credentials, but also a better coordination of supply and demand for qualifications in Germany and "skill deficits" in Britain. On average, the level of stratification by qualifications appears to have decreased slightly across birth cohorts since 1940. In Germany, however, this process originated at a very high level. Moreover, there has been an increasing difference between the quality of (very) first jobs and first stable jobs, which form part of a longer career. This is visible especially for service class positions; in many cases, these positions are obviously entered into after previous entry jobs. The following analyses now look at individual employment subsequent to labor market entry.

Figure 3.4 displays a cohort comparison of the stability of first employment as indicated by the dimensions: median tenure with first employer, median tenure in entry occupation (two-digit International Standard Classification of Occupations 68), and median tenure in entry social class position (11 Erikson-Goldthorpe-Portocarero categories as defined by Erikson & Goldthorpe, 1992), all of them measured in years. These median durations were calculated for a number of successive birth cohorts, whereby "entry conditions" were defined in two different ways: the very first job and the first stable job (with 2 years minimum duration).[2] It should be noted, however, that labor market entry is measured *after* the completion of vocational training. In the case of firm-based training (e.g., the prominent *dual system*

Britain

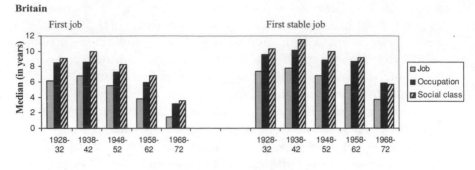

West Germany

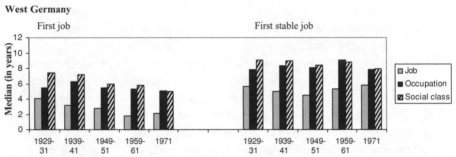

Figure 3.4. Mean duration with first employer/in entry occupation/in entry class: product-limit estimates (medians, in years), by birth cohort product-limit estimations. *Source:* British Household Panel Study; German Life History Study (cf. Hillmert, 2002).

in Germany), overall firm tenure is normally longer. This means that the average stability of German careers is underestimated in these analyses.

In our case, most interesting is a comparison of the various configurations formed by the three dimensions of employment stability.[3] In the UK, the median durations have always been closer together; that is, people have been more likely to leave their occupation and social class when leaving their first employer. In contrast, in Germany, the median episodes of entry occupation (and social class) have been much longer than the equivalent entry jobs: on average, people have stayed in their occupation (and their class position) when leaving their first employer. This obviously means that occupation-specific skills could be transferred between different employers and that strong occupational labor markets do exist. In the British case, human capital has been more closely bound to particular firms.

As one can see, the stability of (very) first jobs has declined across the five birth cohorts that are presented in this chart. For the UK, the trend is similar when one looks at the very first or the first stable job: mobility has increased in all three dimensions, which reflects a major shift from a high proportion of protected employment to an increasingly flexible, deregulated labor market. In West Germany, the pattern of the three median durations has been remarkably stable over time, especially regarding the first stable job. Also, the phase of entry into the labor market has become more extended, and the difference between transitory and stable entry jobs has increased significantly for the younger cohorts. Apart from this period of "settling in," however, the first position at labor market entry has proved to be highly relevant for the quality of the further career, although this career is not necessarily bound to the first employer. This indicates that the impact of the level of formal qualifications and occupational labor markets have remained strong, as has institutional regulation. In separate analyses for men, who have more stable careers than women, these results become even clearer (Hillmert, 2001). It can be seen that, compared to the time in their first job, most German men remained in their initial occupation for a long time.

In sum, these empirical indicators suggest that the importance of formal qualifications at labor market entry has only partly been similar in Britain and West Germany over the past decades. Formal (vocational) qualifications have clearly been more relevant for successful entry and stable early careers in Germany. In Britain, this has been true to a much lower extent with the system of general and academic education being more important than that of vocational training. Moreover, changes in Britain have been more marked.

Consequences for Employers' and Individuals' Rationales

Decisions of skill investment made by both employers and young people can be regarded to be to a larger degree based on expectations concerning the consequences of qualifications in the labor market. Hence, successive cohorts of labor market entrants may be influenced in their behavior by the experiences of preceding cohorts. On the basis of the observed developments in the two skill systems between the World War II and the late 1980s, the actors' situations concerning decisions about vocational education and training in the two systems can be summarized in a stylized way.

In Britain, a comparatively low level of trust and a lack of coordination among employers have prevented long-term strategies of providing standardized vocational training that would be able to send clear signals to potential employers and successive cohorts of applicants. Given an increasingly flexible labor market and further promoted by the weakening of vocational boundaries that were traditionally supported by (occupation-based) trade unions, the time perspectives of individual actors for the investment in skills have been relatively short. Therefore, no thorough collective upgrading of vocational skills could be achieved. As a means of qualifying for higher-level positions, staying in school (and maybe opting for higher education) was likely to be the preferred pathway for young people who met the demands and selection criteria of the schools. However, for many the desirability to stay in school remained limited as long as reasonable employment chances for preceding cohorts of low-skilled workers signaled the lower achieving youth that early dropout was an alternative for them.

In contrast to the British situation, in Germany coordination among employers and other social actors, standardized vocational qualifications, and institutionalized occupational fields have secured a relatively high level of trust concerning the future value of vocational skill investments and allowed for the actors involved to have a long-term time perspective. This has provided incentives for both employers and trainees to invest in vocational training (Soskice, 1994a). High average occupational stability, observable for a number of successive cohorts, supported long-term investments by both individuals and employers in occupation-specific skills that, under such conditions, obviously had a good chance to pay off. Moreover, this helped establish it as a normative standard and permitted the organization of collective interests along these lines. The stratification by qualifications has also been supported by close institutionalized links with various levels of public service employment. Higher education has remained limited as a consequence of a limited expansion of upper secondary education, and the fact that the German production system has heavily relied on vocationally trained workers. Although there have been no formal requirements to enter most of the vocational training programs, changes in the general school system have led to a change in the qualification composition of young people entering vocational training. Training in the dual system has become a reasonable alternative for higher secondary school graduates, somewhat blurring the established hierarchy between vocational and academic training. This change was certainly enforced by popular pessimistic predictions about the future employment perspectives of higher education graduates.

In summary, by the end of the 1980s, fundamental differences in the situations that actors within the skill systems of Britain and Germany faced when making their decisions had evolved that led to the UK being seen as representing a "low skills equilibrium" and West Germany a "high skills equilibrium." Since then, both systems of skill formation have undergone numerous changes. However, the longer-term differences have still had significant consequences for the more recent developments in the two systems of skill formation.

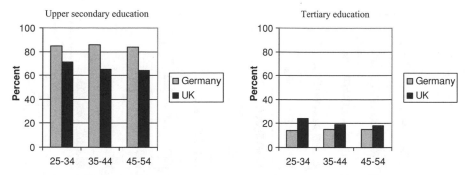

Figure 3.5. Proportion having completed upper secondary education and completed tertiary (degree-level) education, by age group, in Germany and the UK (2003). *Source:* OECD (2005) (data from German Microcensus/British Labor Force Survey).

DEVELOPMENTS SINCE THE EARLY 1990S

At first glance, the present qualification distribution of the population at workforce age (cf. Organisation for Economic Co-operation and Development [OECD], 2005) may confirm traditional perceptions of the skill situation in the two countries, with Germany being a case of a "high skills regime" and Britain more a case of a "low skills regime." One reason for this is that there are still marked differences in the economic structure, with the German economy putting more emphasis on the industrial sector and Britain more emphasis on the trade sector (OECD, 2006). What is masked by such an aggregate analysis, however, is historical change, as a simple breakdown by age group suggests[4] (Figure 3.5). Although the age groups in Germany are relatively similar with regard to educational attainment, in Britain the younger age groups reflect a significantly higher proportion of completed upper secondary and tertiary education than older age groups. Recent graduation rates from tertiary (degree-level) education in Germany hover around 20% (data of 2002); roughly two-thirds of the graduates are from universities, with students enrolled in programs lasting 5 years or more. In the UK, graduation rates approach nearly 40%, with the vast majority of students completing shorter courses of study (OECD, 2005).

These rates suggest that, in recent years, Britain has taken major steps in the direction of a collective upgrading of skill levels, especially in higher education, while there have been no comparable changes in Germany. When looking at youth unemployment rates (Figure 3.6), it should be noted that unemployment rates from different (international) sources are not always consistent. Still, these rates indicate similar levels of youth unemployment, and again, the trend over time looks more favorable in the case of the UK.

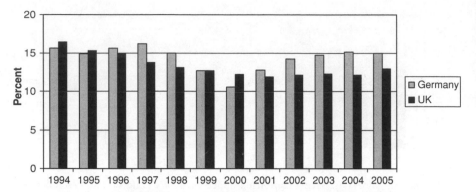

Figure 3.6. Standardized youth unemployment rates (younger than 25 years), 1994–2005. *Source:* Eurostat (2006).

BRITAIN

The widely recognized traditional British "skill deficit" (Layard et al., 1994) led to reforms on various levels of vocational training during the 1990s. Among the developments was, first, the spread of the NVQ/GNVQ system. Although this classification system had been already introduced in the mid-1980s, it was further extended during the 1990s. The basic principles of the NVQ/GNVQ system are modularization and competence-based certification. The idea behind the latter concept is that certification be output oriented rather than a credit for pure "time serving." Although this system was designed according to practical employers' needs, critics have pointed to problems of low acceptance and relatively low rates and long durations of completion. The system did not set standards for training procedures (Deißinger, 1994), and a further weakness appears to have been deficient examination standards; moreover, a modular system may prevent young people from seeking broader transferable skills (Oulton & Steedman, 1994). It seems to still be unclear whether young people are actually in a position to make the appropriate choices necessary and the extent to which this will result in distinguishable skill profiles.

A second reform was the introduction of *(advanced) modern apprenticeships* in an attempt to establish new relationships between collective actors. Introduced in 1995/96, the number of apprenticeship entrants already amounted to approximately 90,000 (increasing) or nearly 14% of the youth population in 1998 (Ryan & Unwin, 2001). Based mainly with larger employers and also supported by public subsidies, modern apprenticeships not only involve a regulation of competencies, but are also closely linked to employment. They were organized first by the *training and enterprise councils* and later the *learning and skills councils*. Again, there were no process requirements such as regulations on duration or the methods of teaching. Among the additional critical points mentioned by observers are still little involvement of many employers, a lack of financial support by employers, problems of initial assessment of entrants, lacking components of general education, informational asymmetry between providers and recipients of training, and relatively low completion rates of less than 50% (Ryan & Unwin, 2001). Traditional major problems of the British skill system – the lack of the power of coordinating intermediate institutions and relatively short time perspectives associated with decisions of skill investment – could obviously not be solved. Also, given the tradition of early employment without training, there are obviously still age barriers for entering apprenticeship training.

A third part of the reforms had even more the character of a training scheme targeting youth unemployment. This was the introduction of the *New Deal for Young People* (since 1998), a mandatory program directed toward young people who were unemployed for more than half a year. Among others, education and training has been one option that young people could choose within this welfare-to-work program. However, *employability* rather than skills attainment has been the major goal of this labor market instrument.

When reviewing the various attempts to reform the system of vocational education and training in Britain, the general impression is that there have been many changes and experiments without finally tackling the deficit in intermediate vocational skills. From the viewpoint of the literature on varieties of capitalism (Hall & Soskice, 2001), the major reason for this is that the institutional (context) structure has just not been adequate for this. As a result, young people in Britain were still facing two major alternatives: either staying on the academic route for higher secondary school qualifications and beyond, or getting to work immediately. However, the trend in economic structure toward services (which so far has been more pronounced in Britain than in Germany), as well as an associated decline in the demand for unskilled manual labor, have made this option less and less acceptable. When the increasing need for a higher skilled workforce became even more urgent in the 1990s, it seemed therefore to be consequential that the UK took an alternative pathway to further attempts of enhancing vocational training: a trend toward mass higher education.

This change in strategy was certainly supported by common experiences of high levels of youth unemployment during the 1980s. Another important step was the introduction of National Targets for Education and Training since the early 1990s, where benchmark proportions for particular skill levels were defined. This initiative was put forward by the government, but had actually been pushed by employers and one of their major associations, the Confederation of British Industry. These targets were, in the first instance,

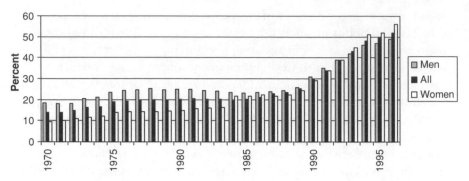

Figure 3.7. Estimated gross enrolment rates in tertiary education,[5] United Kingdom, 1970–1996. *Source:* United Nations Educational, Scientific, and Cultural Organization (1980–1999).

directed at secondary education (e.g., for the year 2000, a 60% proportion was set for A levels or NVQ/GNVQ level 3). However, there were important indirect consequences. Many graduates from upper secondary education were likely to make use of their skill investments, and they wanted to progress further toward qualifications at a higher level. As a consequence of this "supply-side pressure," demand for higher education was rising. In fact, educational expansion in Britain during the 1990s has been remarkable with about 50% of young people born after 1970 holding an A-level degree or above (Smith, 2000: 209). Also the quantitative expansion of tertiary education after 1990 was significant (cf. Figure 3.7).

With regard to academic education, there has clearly been an end to the traditionally elitist character of the higher education system (Halsey, 2000). This is especially true for the time after 1992 when the distinction between traditional universities and the polytechnics (established since the 1960s) was formally abolished. The expansion of higher education was not only, but especially due to the former polytechnics.

At first glance, this development seems to be consistent with the arguments in favor of a radical change toward mass higher education as an economic strategy put forth by authors such as Soskice (1994b). In fact, decomposition estimates indicate that although economic growth has been mainly driven by labor productivity, in the UK this productivity growth can to a considerable extent be attributed to an increase in aggregate human capital (OECD, 2005). When looking more closely, however, it becomes clear that the consequences were somewhat different from the original targets. In particular, the expansion did not take the form of school-based training intermediate (technical) skills, but rather within the "soft" subjects on the BA level of (new) university training, and courses have often been heterogeneous with

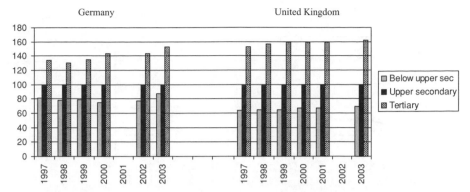

Figure 3.8. Relative earnings (before tax), by qualification level (1997–2003). Index 100 = mean earnings of workers holding upper secondary qualifications. *Source:* OECD (2005) (data from Geman Microcensus/British Labor Force Survey).

respect to content and quality standards. In this regard, it is interesting to compare the fields of study of British and German graduates of higher education. Students in Germany are much more likely to graduate in technical fields such as engineering.

In sum, there is an indication of marked changes in skill supply in Britain during the 1990s. Given the further trend toward a service economy (and also a demographic decline in the number of youth), employers were beginning to change their skill strategies. Having experienced long-term problems with vocational training, they did not opt for the provision of intermediate skills but in favor of graduates from upper secondary school and from institutes of higher education. The ensuing decrease in the demand of young and unskilled workers sent a clear signal to potential school leavers who responded accordingly and now increasingly stayed in school after the end of compulsory schooling. The result was a fairly rapid upgrading in the formal qualification levels attained by young people even in the face of potential overqualification (Brynin, 2002; Roberts, 2004).

Still, in recent years, at least monetary returns to higher levels of education have obviously been relatively stable (cf. Figure 3.8). This again indicates that the expansion of higher education was associated with parallel changes in labor market demand.

GERMANY

The situation in Germany in the 1990s has been different than the British situation. The foremost involvement of employers in the dual system of vocational training, a high level of institutionalized coordination between

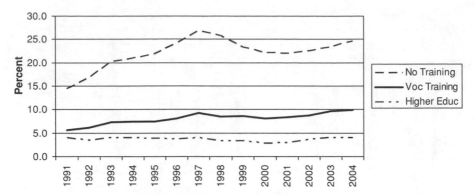

Figure 3.9. Qualification-specific unemployment rates, West Germany, 1991–2004.
Source: IAB (2005).

collective actors, and deeply rooted occupational structures of the German labor market supported a strong emphasis on the creation of medium-level vocational skills as both a collective and an individual goal. The expansion of higher education has remained limited, not least to a limited expansion of the higher secondary school tracks that preselect university entrants. There have definitely been enormous challenges for firms as potential providers of training: increasing international competition with a need to reduce costs and to accelerate innovation, the trend toward services, declining coordination among employers, and, moreover, the economic demands following German unification. However, these challenges were to be met within the conventional structures of the skill system. There have been a number of innovations (e.g., the introduction of new vocational profiles), but structural change in the German education and training system in general has been limited, and participation in higher education had remained relatively stable.

Over the past decades, the unemployment levels of unskilled workers have been relatively high, emphasizing the relative advantage of vocational training. However, after 1990, there has also been an increasing difference between the unemployment risk of graduates from higher education – whose unemployment rate remained fairly stable – and workers with medium-level vocational training – whose unemployment rate almost doubled (cf. Figure 3.9).

When looking at young people, it is remarkable that, in addition to the unemployed, there is also a substantial proportion of young people in the "transition system" (i.e., state measures of qualifying below apprenticeship level and labor market integration); in fact, it has become the most common experience for school leavers with no or lower-level school qualifications (Konsortium Bildungsberichterstattung, 2006).

Together these indicators suggest that the German experience after 1990 is not just an example of "efficient path dependency" of skill production and employment, but that there are also signs of dysfunctional rigidities (cf. also Mayer & Hillmert, 2003). They concern not least the core of the German skill formation system, the dual system of vocational training. The central position of vocational education and training within the German skill system makes its successful development crucial for school-to-work transitions and the overall labor market situation of German youth. In 2003, nearly one-third of young people leaving the dual system experienced at least a short period of unemployment after having completed training (Bundesministerium für Bildung und Forschung [BMBF], 2005: 232).

These figures may reflect a worsening of the relative position of these skilled workers in the "labor queue" (in the sense of Thurow, 1975) rather than absolute skill deficits. However, there are also other indicators that are more directly related to the functional capability of the vocational training system. The overall number of training places within the dual system has declined over recent years. While in the 1980s and early 1990s, this was also demographically induced; since then, there has obviously been a decreasing willingness of employers to provide training. There has also been an increasing awareness of the heterogeneity among apprenticeships as reflected by different financial investment and individual employment chances after completion.

Long-term calculations of the number of employed and registered unemployed at various qualification levels (Institut für Arbeitsmarkt- und Berufsforschung [IAB], 2005) suggest that since the early 1990s, high skilled jobs were the only category that still expanded, while intermediate skill levels stagnated (or people with intermediate skills were increasingly displaced) and demand for low-skilled jobs showed a moderate decline. Hence, higher education has become an increasingly attractive alternative for young people finishing school (even if the expected wage premium has been smaller than in many other countries). Additional pressure on the system of vocational training comes from the move toward a system of BA/MA courses in higher education in accordance with the Bologna Process launched by the European Union. Structural change has been associated with a considerable reduction of absolute employment in manufacturing during the 1990s, which has traditionally been the core area of the dual system and which still accounts for a comparatively high share of total employment in Germany. The service sector has been the only sector with employment growth, but its share is still smaller than in Britain.

Open to debate is the extent to which the conditions for the "German model" to operate successfully still exist (Streeck, 1997; Culpepper, 1999).

Some indicators, such as the fact that a larger number of school leavers from upper secondary tracks do enter apprenticeships, suggest that (higher levels of) apprenticeships have remained attractive. The reported problems of vocational training, therefore, do not necessarily imply a suggestion for Germany to follow the British way; given the variety of training systems (cf. Lauterbach, 2000) and their dependencies on specific institutional contexts, an international transfer of particular elements of skill systems is often unrealistic. However, these problems indicate that the German vocational training system is in urgent need of adaptation.

Special problems for the dual system have arisen, especially from the economic situation in East Germany, where, as yet, no adequate structure of enterprises that may provide training has been established, and where a good deal of training is state-supported, out-of-firm training. Even when leaving the problems in East Germany aside, scientific observers have mentioned a number of current deficiencies of the German vocational training system. Among them are (Geißler, 1991; Rothe, 2001; Baethge, 2003) the insufficient adaptation to the changing occupational structure (especially in the service sector) and the insufficient "permeability" between general and vocational education. Although there is no early differentiation into "vocational tracks" within the school system, there is early selection among secondary school tracks within the general school system that, for many, entails clear restrictions for later stages of training.

The problematic situation of low-skilled youth is further intensified by the fact that an increasing proportion of graduates from higher secondary schools has entered the dual system of vocational training, often in combination with higher education (Hillmert & Jacob, 2004; Jacob, 2004). Although this indicates that (higher-level) vocational training courses have been successfully adapted to contemporary demands, lower educated school dropouts are in increasing danger of being displaced by the higher qualified. Measures of requalifying low-skilled and unemployed youth according to an idea of standardized "normal biographies," as expected by the German skill system, have often proved to be ad hoc, protracting individual transitions ("measurement careers") and not leading to enduring labor market integration (Solga, 2005). The considerable volume of these measures has certainly masked rising youth unemployment. Moreover, an upgrading of training may cause structural problems of insufficient supply of apprenticeships, especially if small firms cannot meet the higher standards of more theory-oriented training within primarily firm-based training.

Given the increasing need for continuing education and retraining along the life course, occupational boundaries and the organization of the training system along lines of sectors and industries may present yet another obstacle. So far, a standardized system of high-quality retraining has not been established. Such a system would probably be a complement to the existing vocational training system, but rising skill demands will probably also lead to a larger differentiation within the system of initial vocational education and training. Recent reforms such as the amendment of the Vocational Training Act (Berufsbildungsgesetz) in 2005 may have led to some improvements to the problems mentioned. For example, it facilitates crediting prequalificational phases in the course of acquiring vocational training certificates. Still, the development of links, as well as the competition between general and vocational education, will be crucial for the future performance of the German vocational training system.

BRITAIN VERSUS GERMANY

In sum, the 1990s made the different "strategies" to meet the skill demands in the two countries even more explicit. Both systems have shown a considerable capacity of adaptation, whereby Britain has shown more *radical* change and Germany rather *incremental* change.

Britain has experienced long-term difficulties with the provision of (intermediate) vocational training. Therefore, a strategy of a "gradual" upgrading of skills could not be successfully implemented when there was decline in the demand for low-skilled labor and the skill deficit became urgent. In effect, Britain took a more radical change in its skill policy with an emphasis on mass higher education. The "success" of upgrading skills has been mixed if one takes forms of intermediate vocational training into account, but a combination of deliberate political strategies and individual responses has changed the overall skill composition considerably.

In contrast, the skill situation in Germany has, at least at first glance, been much more stable. Relying on long-established practices and relationships involved in the training process, the German skill system has tried to adapt within the given skill strategy. This has, however, obviously led to rigidities and increasing problems for skill provision and individual labor market chances, especially at the lower quality end of the vocational training system. It is not easy to assess how functional the adaptations that both skill systems have undergone have been. However, in Germany, labor market problems of many young people on the one hand and a comparatively slowly growing service sector on the other hand may indicate a dysfunctional momentum in the way in which preceding institutional conditions put constraints on future changes.

CONCLUSION AND OUTLOOK

As a comparative case study, this chapter looks at empirical developments within two specific training systems, the German and the British, but it may also help to answer the more general questions that appear in the first section. Looking at both indicators of output and efficiency, the results can be summed as follows:

1. In principle, vocational training systems can be organized successfully in very different ways, but their structures entail specific advantages and disadvantages. Moreover, this general conclusion might have to be modified when better (comparative) evidence on the quality of training becomes available. It should also be noted that the results of an evaluation always depend on the relative weight that is put to specific criteria of efficiency and the values behind them. These may also relate to the more latent functions of training systems such as social integration.
2. As the case of Britain demonstrates, skill systems are not necessarily stable over time but may adapt to specific challenges. There are marked long-term *historical changes* in skill formation. In Britain, this applies, in particular, to labor market–related context factors such as the weakening of occupational boundaries and the decline of traditional sectors offering apprenticeships. In recent years, fundamental changes have affected the quantitative composition of various tracks of the educational system, indicating a change in the dominant strategy of skill formation.
3. Relative advantages and disadvantages of training systems may change over time as a result of changes in the economic environment in which these systems operate, and traditional virtues may become obstacles. The highly differentiated and regulated German system of primarily firm-based vocational training seems to come under particular pressure by ongoing trends such as the development of the occupational structure toward services.
4. At the same time, policies of intervention are, at least in middle-range perspective, constrained by the specific configurations of institutions and the typical strategies of the actors that are associated with them. Both historical change and the salience of contexts in the sense of national configurations of institutions can be regarded as manifestations of system-specific historical path dependencies. Path dependency

in this sense is not to be equated with overall stability, but rather with specific developments that *depend* strongly on previous conditions and that are also *constrained* by them.

Future evaluation research (cf. also Descy & Tessaring, 2005) will have to focus more on both empirical indicators of *quality* (i.e., individual competencies) and on the (net) *impact* of skill formation, particularly on economic performance. The second important area of research is concerned with the connections between the collective skill output and individual-level life chances. Such aspects of social inequality manifest themselves in individual chances of access to training and in the permeability of qualification tracks. However, a collective upgrading of skills will probably not be a sufficient solution of problems of (youth) unemployment (Crouch et al., 1999). One way or the other, all advanced societies take part in a positional competition of educational expansion, and it is in particular the lower skilled that will continue to be in need of better-targeted training and social policy.

Finally, the question arises as to which way forward can be expected for the two skill systems. Common economic trends such as the recognized need for more frequent retraining and lifelong learning may make the recent British way of mass higher education increasingly attractive. Together with an international standardization of higher education, this will further increase the pressure of adaptation on a training system such as the German one, with a traditionally strong emphasis on medium-level, occupation-specific vocational qualifications. This form of education and training will adapt to perceived rising skill demands only if it offers institutionalized links with forms of higher education and continuing education.

Notes

1. Although not explicitly mentioned in this chapter, one should also be aware of important institutional and structural differences among the various parts of the UK and among the German *Länder*. The examples given in this section concentrate on England and Wales; the discussion of the German system is confined to West Germany.
2. This "stronger" criterion shifts the point of labor market entry beyond periods of exclusively short-term employment that may, for example, still represent temporary work episodes during training.
3. In contrast to the absolute level of mobility, the relative differences between the three dimensions are probably biased to a minor extent by recall error, an aspect

that may contribute to unusually high employment stability in the older cohorts, especially in the British case.

4. This interpretation of age group comparisons as cohort change leaves aside some data problems with "censored" observation (i.e., the fact that, especially in Germany, people in the younger age group are still likely to attain higher-level qualifications).

5. Gross enrollment ratios are defined as "all students enrolled in tertiary education/population ages 19 to 23." This definition leads to an overestimation of absolute enrollment rates because there are also students of other ages, but in the case of the UK, where student populations have traditionally been rather standardized with regard to age, this estimation may still be useful.

References

Albert, M. (1992). *Kapitalismus contra Kapitalismus.* Frankfurt/Main: Campus.

Allmendinger, J. (1989). Educational systems and labor market outcomes. *European Sociological Review,* 5, 231–250.

Ashton, D. N., Maguire, M., & Spilsbury, M. (1990). *Restructuring the labour market: the implications for youth.* London: Macmillan.

Baethge, M. (2003). Das berufliche Bildungswesen am Beginn des 21. Jahrhunderts. In K. S. Cortina, J. Baumert, A. Leschinsky, K. U. Mayer, & L. Trommer (Eds.), *Das Bildungswesen in der Bundesrepublik Deutschland. Strukturen und Entwicklungen im Überblick* (pp. 525–580). Reinbek, Germany: Rowohlt.

Blossfeld, H.-P., & Mayer, K. U. (1988). Labor market segmentation in the Federal Republic of Germany: An empirical study of segmentation theories from a life course perspective. *European Sociological Review,* 4, 123–140.

Brauns, H., Müller, W., & Steinmann, S. (1997). *Educational expansion and returns to education: A comparative study on Germany, France, the UK, and Hungary.* MZES Working Paper I/23, University of Mannheim.

Breen, R., & Goldthorpe, J. H. (1997). Explaining educational differentials: Towards a formal rational action theory. *Rationality and Society,* 9, 275–305.

British Household Panel Survey (1995). Colchester: Institute for Social & Economic Research.

Brown, R. K. (1990). A flexible future in Europe? Changing patterns of employment in the United Kingdom. *British Journal of Sociology,* 41, 301–327.

Brynin, M. (2002). Overqualification in employment. *Work, Employment and Society,* 16, 637–654.

Bundesministerium für Bildung und Forschung (BMBF). (2005). *Berufsbildungsbericht 2005.* Bonn, Germany: Author.

Bynner, J., & Roberts, K. (Eds.). (1991). *Youth and Work: Transition to Employment in England and Germany.* London: Anglo-German Foundation for the Study of Industrial Society.

Coffield, F. (1995). Always the trainee, never the employee? Increasingly protracted transitions in the U. K. In A. Cavalli & O. Galland (Eds.), *Youth in Europe* (pp. 45–62). New York: Pinter.

Crouch, C., Finegold, D., & Sako, M. (1999). *Are Skills the Answer? The Political Economy of Skill Creation in Advanced Industrial Countries.* Oxford, UK: Oxford University Press.

Culpepper, P. D. (1999). The future of the high-skill equilibrium in Germany. *Oxford Review of Economic Policy*, 15, 43–59.

Deißinger, T. (1994). Das Reformkonzept der 'Nationalen beruflichen Qualifikationen'. Eine Annährung der englischen Berufsbildungspolitik an das 'Berufsprinzip'? *Bildung und Erziehung*, 47, 305–328.

Descy, P., & Tessaring, M. (2005). *The Value of Learning: Evaluation and Impact of Education and Training*. Luxembourg: European Centre for the Development of Vocational Training.

Dingeldey, I. (1996). Wandel gewerkschaftlicher Strategien in der britischen Berufsbildungspolitik der 1980er und 1990er Jahre. *Politische Vierteljahresschrift*, 37, 687–712.

Doeringer, P. B., & Piore, M. J. (1971). *International Labor Markets and Manpower Analysis*. Lexington, MA: Heath Lexington Books.

Erikson, R., & Goldthorpe, J. H. (1992). *The Constant Flux: A Study of Class Mobility in Industrial Societies*. Oxford, UK: Clarendon Press.

Esping-Andersen, G. (1990). *The Three Worlds of Welfare Capitalism*. Princeton, NJ: Princeton University Press.

Eurostat. (2006). *Langfristindikatoren Bevölkerung und soziale Bedingungen*. Available at: http://epp.eurostat.ec.europa.eu.

Finegold, D., & Soskice, D. (1988). The failure of training in Britain: Analysis and prescription. *Oxford Review of Economic Policy*, 4, 21–53.

Geißler, K. (1991). Das Duale System der industriellen Berufsausbildung hat keine Zukunft. *Leviathan*, 19, 68–77.

German Microcensus (2000). Wiesbaden: Statistisches Bundesamt.

Hall, P. A., & Soskice, D. (Eds.). (2001). *Varieties of Capitalism: The Institutional Foundations of Comparative Advantage*. Oxford, UK: Oxford University Press.

Halsey, A. H. (2000): Further and higher education. In A. H. Halsey & J. Webb (Eds.), *Twentieth Century British Social Trends* (pp. 221–253). Basingstoke, UK: Macmillan.

Hillmert, S. (2001). *Ausbildungssysteme und Arbeitsmarkt. Lebensverläufe in Großbritannien und Deutschland im Kohortenvergleich*. Wiesbaden, Germany: Westdeutscher Verlag.

Hillmert, S. (2002). Labour market integration and institutions: An Anglo-German comparison. *Work, Employment and Society*, 19, 675–701.

Hillmert, S., & Jacob, M. (2004). *Multiple Episodes: Training Careers in a Learning Society*. GLOBALIFE Working Paper 64. Bamberg, Germany.

Institut für Arbeitsmarkt- und Berufsforschung (IAB). (2005). *IAB Zahlenfibel*. Available at: www.iab.de/asp/fibel.

Jacob, M. (2004). *Mehrfachausbildung in Deutschland: Karriere, Collage, Kompensation?* Wiesbaden, Germany: VS Verlag für Sozialwissenschaften.

Kerckhoff, A. C. (1990). *Getting Started: Transition to Adulthood in Great Britain*. Boulder, CO: Westview Press.

Konsortium Bildungsberichterstattung. (Ed.). (2006). *Bildung in Deutschland: Ein indikatorengestützter Bericht mit einer Analyse zu Bildung und Migration*. Bielefeld, Germany: Bertelsmann.

Lauterbach, U. (2000). *Internationales Handbuch der Berufsbildung*. Baden-Baden, Germany: Nomos.

Layard, R., Mayhew, K., & Owen, G. (Eds.). (1994). *Britain's Training Deficit: The Centre for Economic Performance Report*. Aldershot, UK: Avebury.

Lessenich, S. (1995). Wohlfahrtsstaatliche Regulierung und die Strukturierung von Lebensläufen. Zur Selektivität sozialpolitischer Interventionen. *Soziale Welt*, 46, 51–69.

Mayer, K. U. (1997). Notes on a comparative political economy of life courses. *Comparative Social Research*, 16, 203–226.

Mayer, K. U. (2001). The paradox of global social change and national path dependencies: Life course patterns in advanced societies. In A. Woodward & M. Kohli (Eds.), *Inclusions and Exclusions in European Societies* (pp. 89–110). London: Routledge.

Mayer, K. U., & Hillmert, S. (2003). New ways of life or old rigidities? Recent changes in social structures and life courses in Germany and their political impacts. In H. Kitschelt & W. Streeck (Eds.), *Germany: Beyond the Stable State*. West European Politics 26, 4/2003 (Special Issue), 79–100.

Mincer, J. (1974). *Schooling, Experience and Earnings*. New York: Columbia University Press.

Müller, W., & Shavit, Y. (1998). The institutional embeddedness of the stratification process: A comparative study of qualifications and occupations in thirteen countries. In Y. Shavit & W. Müller (Eds.), *From School to Work: A Comparative Study of Educational Qualifications and Occupational Destinations* (pp. 1–48). Oxford, UK: Clarendon Press.

Organisation for Economic Co-operation and Development (OECD). (2005). *Education at a Glance: OECD Indicators 2005*. Paris: OECD.

Organisation for Economic Co-operation and Development (OECD). (2006). *OECD Factbook 2006 – Economic, Environmental and Social Statistics*. Available at: http://www.sourceoecd.org/factbook.

Oulton, N., & Steedman, H. (1994). The British system of youth training: A comparison with Germany. In L. M. Lynch (Ed.), *Training and the Private Sector: International Comparisons* (pp. 61–76). Chicago: The University of Chicago Press.

Roberts, K. (1995). *Youth and Employment in Modern Britain*. Oxford, UK: Oxford University Press.

Roberts, K. (2004). School-to-work transitions: Why the United Kingdom's educational ladders always fail to connect. *International Studies in the Sociology of Education*, 14, 203–215.

Rothe, G. (2001). *Die Systeme beruflicher Qualifizierung Deutschlands, Österreichs und der Schweiz: Eine finanzpolitische Analyse und ihre ordnungspolitischen Konsequenzen*. Villingen-Schwenningen, Germany: Neckar.

Ryan, P., & Büchtemann, C. F. (1997). The school-to-work transition. In G. Schmid, J. O'Reilly, & K. Schömann (Eds.), *International Handbook of Labour Market Policy and Evaluation* (pp. 308–347). Cheltenham, UK: Elgar.

Ryan, P., & Unwin, L. (2001). Apprenticeship in the British 'training market'. *National Institute Economic Review*, 178, 99–114.

Smith, G. (2000). Schools. In A. H. Halsey & J. Webb (Eds.), *Twentieth Century British Social Trends* (pp. 179–220). Basingstoke, UK: Macmillan.

Solga, H. (2005). *Ohne Abschluss in die Bildungsgesellschaft: die Erwerbschancen gering qualifizierter Personen aus soziologischer und ökonomischer Perspektive*. Opladen, Germany: Budrich.

Sørensen, A. B., & Kalleberg, A. L. (1981). Outline of a theory for the matching of persons to jobs. In I. Berg (Ed.), *Sociological Perspectives on Labor Markets* (pp. 49–74). New York: Academic Press.

Soskice, D. (1994a). Reconciling markets and institutions: The German apprenticeship system. In L. M. Lynch (Ed.), *Training and the Private Sector: International Comparisons* (pp. 25–60). Chicago: The University of Chicago Press.

Soskice, D. (1994b). Social skills from mass higher education: Lessons from the US. In R. Layard, K. Mayhew & G. Owen (Eds.), *Britain's Training Deficit: The Centre for Economic Performance Report* (pp. 314–338). Aldershot, UK: Avebury.

Spence, M. (1973). Job market signalling. *Quarterly Journal of Economics*, 87, 355–374.

Streeck, W. (1989). Skills and the limits of neo-liberalism: The enterprise of the future as a place of learning. *Work, Employment and Society*, 3, 89–104.

Streeck, W. (1997). The German model: Does it exist? Can it survive? In C. Crouch & W. Streeck (Eds.), *Political Economy of Modern Capitalism: Mapping Convergence and Diversity* (pp. 33–54). London: Sage.

Streeck, W., & Thelen, K. (Eds.). (2005). *Beyond Continuity: Institutional Change in Advanced Political Economies*. Oxford, UK: Oxford University Press.

Thelen, K. (2004). *How Institutions Evolve: The Political Economy of Skills in Germany, Britain, the United States, and Japan*. Cambridge, UK: Cambridge University Press.

Thurow, L. C. (1975). *Generating Inequality: Mechanisms of Distribution in the US Economy*. New York: Basic Books.

United Nations Educational, Scientific, and Cultural Organization (UNESCO). (1980–1999). *Statistical Yearbook*. Paris: UNESCO.

Windolf, P. (1984). Formale Bildungsabschlüsse als Selektionskriterium am Arbeitsmarkt: Eine vergleichende Analyse zwischen Frankreich, der Bundesrepublik Deutschland und Großbritannien. *Kölner Zeitschrift für Soziologie und Sozialpsychologie*, 36, 56–74.

Windolf, P., & Wood, S. (1988). *Recruitment and Selection in the Labor Market: A Comparative Study of Britain and West Germany*. Aldershot, UK: Avebury.

PART TWO

THE ECONOMICS AND SOCIOLOGY OF SKILL FORMATION

Access, Investments, and Returns to Training

4   Why Does the German Apprenticeship System Work?[1]

Christian Dustmann and Uta Schoenberg

Competitiveness and performance of national economies is inherently linked to the productivity of their workforces. Some of this productivity is created by full-time primary, secondary, and postsecondary education. A significant part is built up later when workers participate in the workforce. With strong complementarities between technology and skills, training and education is now being considered as a key factor in global competitiveness. Industrialized countries seek to improve, and are willing to substantially invest in, their education and training institutions.

Only recently, the Organisation for Economic Co-operation and Development (OECD) Programme for International Student Assessment study has led to critical scrutiny of primary and secondary education systems in those countries that achieved relatively low scores, and triggered a wave of research and reform suggestions (see, e.g., Fertig & Schmidt, 2002; Fertig, 2003). At least equally important are postsecondary education schemes. Although primary and secondary education provides skills that are largely general and provide mostly academic knowledge, postsecondary schemes are tailored toward specialization, and often toward provision of skills that are specific to the needs and requirements of particular labor markets.

There are large differences between postsecondary education systems across industrialized countries. For instance, in the Anglo-Saxon countries, postsecondary education is usually state provided, through universities, colleges, and vocational schools. There is some concern about the emphasis on the academic bias of this system, with school-based vocational training schemes and specialized colleges not being able to provide workers with the "hands-on" skills the labor market requires. In contrast, in countries such as Germany and Austria, only a relatively small fraction of each cohort enrolls in vocational schools, colleges, or universities. The largest part of each cohort undergoes training within apprenticeship schemes. In the case of Germany, about 60% of each cohort obtains postsecondary training customized for particular professions (there are about 370 recognized occupations) through a combination of firm- and state-provided education.[2]

This so-called apprenticeship system has many obvious advantages. First, it combines state-provided, more academically oriented school-based education with training on the job, providing young trainees with important knowledge and expertise of how a job is done. This seems particularly important in the crafts sector, where experienced craftsmen are likely to be better teachers in practical applications than classroom teachers. However, such training schemes are also providing useful skills in white collar professions. In fact, although the apprenticeship system is often considered as a provider for training in craft-related professions, only one in three individuals on apprenticeship training schemes are in this sector, with the remaining positions in predominantly white collar professions, such as nurses, medical assistants, and bank clerks. Firsthand experience of how an entire firm or organization is run, how to interact with customers and other traders, and how jobs are conceptualized and implemented is a valuable knowledge that is unlikely to be taught similarly efficiently in the classroom.

A second advantage is that the training scheme provides structured postsecondary training options for individuals who are less academically inclined and would otherwise enter the labor market without further preparation. In fact, the proportion of individuals who enter the labor market without postsecondary training is considerably higher in the United States than in Germany. According to the Bureau of Labor Statistics, 38% of high school graduates in the United States did not attend colleges after graduation in 2001. In Germany, in contrast, the percentage of individuals between 20 and 24 years old without postsecondary education was 14% in 2000 (Bundesinstitut für Berufsbildung [BIBB], 2006).

At the same time, the apprenticeship system provides training for many occupations that is college provided in the United Kingdom (UK) or in the United States. As a consequence, although about 45% of each cohort in the United States holds at least a bachelor's degree, only 25% in Germany receive university education. This suggests another interesting aspect when comparing the two systems: although in the United States and the UK a large fraction of postsecondary education is college based and worker or tax financed, apprenticeship schemes are firm based and to a significant degree firm financed (see Table 4.1 for evidence).

Finally, the apprenticeship training scheme has the added benefit of allowing for smooth transitions of new labor market entrants into the labor market, thus reducing youth unemployment (see, e.g., Ryan, 2001, for evidence;

Jimeno & Rodríguez-Palenzuela (2003) illustrated substantially lower youth unemployment rates in Germany and Austria than in all other European OECD countries). Some academic papers suggest therefore the German apprenticeship system as a role model for similar schemes in other countries (see, e.g., Gospel, 1998; Steedman et al., 1998; Lehmann, 2000).

Not surprisingly, many industrialized economies have attempted to introduce similar schemes, or to remobilize schemes that have in the past seen their support withdrawn in favor for more academically oriented postsecondary education schemes (see, e.g., Steedman & West, 2003, for details on the UK vocational training system and directions for improvement).

Why does the apprenticeship system work so well in Germany? What are the main aspects to be considered when attempting to introduce similar schemes to other economies? A key question concerns the financing of the scheme. As mentioned previously, in the German case, it is both workers and firms who contribute, through forgone earnings as unskilled workers, and investment in training personal and training facilities. As we show, both worker and firm contributions are indeed significant. Workers are only willing to accept reduced wages over the training period if there is a worthwhile advantage of obtaining apprenticeship education over the life cycle. Firms are only willing to offer apprenticeship training if the benefits of doing so outweigh the costs of the investment. Some attempts (e.g., recently in Australia) to implement similar training schemes have not created sufficient interest on the side of potential trainees, despite highly subsidized wages. This suggests that the value of training within such schemes is not always evident for the worker. On the side of the firm, economic theory suggests that firms are not willing to sponsor training that is largely general in nature because they cannot recoup the costs of training. It is therefore quite remarkable that Germany manages to remain in a training equilibrium, where about 60% of each cohort is trained within the apprenticeship system, and firms significantly contribute to the system.

In this chapter, we address two issues that we believe are at the core of the German apprenticeship scheme. First, why workers are willing to undergo training, and what is the return to training. Second, why firms are willing to bear part of the training costs even though apprenticeship training is mostly general. We draw on detailed and in-depth analysis in three other publications (Dustmann & Schoenberg, 2004, 2006; Adda et al., 2006).

We first discuss possible reasons for why firms would be willing to pay for apprenticeship training. As mentioned previously, simple models of human capital investment imply that firms have no incentive to invest in general skills. Recent models of human capital investment, in contrast, show that firms are willing to train if wages are compressed (i.e., if training increases workers' productivity by more than workers' [outside] wages). We discuss three possible reasons for wage compression. The first relates to labor market institutions, in particular, unions. The second is possible complementarities between firm-specific and general human capital; the third is asymmetric learning. We briefly discuss the empirical implications of each of the three explanations. Drawing on Dustmann and Schoenberg (2004), we then provide some evidence that is compatible with the first explanation. Finally, drawing on recent research by Dustmann and Schoenberg (2006), we report additional evidence in favor of the last two explanations.

A second important question is the return to enrolling in such training schemes for the worker. If this return is too low, potential trainees may not be willing to enroll in training schemes that pay lower wages than they could obtain as unskilled workers. Establishing how large the returns to apprenticeship are is not trivial. Comparisons of life cycle incomes of individuals who underwent training and individuals who did not may be misleading because there is selection into training schemes. Moreover, apprenticeship training may lead to lower unemployment probabilities or create other nonmonetary benefits. Adda et al. (2006) investigated the returns to apprenticeship training within a dynamic life cycle and educational choice. We discuss the main advantages of this approach, as well as the main findings of their research.

We conclude with a discussion about the future of the German apprenticeship system and the difficulties of implementing similar training schemes in other economies.

BACKGROUND

The Apprenticeship System

The German apprenticeship system is a vocational training program that combines on-the-job training, provided by the firm, with school-based education, provided by the state. This organizational separation between the state education system and the firm in training the worker is quite unique to German-speaking countries. It is often termed *dual system* because of the contributions made by two independent bodies to the individual's education.

The apprenticeship system has a long history. Its roots can be traced back to the Middle Ages, when the guilds regulated journeymanship-type training schemes and issued training certificates. Entry into training schemes was at that time highly regulated, and there were strict requirements on entry age, duration of training, and family background (e.g., children had to be

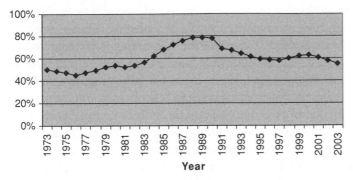

Figure 4.1. Percent of individuals in apprenticeship training over population in the age range of 15 to 18 years, various years. *Source:* Own calculations; based on Berufsbildungsstatistik and Population Statistics, German Statistical Office. The apprenticeship quota is calculated as the ratio of the number of individuals on apprenticeship schemes in a particular year over the population in the age range of 15 to 18 years.

legitimate) (see Muench, 1992). These early training schemes already shared many characteristics of today's apprenticeship system. For instance, training was provided only in recognized occupations, a requirement was tenure in the company of the master, and a regular examination had to be set (see Kempf, 1985, for further details).

The decline of the guilds from the sixteenth century onward – which went along with economic liberalism – led to a disintegration of organized vocational training. As a response, during the Industrial Revolution in the nineteenth century, the demand for qualified workers let the industry adopt vocational training schemes that had been successful in the crafts sector (see Muench, 1992). At the same time, compulsory school laws were introduced. This contributed to the development of the dual apprenticeship system, as school- and workplace-based apprenticeship training was considered to satisfy the compulsory school attendance requirement.

Today, about 60% of each cohort in Germany goes through the apprenticeship system (see Figure 4.1 for the trend since 1973). Individuals enter the apprenticeship system after completion of secondary schools. Apprenticeship training schemes last between 2 and 3 years (and since 1990, 3.5 years in some occupations).

During this time, apprentices attend vocational state schools (typically 1 or 2 days a week), where they acquire general knowledge, as well as knowledge that is specific to their occupation. The remaining days they are on specific on-the-job training schemes of the training firm. Within the firm, qualified

personnel are responsible for the apprentice and allocate apprentices to particular tasks. Larger firms also run specific classes or seminars for apprentices.

There are two examinations, one midterm exam, and one final exam (see
Muench, 1992). The final exams are unified and organized by an independent
body – the so-called chambers. Examinations are in both written and oral
form, and are occupational specific as well as general. In craft occupations,
there is also a practical exam. After having successfully completed the final
examination, the apprentice is issued a certificate that ascertains that he or
she is a skilled worker. Successful graduates are graded on a scale of 1 to 4
(excellent to pass), with achievements in particular areas separately listed and
graded. Examination results are important for later job interviews. Trainees
who fail the exam can resit. Certificates are accepted as skill qualification.

The Cost of Training

A key feature of the apprenticeship system is that firms and workers share
the cost of training. While on the scheme, apprentices accept wages that are
substantially lower than the wage of an unskilled worker in the occupation
the apprentice has chosen (see details in the next section). Over the training
period, apprenticeship wages increase, possibly reflecting the increasing productivity of trainees. At the same time, firms invest considerably in training
personnel and training facilities. In Table 4.1, we display information on the
cost of training, as well as the share of the cost that is borne by the worker and
the firm. The numbers on the firm's share are based on calculations in Beicht
et al. (2004); the numbers on apprenticeship wages and ages for unskilled
workers with the same characteristics are our own calculations, based on data
from the Institut für Arbeitsmarkt- und Berufsforschung (IAB) social security sample for the year 2001 (see Dustmann & Schoenberg, 2006, for more
details). The direct net cost of training, such as personnel costs for trainers,
plant and material costs, and teaching materials, amount to about €2,663 per
year (column 2). The productivity of an apprentice during training is estimated to be €7,730. In a competitive world in which workers bear all the training costs, workers should receive an apprenticeship wage of €5,067 (calculated
as the difference between €7,730 and €2,663). However, the average apprenticeship wage is €7,031, suggesting that firms bear at least some of the training
costs. In contrast, apprenticeship wages are about 56% of the average wage of
an unskilled worker without experience, suggesting that firms and workers
share the costs of apprenticeship training.

Note that the total cost of apprenticeship training is the sum of the direct
cost of training (column 2) and the opportunity cost of training (i.e., the

Table 4.1. The cost of apprenticeship training

1	2	3	4	5	6
Returns	Direct Cost	Apprenticeship Wage	Wage Unskilled Worker	Total Cost	Worker's Share
€7,730	€2,663	€7,031	€11,973	€6,906	71.6%

Column 1: estimates for workers' (annual) productivity during apprenticeship training. Column 2: estimates for the direct cost of training, such as personnel costs for trainers, plant and material costs, as well as textbooks, teaching software, etc. (Beicht et al., 2004). Columns 3 and 4: average annual apprenticeship wage; average annual wage of untrained workers with zero labor market experience (calculated from the IAB-Beschaeftigtenstichprobe for the year 2000). Column 5: total cost of apprenticeship training as difference between wage of untrained workers and the productivity of apprentices plus the "variable" cost of training, that is, column 4 − column 1 + column 2. Workers' share of training costs: ratio of the average wage of an untrained worker minus the average apprenticeship wage and the total training cost, that is, (column 4 − column 3)/column 5.

difference between the productivity of unskilled workers and workers in training). Because we have no estimate for the productivity of unskilled workers, we approximate it by their wage. Column 5 shows our estimates for the total cost of apprenticeship training, and column 6 shows worker's share of training as the ratio between the difference of the wage of unskilled workers and the apprenticeship wage and the total cost of training. According to this calculation, workers bear about 70% of the total training cost.[3]

Who Trains?

Do all firms in Germany train workers, or is training intensity distributed unequally across firms? Table 4.2 provides information on training intensity in firms. The numbers in the table are drawn from the firm panel of the IAB, and refer to the year 1999.

The perhaps most surprising figure in Table 4.2 is the overall percentage of firms that train apprentices: less than one in three firms trains young

Table 4.2. Firms and training firms, 1999

Percentage of firms that train workers on apprenticeship schemes	29.63%
Proportion of workers that work in firms that train	60.37%
Proportion of apprentices, all firms	5.37%
Proportion of apprentices in firms that train	18.13%

Source: Own calculations based on the IAB Firm-panel, year 1999.

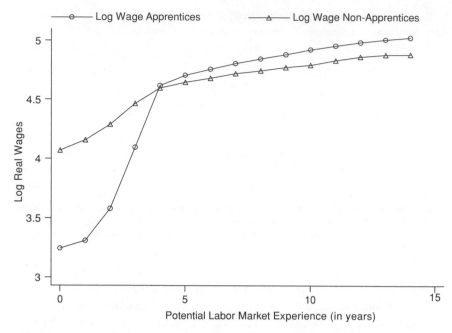

Figure 4.2. Log real wages, apprentices/nonapprentices, by potential experience.

workers on apprenticeship schemes. Because these firms are predominantly large firms, they employ approximately 60% of all workers. On average, 5.4% of all workers in firms are on apprenticeship training schemes. This number is compatible with the average percentage of skilled workers in the workforce: because apprenticeship education takes approximately 3 years and about 65% of workers are trained on these schemes, with a remaining time in the labor force of about 40 years after training, the average training intensity in the economy should be close to 5%. However, this training "burden" is unequally distributed: those firms that train have about 18% of workers employed on apprenticeship schemes.

The Returns to Training

What are the returns to training for workers? As illustrated previously, there are not only costs for firms, but also substantial costs for workers in terms of forgone earnings during the apprenticeship period because the wages of unskilled workers are substantially higher. This is illustrated in Figure 4.2. Based on data from the IAB social security records, we display the wages of skilled and unskilled workers during the first 15 years of potential labor market experience. Figure 4.2 clearly shows a large wage disadvantage during the first 3 years when apprentices are on training schemes. This disadvantage decreases as apprenticeship wages increase during the training period. Wages of apprentices rise steeply after about 3 to 4 years, when apprentices start working as regular skilled workers. Wages of unskilled workers likewise rise steeply during the first years in the labor market. Wages of apprentices catch up with wages of unskilled workers after about 4 years of potential experience; after that, they continue to rise slightly more steeply.

Of course, these figures are not indicative of the benefit apprenticeship training may have for a randomly selected worker, for various reasons. Those who enroll on training schemes may be a selected population. Apprenticeship training may have benefits other than wages, as apprentices may face different job destruction rates, a different wage offer distribution, or may select into firms that are more productive.

Some of these differences are illustrated in Figure 4.3, where we display the accumulation of labor market experience (left figure) and job tenure (right figure) for the two groups. In both figures, the diagonal line refers to potential experience. If individuals would remain continuously in the labor market after entry, potential experience would be equal to actual experience and all the entries would be on the diagonal line. Likewise, if individuals would be with the same firm after labor market entry, all entries in the left figure would be on a diagonal line. The figure on the right-hand side indicates a high labor market attachment of apprentices during the first 3 years in the labor market; this period coincides with the training period. Apprentices continue to have a higher labor market attachment than unskilled workers in later years. Likewise, apprentices accumulate more tenure during the training period and in later years, as the gap between the two groups is slightly increasing. This suggests that apprentices switch firms less often than nonapprentices.

When deciding whether to enroll in training schemes, apprentices consider the impact apprenticeship training may have on labor market attachment and firm tenure, and make choices based on their own assessments of their abilities. Hence, a full understanding of the decision-making process of young workers who have the choice to enter the labor market as unskilled workers or to undergo apprenticeship training cannot be achieved by investigating simple descriptive evidence, but requires the formulation and estimation of a fully structural model. This is done in Adda et al. (2006) and discussed in more detail later in this chapter.

WHY DO FIRMS PAY FOR TRAINING?

We now address our first key question: Why are firms willing to pay for training workers in skills that are largely general rather than specific? Standard

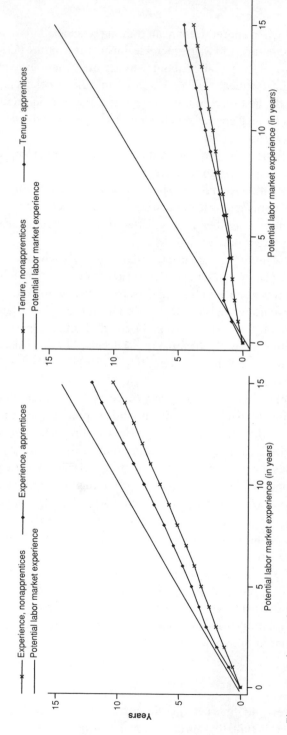

Figure 4.3. Labor market experience and job tenure for apprentices and nonapprentices.

94

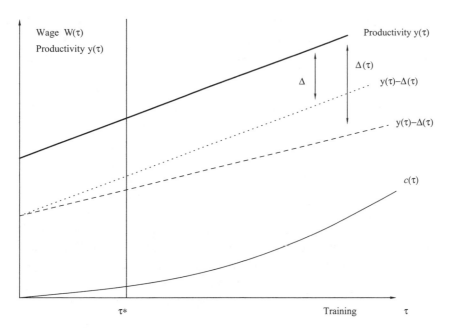

Figure 4.4. Training and compressed wage structures. *Note:* A similar figure can be found in Acemoglu and Pischke (1999b, Figure 1).

human capital theory predicts that firms do not invest into general training of their workers because the worker is the sole recipient of that investment (Becker, 1964).

Acemoglu and Pischke (1999a, 1999b) demonstrated that these predictions rest on the assumption that labor markets are perfectly competitive. If, in contrast, labor market imperfections lead to a compressed wage structure, firms have an incentive to sponsor training even if training is completely general. The reason is that under a compressed wage structure, training increases workers' productivity by more than workers' outside option, enabling firms to increase profits by training.

The key ideas are demonstrated in Figure 4.4. A similar figure can be found in Acemoglu and Pischke (1999b, Figure 1). The vertical axis displays wages and productivity. The horizontal axis carries the amount of training a worker receives. The solid line is the productivity of a worker for a given level of training, $y(\tau)$. Now suppose that there are some imperfections that lead to wages being below productivity. One such mechanism could be mobility costs, or nonmonetary benefits of particular jobs. Assume that the difference between wages and productivity is given by Δ, which is the (ex post) profit the firm makes on each worker, and that this profit is the same for each level of training. In this case, the firm has no incentive to train workers: the profit made on workers is the same regardless of the workers' level of training. Labor market imperfections themselves are therefore not sufficient to induce firms to sponsor training.

Now assume that there is some additional mechanism that creates larger profits of firms at larger levels of workers' training, so that $\frac{\partial \Delta(\tau)}{\partial \tau} > 0$. In this case, it is advantageous for firms to train workers: The higher the level of training, the higher is the profit the firm makes. The panel $c(\tau)$ represents the costs of training. If this is convex in training intensity (which is suggested by any human capital model), then there will be an optimal level of training provision for the firm, which we have denoted by τ^*. The increase in the profit that firms make on workers at higher levels of training (and the according increase in the gap between productivity and wages) is usually referred to as *wage compression.* Wage compression may create an incentive to train workers in human capital that is general. Different hypotheses have been brought forward in the literature for why wages may be compressed. We discuss the empirical relevance of three alternative explanations.

Unions

One explanation for wage compression – and thus firm-financed training – is unions. This explanation seems particularly relevant in Germany and Austria, where the majority of workers are covered by collective bargaining agreements. Dustmann and Schoenberg (2004) developed a model that takes into account the particular structure of collective bargaining in Germany. The hypothesis that unions, through imposing wage floors that lead to wage compression, increase on-the-job training is then tested, using matched employer–employee data.

BACKGROUND AND THEORY

Standard human capital theory predicts that unions or minimum wages reduce on-the-job training. A minimum wage reduces training investments because it prevents workers from taking a wage cut during the training period to finance training (Rosen, 1972; Hashimoto, 1982). If unions lead to wage compression so that training increases workers' productivity more than workers' wages, then workers will not capture the full return to the training investment. Hence, unions may likewise decrease training in the economy (e.g., Mincer, 1983). However, these arguments ignore that minimum wages and unions also alter firms' incentives to finance training. In particular, if minimum wages or unions compress the wage structure, firms have a stronger incentive to finance general training in a unionized than in a nonunionized economy, and whether unions increase or decrease training is no longer clear.

Germany's collective bargaining system provides a unique opportunity for testing the hypothesis that unions increase training. This system differs in many aspects from those in the United States and the UK. Most important, in Germany union agreements are binding only in firms that belong to an employer federation (Arbeitgeberverband). Membership in an employer federation is voluntary. In firms that choose to belong to an employer federation, union agreements apply to all employees, independently of their union status.

In contrast, in firms that do not belong to an employer federation, union agreements are not binding. This divides firms and their workers into a unionized and a nonunionized sector. A further crucial feature of the German collective bargaining system is that wage negotiations occur on a yearly basis at the regional and industry level between unions and employer associations, and these negotiations determine wages for different education groups. Union wages act as minimum wages. Unions and employer federations do not directly bargain over apprenticeship training (Bispinck, 2001; Bispinck et al., 2002).

Dustmann and Schoenberg (2004) developed a model of firm-financed training that captures the key elements of this system. The model extends previous work by Booth and Chatterji (1998), Acemoglu and Pischke (1999a, 1999b), Acemoglu et al. (2001), Booth and Bryan (2002), and Booth et al. (2003) in various directions. First, unionized and nonunionized firms coexist in equilibrium, and only unionized firms are bound to pay union wages. Second, union agreements act as minimum wages, and unionized firms are allowed to pay wages above the union wage. Third, workers are allowed to be heterogeneous and mobility to be endogenous.

There are three types of labor market imperfections in this model: limited commitment to training provision, the infeasibility of long-term contracts, and rents, allowing firms to pay wages below productivity. Because firms cannot commit to training, workers are not willing to accept a wage cut to finance training. Consequently, because wages are not compressed in nonunionized firms, these firms do not offer training. In unionized firms, in contrast, the union wage compresses wages for workers with productivity around the union wage, inducing them to train these workers. This argument crucially depends on firms paying wages below (marginal) productivity. In the model, this is because of nonpecuniary job characteristics. The same arguments would apply if wages were below productivity for other reasons, such as mobility costs.

Dustmann and Schoenberg (2004) interpreted the guarantee of unionized firms to pay at least the union wage in the future as a special form of long-term wage contract. Although, in principle, firms do not have to join an employer federation in order to commit to a wage guarantee, such a commitment is not self-enforceable because firms have an incentive to offer a lower wage in case a negative productivity shock arrives. Hence, in their model, unions serve as a commitment device: unionized firms credibly signal to workers that they will pay at least the agreed union wage in the future.

DATA AND RESULTS

The empirical analysis in Dustmann and Schoenberg (2004) is based on three data sets: (1) a panel of establishments for the years 1995 to 1999; (2) an administrative data set for workers based on social security records; and (3) a matched data set, combining firm information from the first data source with information on employees from the second data source.

The analysis begins with a number of tests of the key assumptions of the model. First, there are binding wage floors in unionized, but not in nonunionized firms. Consequently, wages are more compressed in unionized than in nonunionized firms. Comparing the variance of log-wages and education wage differentials in unionized and nonunionized firms, conditional on worker and firm characteristics and firm fixed effects, they find strong evidence for a more compressed wage structure in unionized than in nonunionized firms.

They then test for two implications that are a direct consequence of wage floors. First, layoffs should occur more frequently in unionized firms. Second, wage cuts should be observed more often in nonunionized firms because unionized firms respond to negative productivity shocks by firing workers, whereas nonunionized firms cut wages. Again, they find empirical support for both implications, particularly for the low educated workers for whom wage floors should be most binding.

They then test directly for training differences between unionized and nonunionized firms. The identification strategy exploits the changes in union status over time. This allows controlling for unobserved time-invariant firm (and worker) heterogeneity. The results consistently suggest that unions increase training. Thus, the empirical evidence is consistent with their hypothesis that membership of firms in employer federations, via imposing minimum wages and wage compression, increases training in apprenticeship programs. However, the results also suggest that unions are not the only reason for firm-financed apprenticeship training because nonunionized firms also train workers.

Asymmetric Information and Firm-Specific Human Capital

In Dustmann and Schoenberg (2006), they therefore re-examine the question of why firms train workers within the German apprenticeship system, concentrating on two further motives: asymmetric information (Acemoglu & Pischke, 1998) and firm-specific human capital (e.g., Franz & Soskice, 1995; Acemoglu & Pischke, 1999a, 1999b).

As our descriptive statistics suggest, only a minority of firms in Germany train workers on apprenticeship-type schemes; firm size is the most important predictor for whether a firm trains or not. It is possible that the motives behind firm-financed training differ between small and large firms. Dustmann and Schoenberg (2006) therefore also investigated whether the degree of informational asymmetries and the degree of specificity varies by firm size.

BACKGROUND AND THEORY

To structure the analysis, Dustmann and Schoenberg (2006) developed a simple theoretical framework of firm-financed training. The benchmark model is one where firms earn (ex post) positive profits (due to mobility costs on the side of the worker), but have no incentive to finance training. This model is then extended to incorporate both firm-specific human capital and asymmetric information. This changes the firm's optimization problem: similar to our previous graphical exposition, both explanations lead to wage compression and thus firms making larger profits on trained workers.

Dustmann and Schoenberg (2006) then explored various empirical predictions of each explanation. A key implication of asymmetric information between incumbent and outside firms is adverse selection: workers who leave the firm after training are of lower quality than workers who stay with the training firm. Dustmann and Schoenberg (2006) tested for an adverse selection of movers by comparing wages of workers who leave the training firm for endogenous reasons (endogenous movers) with wages of workers who initially stay with their training firm (stayers) and who are displaced from their training firm because of plant closure (exogenous movers). They interpret persistently lower wages of endogenous movers than of stayers and exogenous movers as evidence in favor of an adverse selection. In the second step of the analysis, they test for alternative explanations for an adverse selection of movers, such as the sorting of workers into firms, wage floors, and the complementarity between ability and firm-specific human capital.

In a final step, they use a model of firm-financed training to simulate what their estimates for the adverse selection of movers and the degree of specificity imply for firms' willingness to finance training.

DATA AND RESULTS

Dustmann and Schoenberg (2006) used two data sets for their analysis. The first data set is a 1% sample of administrative social security records in Germany from 1975 to 1995. The administrative nature of these data ensures that wages are measured more precisely than in typical survey data. Another advantage of these data is that they contain information on plant size for every year between 1980 and 1995, even if the worker is no longer employed with the plant, which they use as a measure for plant closure.

The second set of data comes from the repeated cross-section German Qualification and Career Survey, which is conducted jointly by the BIBB and the IAB. They use this survey to estimate the degree of specificity of apprenticeship training. The survey is available for four different years: 1979, 1985, 1991/92, and 1998/99.

The main results are as follows. In line with Acemoglu and Pischke (1998) and Wachter and Bender (2006), Dustmann and Schoenberg (2006) found strong evidence for an adverse selection of workers who move away from their training firm after apprenticeship training, even if controlling for the sorting of workers into training firms. They consider two alternative explanations for the adverse selection of movers: wage floors and the complementarity between ability and firm-specific human capital accumulation. Although these explanations may contribute to the wage disadvantage of movers, they cannot fully explain it. They thus conclude that asymmetric information between incumbent and outside firms is one reason for the adverse selection of movers. They also find important differences between small and large training firms: adverse selection of movers is substantially greater in large than in small firms.

The analysis on the specificity of apprenticeship skills suggests that these are mostly general; however, there is a large occupation-specific component. Some approximate calculations suggest that workers who have left the apprenticeship firm but not the apprenticeship occupation can employ 4.5% less of their skills than workers who are still employed at the apprenticeship firm and apprenticeship occupation, compared to 8.6% for workers who are still employed at the training firm but have left the training occupation, and

34.2% for workers who left both the training firm and occupation. Again, there are important differences between small and large firms, with training appearing to be more firm and occupation specific in small firms.

Based on the theoretical model, they simulate what the estimates for the adverse selection of movers and the degree of specificity of training imply for firms' willingness to finance training. They find that firm-specific human capital accumulation contributes little to firm-financed apprenticeship training. Asymmetric information, in contrast, can explain up to two-thirds of firms' share of the training costs.

WHY DO WORKERS CHOOSE APPRENTICESHIP TRAINING SCHEMES?

A further key question is why should workers choose apprenticeship training schemes? As we demonstrate, wages of apprentices are considerably lower than wages of unskilled workers in the same age and education group. The opportunity costs of undergoing apprenticeship training are therefore substantial.

Adda et al. (2006) investigated the life cycle returns to formal training relative to informal training implicitly obtained while on the job. They compare the long-run value of education choices and subsequent labor market outcomes for apprentices and nonapprentices. This is done within a dynamic discrete choice model of career progression and educational choice. The model is then estimated on a large administrative data set that describes career progression from the end of secondary schooling. In the next section, we briefly discuss the basic idea of the model and some of the key findings of their analysis.

BACKGROUND AND THEORY

Understanding the choice of young workers between entering the labor market directly after secondary schooling and enrolling first in an apprenticeship scheme requires modeling education choices and labor market careers within a complete life cycle setting. Adda et al. (2006) specified and estimated a life cycle model of education choice and labor market careers for men who complete standard schooling at about age 16. These individuals have already decided not to attend college (by way of their secondary school choice at about age 10), and they now face the choice between formal apprenticeship training and entering the labor market as unskilled workers.

When deciding whether to enroll in apprenticeship training or to enter the labor market without formal postsecondary training, individuals forgo higher current wages they would obtain as an unskilled worker in return for higher future wages as a skilled worker. A key aspect of the model in Adda et al. (2006) is that apprenticeship training does not only affect wages, but also other career characteristics, such as the probability of receiving a job offer while employed or unemployed, the exogenous job destruction rate, the return to general and specific human capital accumulation, the income while unemployed, the dispersion of wage offers, and the distribution of aggregate shocks that affect the evolution of relative wages in the two skill categories.

While working as skilled or unskilled workers, wages grow by experience and tenure due to informal accumulation of general and specific human capital. Once in the labor market, workers can search to improve the quality of their job match.

After estimating the parameters of the model, Adda et al. (2006) then used the model to simulate the career paths of apprentices and nonapprentices, as well as to study the mechanisms that affect the choice of workers in favor of or against apprenticeship education. Finally, they used the model to simulate labor market policies and their impact on educational choice.

DATA AND RESULTS

Estimation of the model requires data on complete work and earnings histories, including information on job mobility. These data are drawn from the IAB social security records – the same data used by Dustmann and Schoenberg (2004, 2006). Individuals are observed from the moment they enter the labor market to up to 15 years in the labor market. The sample consists of West German males, who end formal education after lower or intermediate secondary school, and who either enter the labor market directly or enter and apprenticeship.

Adda et al. (2006) first computed the *wage* returns to apprenticeship by simulating wage profiles under the two education states, distinguishing between the average treatment effect (ATE) and the average treatment on the treated effect (ATTE). Comparing these to the profile that is obtained when endogenous selection is ignored (which is equivalent to straightforward Ordinary Least Squares (OLS) estimation) shows a substantial bias in the latter due to self-selection. Although ATTE is higher than ATE, they both grow more rapidly than the OLS returns, reaching about 27% by age 35, compared to the OLS estimate of 17%. Not surprisingly, the ATTE is higher than ATE. Their simulations also show that the wage returns to apprenticeship only provide a partial picture of the relative advantages of the two careers. These differ in a number of other dimensions, such as job destruction rates, income while unemployed, job arrival rates, sensitivity to business cycle fluctuations, and dispersion of new job opportunities. In addition, there are both direct utility costs and opportunity costs of apprenticeship training.

When taking into account these nonwage returns to apprenticeship training, they obtain the following results. First, taking all individual costs into account, the average return to apprenticeship (ATE) is negative (at about –1.7%). The negative return is due primarily to the opportunity cost of apprenticeship training. However, for those who choose to undergo apprenticeship training, the returns are far larger (at about 8%). Considering the full (i.e., wage plus nonwage) returns at age 18 (which eliminates the opportunity costs of training), the ATEs are 14%. Thus, the average wage returns estimated are similar to those implied by 2 to 3 years of full-time schooling.

CONCLUSION AND DISCUSSION

In this chapter, we investigate reasons why the German apprenticeship system works. A key feature of the system is that workers and firms share the costs of training, through forgone earnings as unskilled workers, and investment in training personal and training facilities. Thus, the two questions we pose in this chapter are as follows: Why are firms willing to sponsor apprenticeship training? Why are workers willing to enroll in the system, despite a substantial opportunity cost during the training period?

Recent models of training indicate that firms only have an incentive to pay for training if the gap between productivity and (outside) wages is increasing in training. This is widely known in the literature as "wage compression."

Drawing on earlier studies (Dustmann & Schoenberg, 2006), we investigate three explanations for wage compression – and thus firm-financed training – in Germany. The first relates to labor market institutions, in particular, unions. There is empirical support for this explanation: wage compression is indeed higher in firms that recognize unions, compared to firms that do not; and the effect of union recognition on training is substantial and positive. Thus, labor market institutions appear to be one reason for firm-financed apprenticeship training in Germany.

However, because nonunionized firms also finance training, unions cannot be the only explanation. Drawing on work by Dustmann and Schoenberg (2006), we argue that asymmetric information between incumbent and outside firms is an important additional reason for firm-financed training, especially in large firms. Firm-specific human capital accumulation, in contrast, contributes little to firm-financed training in Germany.

The other key question is why workers enroll in apprenticeship schemes. Drawing on work by Adda et al. (2006), we argue that workers' costs of apprenticeship training in terms of forgone earnings are substantial. In fact, the average effect of apprenticeship training on overall earnings, if evaluated over a 40-year period, is slightly negative. However, when excluding the years of training, the overall return turns positive and is similar to the effect of 2 to 3 years of full-time schooling. The analysis also shows that simple comparisons between individuals who enroll in apprenticeship schemes and those who do not are inappropriate because there is a strong selection into apprenticeship training. Furthermore, apprenticeship training improves various labor market outcomes other than wages, such as the job arrival rate, the job destruction rate, and income while unemployed.

What do our results imply for the future of the German apprenticeship system? As we argue, an important reason why German firms are willing to sponsor apprenticeship training is wage compression due to unions. Since the mid-1990s, Germany has witnessed an unprecedented decline in unionization rates: the percentage of firms that neither recognize industrywide nor firmwide agreements has risen from 38.4% in 1995 to 52.4% in 1999 (own calculations based on the IAB Establishment Panel). Our results imply that this erosion of the German collective bargaining system has undesired effects on the apprenticeship system.

Although there is still a lot of praise for the German apprenticeship system, there is also a growing concern that the system provides workers with skills that are too specific, thus locking workers into jobs and reducing later mobility (see, e.g., Heckman et al., 1994; Neal, 1999). This could have far-reaching consequences for the performance of the economy. For example, reallocation costs of worker displacement and the speed of adjustment to technological change depend crucially on how transferable skills are across jobs (e.g., Krüger & Kumar, 2004; Wasmer, 2006). Our results indicate that the firm-specific component of training is small; concerns that apprenticeship training provides workers with skills that are too firm specific may thus not be warranted. We do, however, find that the occupation-specific component of apprenticeship training is substantial and may be as high as 35%. How does the degree of occupation specificity compare with other forms of postsecondary training? Table 4.3 investigates this issue. Results are based on the German Qualification and Career Survey. In 1986, workers who switched occupations were asked how much of the skills used at their previous occupation can be applied at the current occupation. Respondents had five choices: very much, a lot, some, not too much, and very little. We code this variable to be equal to 1 if workers can transfer a lot or very much of the skills, and 0 otherwise. The entries in Table 4.3 report the difference in the mean of this variable between the base category of workers who undergo no postsecondary training and

Table 4.3. Postsecondary education and occupation specificity

Base category: no postsecondary education *Relative to base category:*	Column A: unconditional differences	Column B: differences conditional on worker's age and current occupation
Vocational training	0.0365 (0.0444)	0.0410 (0.0451)
Apprenticeship training	0.1529 (0.0277)	0.1380 (0.0288)
Technician	0.3659 (0.0497)	0.2784 (0.0533)
Community college	0.3202 (0.0570)	0.1898 (0.0615)
University	0.3473 (0.0559)	0.2566 (0.0650)

Source: Own calculations based on the German Qualification and Career Survey, year 1986. Entries in column 1 are differences between responses of workers who change occupation and who obtained the respective postsecondary training and workers who change occupation, but have not received any postsecondary training, to the question of whether they can transfer a lot or very much of their skills to the new occupation. Column A reports unconditional differences; column B reports differences, conditional on current occupation, age, and age squared.

workers who enrolled in vocational training, apprenticeship training, technician, community college, or university.

Column A reports the raw difference in means across education groups; columns B reports the conditional mean, where we control for observable worker and firm characteristics, such as current occupation (ten dummies), age, and age squared. Among workers who entered the labor market without any postsecondary education, only 8.6% say that they can transfer very much or a lot of the skills to their new occupation. The fraction is about 3.6 percentage points higher for workers who attended a vocational school. Interestingly, the fraction is about 15 percentage points higher for workers who completed an apprenticeship, regardless of whether we condition on observable characteristics or not. However, apprentices can transfer fewer skills to their new occupation than workers with a college or university degree. According to our interpretation, these results do not lend strong support to the concern that the apprenticeship system provides workers with skills that are "too" specific.

What do our results imply for why it has proven difficult to implement similar training schemes in other countries? In our opinion, the German apprenticeship system works because two conditions hold: first, firms have incentives to bear part of the training costs. Second, the returns to apprenticeship training are high enough to encourage workers to participate. Our results suggest that one reason why German firms are willing to sponsor apprenticeship training is related to the particular institutional structure of the German labor market. This may imply that firms in less regulated labor markets, such as the UK, the United States, or Canada, have fewer incentives to participate in similar training schemes. However, our results also suggest that labor market institutions are not the only reason for firm-financed apprenticeship training. Asymmetric information between incumbent and outside firms is an important additional reason and should equally apply in less regulated labor markets.

The second prerequisite for apprenticeship schemes to work is that workers have sufficient financial incentives to participate in such schemes. One problem of the recent attempt to implement a similar training scheme in Australia was that it simply did not create enough interest on the side of potential trainees, although training wages were heavily subsidized. The full return to apprenticeship training in Germany, in contrast, is comparable to that of full-time schooling in the United States or the UK. Why is this so? We believe that the fact that apprentices take centralized exams that are organized by an independent body – chambers – plays a key role here. Moreover, after having successfully completed the final examination, apprentices are issued a certificate that does not only list in detail the subjects an apprentice has taken, but also his or her performance in each subject. This makes it easier for nontraining firms to evaluate the quality of apprenticeship training. Our recommendation is that when implementing similar schemes in other countries, policy makers should pay careful attention to these aspects of the German apprenticeship system.

Notes

1. We are grateful to the Anglo-German Foundation and the Deutsche Forschungsgemeinschaft for funding this research.
2. See Soskice (1994) and Winkelmann (1996) for more details. In 2004, the overall quota was 59.5%. This quota is calculated for each age group i between 16 and 24 in a particular calendar year (in this case, 2004) as $\sum_{i=16}^{24} \frac{Apprenticeship - takeups_i}{Population_i}$.
3. Our approach neglects possible selection into apprenticeship training.

References

Acemoglu, D., Aghion, P., & Violante, G. (2001). Deunionization, technical change and inequality. *Carnegie-Rochester Conference Series of Public Policy*, 55, 229–264.

Acemoglu, D., & Pischke, S. (1998). Why do firms train? Theory and evidence. *Quarterly Journal of Economics*, 112, 79–119.

Acemoglu, D., & Pischke, S. (1999a). Beyond Becker: Training in imperfect labour markets. *Economic Journal Features*, 109, F112–F142.

Acemoglu, D., & Pischke, S. (1999b). The structure of wages and investment in general training. *Journal of Political Economy*, 107, 539–573.

Adda, J., Dustmann, C., Meghir, C., & Robin, J. M. (2006). *Career Progression and Formal versus On-The-Job Training*. IZA Discussion Paper No. 2260.

Becker, G. (1964). *Human Capital*. Chicago: The University of Chicago Press.

Beicht, U., Walden, G., & Herget, H. (2004). *Cost and Benefits of In-Company Vocational Education and Training in Germany*. Bielefeld, Germany: Federal Institute for Vocational Training.

Bispinck, R. (2001). Qualifizierung und Weiterbildung in Tarifvertraegen – Bisherige Entwicklung und Perspektiven. In R. Dobischat & H. Seifert (Eds.), *Lernzeiten neu organisieren: Lebenslanges Lernen durch Integration von Bildung und Arbeit* (pp. 153–180). Berlin: Edition Sigma.

Bispinck, R., Dorsch-Scweizer, M., & Kirsch, J. (2002). Tarifliche Ausbildungsfoerderung – begrenzt erfolgreich. Eine empirische Wirkungsanalyse. *WSI-Mitteilungen*, 4.

Booth, A., & Bryan, M. L. (2002). *Who Pays for General Training? New Evidence for British Man and Women*. IZA Discussion Paper No. 464.

Booth, A. L., & Chatterji, M. (1998). Unions and efficient training. *Economic Journal*, 108, 328–343.

Booth, A. L., Francesconi, M., & Zoega, G. (2003). Unions, work-related training, and wages: Evidence for British men. *Industrial and Labor Relations Review*, 57, 68–91.

Bundesinstitut für Berufsbildung (BIBB). (2006, February). *Schaubilder zur Berufsbildung – Strukturen und Entwicklungen*. Bonn, Germany: Author.

Dustmann, C., & Schoenberg, U. (2004). *Training and Union Wages*. IZA Discussion Paper No. 1435.

Dustmann, C., & Schoenberg, U. (2006). *Apprenticeship Training, Firm-Specific Human Capital, and Asymmetric Information*. Mimeograph, University College London.

Fertig, M (2003). *Who's to Blame? The Determinants of German Students' Achievement in the PISA 2000 Study*. IZA Discussion Paper No. 739.

Fertig, M., & Schmidt, C. M. (2002). *The Role of Background Factors for Reading Literacy: Straight National Scores in the PISA 2000 Study*. CEPR Discussion Paper No. 3544.

Franz, W., & Soskice, D. (1995). The German apprenticeship system. In F. Buttler, W. Franz, R. Schettkat, & D. Soskice (Eds.), *Institutional Frameworks and Labor Market Performance* (pp. 206–234). London: Routledge.

Gospel, H. (1998). The revival of apprenticeship training in Britain? *British Journal of Industrial Relations*, 36, 435–457.

Hashimoto, M. (1982). Minimum wage effects on training on the job. *American Economic Review*, 72, 1070–1087.

Heckman, J. J., Roselius, R., & Smith, J. (1994). US education and training policy: A re-evaluation of the underlying assumptions of the 'new consensus'. In L. Solomon & A. Levenson (Eds.), *Labour Markets, Employment Policy and Job Creation* (pp. 83–121). Boulder, CO: Westview Press.

Jimeno, J. F., & Rodríguez-Palenzuela, D. (2003). *Youth Unemployment in the OECD: Demographic Shifts, Labour Market Institutions and Macroeconomic Shocks*. European Network of Economic Policy Research Institutes Working Paper No. 19.

Kempf, T. (1985). *Theorie und Empirie betrieblicher Ausbildungsplatzangebote*. Frankfurt/Main: Lang.

Krüger, D., & Kumar, K. B. (2004). Skill-specific rather than general education: A reason for US-Europe growth differences? *Journal of Economic Growth*, 9, 167–207.

Lehmann, W. (2000). Is Germany's dual system still a model for Canadian youth apprenticeship initiatives? *Canadian Public Policy*, 26, 225–240.

Mincer, J. (1983). Union effects: Wages, turnover, and job training. *Research in Labor Economics*, 7, 217–252.

Muench, J. (1992). *Das Berufsbildungssystem in der Bundesrepublik Deutschland*. Berlin: European Centre for the Development of Vocational Training.

Neal, D. (1999). The complexity of job mobility amongst young men. *Journal of Labor Economics*, 17, 237–261.

Rosen, S. (1972). Learning and experience in the labor market. *Journal of Human Resources*, 7, 326–342.

Ryan, P. (2001). The school-to-work transition: A cross-national perspective. *Journal of Economic Literature*, 39, 34–92.

Soskice, D. (1994). Reconciling markets and institutions: The German apprenticeship system. In L. M. Lynch (Ed.), *Training and the Private Sector, International Comparisons* (pp. 1–24). NBER Series in Comparative Labor Markets. Chicago: The University of Chicago Press.

Steedman, H., Gospel, H., & Ryan, P. (1998). *Apprenticeship: A Strategy for Growth*. CEP Discussion Paper No. CEPSP11, London.

Steedman, H., & West, M. (2003). *Finding Our Way: Vocational Education in England*. CEP Discussion Paper No. CEPOP18, London.

Wachter, T., & Bender, S. (2006). In the right place at the wrong time: The role of firms and luck in young workers' careers. *American Economic Review*, 96(5), 1679–1705.

Wasmer, E. (2006). Interpreting Europe-US labor market differences: The specificity of human capital investments. *American Economic Review*, 96(3), 811–831.

Winkelmann, R. (1996). Employment prospects and skill acquisition of apprenticeship-trained workers in Germany. *Industrial and Labor Relations Review*, 49, 658–672.

5   What Do We Know About Training at Work?

Philip J. O'Connell and Jean-Marie Jungblut

The resurgence of interest in recent years in the importance of education and training in furthering the goals of economic progress, fuller employment, and social integration coincides with a new emphasis on the need for "life-long learning," both to respond to current changes in the organization and technology of production and service delivery and to counter the socially disruptive effects of increased labor market flexibility.

Although there has been a great deal of interest in and research on initial education prior to labor market entry, continuing job-related training is also believed to be highly influential in determining both corporate or organizational performance as well as individual earnings and career development, although the empirical research on this topic is much more limited. Given that the impact of initial educational attainment on both labor market entry and on subsequent career development is already well established in the research literature, we focus in this chapter on continuing education and training of employed workers.

It should be noted that there has also been a parallel interest in the effects of education and training targeted on the unemployed, and that this field has generated a substantial body of sophisticated empirical research that has already been extensively reviewed (see, e.g., Fay, 1996; Friedlander et al., 1997; Heckman et al., 1999). Most empirical work has been confined to relatively short-term employment and earnings effects. The results of this research are inconclusive and largely negative, suggesting, at best, that the effects of active labor market programs on the labor market prospects of unemployed workers are quite limited (see, for Germany, Wingens et al., 2000; for France, Checcaglini, 2000). However, positive effects have been found for carefully targeted programs and those delivered to particularly disadvantaged participants (Fay, 1996) and in respect of programs with close linkages to the open labor market (O'Connell, 2002a).

Table 5.2. Participation of the labor force in nonformal job-related continuing education and training by level of educational attainment, selected countries, 2003

	Lower secondary (%)	Upper secondary (%)	Tertiary (%)	All (%)	Tertiary:lower secondary ratio
Denmark	31	42	59	46	1.9
Sweden	27	41	62	45	2.3
Finland	28	38	60	44	2.1
United States	14	37	61	44	4.4
Switzerland	11	37	63	41	5.7
United Kingdom	12	31	50	34	4.2
Canada (2002)	9	24	40	29	4.4
France	14	22	37	23	2.6
Belgium	11	19	35	22	3.2
Germany	4	12	26	14	6.5
Ireland	7	12	22	14	3.1
Poland	3	9	33	12	11.0
Italy	2	8	14	6	7.0

Source: The indicator examines the participation of adults in lifelong learning, For the European countries the data are compiled from the ad hoc module on Lifelong Learning of the 2003 EU Labour Force Survey. See OECD, *Education at a Glance*, 2005, table C6.1a.

training are likely to exacerbate rather than mitigate labor market inequalities. Of interest here, however is that the training gap between those with low and high levels of educational attainment tends to be smaller in countries characterized by comparatively high overall rates of training participation. This raises the policy question of whether interventions to increase the overall national rate of training would increase training among those with lower qualifications, or whether interventions to redistribute training opportunities to those currently exhibiting low participation would lead to an increase in the overall rate of training participation.

In general, there is little evidence to suggest any marked gender differences in access to training. For example, O'Connell (1999) showed that the incidence of training is similar for men and women across a range of OECD member countries. However, Evertsson (2004) showed that in Sweden women are less likely than men to participate in formal on-the-job training. Moreover, there is some evidence that the characteristics of female employment in France, where the combination of part-time paid work with domestic work may have a negative impact on women's access to training (Fournier,

2001; Trautmann, 2002; Méhaut, 2003). Moreover, in terms of training accumulation over the life course, women tend to be disadvantaged relative to men due to tension between work and family life (Fournier, 2003).

Participation in training has also been found to decline over the life course. This may be due to the difficulty in recouping the costs of training in either wages or productivity among older workers, given that the time span for cost recovery is shorter among older workers (see Gelderblom & de Koning, 2002, for Dutch data). Much training in France is used to integrate young labor market entrants into their workplaces because the *lycées professionels* are primarily focused on general theoretical education (Germe & Pottier, 1996). Similarly, in the United Kingdom (UK), a great deal of training has been found to be induction training of new recruits (Booth & Bryan, 2002).

This age-related pattern in training participation may differ among occupational groups. For example, Fournier (2003) found that in France the incidence of training declines more rapidly with age among elementary occupations than among managerial and intermediate occupations.

The dominant theoretical framework informing most of the research attempting to understand the observed patterns in participation in training has been the human capital approach. This approach, deriving from Becker (1975), situates the training participation decision in a classical utility maximizing framework within competitive labor markets: individual workers undertake training and employers invest in training on the basis of their estimates of future returns (including employment prospects, wages, and productivity gains). Access to training is thus not regarded as problematic, although market failures and barriers to training (e.g., imperfect capital markets and/or imperfect information) may lead to suboptimal investment in training.

With regard to continuing vocational training of employees, the human capital approach emphasizes the distinction between "general" and "specific" training. General training is defined in terms of its transferability: general training may be of use to current and subsequent employers, whereas specific training is of use only to the current employer. In this approach, employers will not pay for general training. If employers were to pay for general training, they would have to recoup the cost by paying a wage below marginal productivity after training, and in a competitive labor market, the workers would leave to earn their full marginal product with another employer. This gives rise to the poaching problem, whereby "nontraining" employers can pay higher rates to workers who have received general training from a previous employer. This has obvious implications for whomever bears the cost of training, and a consequence of this market failure is that there is underinvestment in training.

A key hypothesis arising from the human capital approach is that employers will not pay for general training, and extensions of the theory suggest that employees pay for general training, either directly or in the form of lower wages during the training period. This hypothesis does not receive much support from the empirical literature, which has found (1) that the theoretical distinction is difficult to operationalize, and (2) that many employers pay for both general and specific training. Most job-related training appears to be employer paid, at least partially, even when it occurs at the workplace or in the employer's training center. These patterns summarize the findings from Booth and Bryan (2002) in relation to the UK, Pischke (2000) in relation to Germany, and Loewenstein and Spletzer (1999) and Bishop (1996) in relation to the United States. For example, Booth and Bryan (2002) found that about 85% of respondents to the British Household Panel Survey considered their training to be general in nature, and 89% reported that it was employer financed. O'Connell (2004) showed that almost 80% of surveyed employees who received employer-sponsored training considered that the training was general and could be used both in their current job or be of use to another employer. Evertsson's (2004) analysis of an employee survey in Sweden showed that only about 5% of training is regarded as firm specific in Sweden, another 38% is industry but not firm specific, and more than half is general and fully portable across sectors and firms.

A key assumption of the human capital approach is that labor markets are perfectly competitive, which is, of course, an idealized notion. This assumption underpins the idea that employees can capture the full return on the investment in (general) training, either by earning their marginal product with their current employer or by moving to a different employer. Much of the recent literature has challenged this assumption. Acemoglu and Pischke (1999) argued that compressed wage structures, which may arise due to trade union organization or due to collective bargaining at sectoral or national levels, alter the incentive structure and give rise to a situation in which employers can capture at least some of the returns to training. Other reasons advanced for why employers may pay for general training also emphasize departures from perfect competition in the labor market, including transaction costs (e.g., asymmetric information) and institutional factors, and labor market regulation, such as employment protection legislation or minimum wages (Acemoglu & Pischke, 1999). Loewenstein and Spletzer (1999) developed a model in which training is determined within long-term contracts, including minimum wage guarantees. Bassanini et al. (2005) argued that employers may exercise market power in setting wages, for example, when employees face search frictions entailing imperfect information, mobility costs in changing jobs, and preferences regarding a range of nonwage characteristics of jobs (e.g., location, commuting, working time flexibility). This "new oligopsony" approach allows for situations in which the wage returns to training may be less than the productivity effects, providing a rationale for employers to pay for general training.

A key issue in this debate is whether wage compression induced by imperfect labor market competition may provide an incentive for employers to pay for general training. Bassanini and Brunello (2003), in an analysis of European Community Household Panel Survey data for seven countries, found that the incidence of general training (proxied by off-site training) is higher in clusters with a lower differential between wage growth of trained versus untrained workers. They find no evidence of a relationship between firm-specific training and the training wage premium. More detailed information on the importance of labor market institutions comes from Brunello (2001), who found that institutions do influence training incidence: countries with higher union density, stronger employment protection, and lower minimum wages (relative to the average wage) tend to show higher incidence of training. He also found that individuals with higher education are more likely to participate in training, and that training is higher in countries with more comprehensive school systems (e.g., Ireland or the UK) than in countries with highly stratified school systems (e.g., Germany), suggesting that continuing training after labor market entry is used to compensate for lack of specialization in initial education. The probability of getting a job is much higher for highly skilled young labor market entrants. The explanation for this is that those with higher levels of educational attainment are more likely to participate in training and employment schemes and are likely to learn new skills on the job more rapidly (Müller et al., 2002). Müller et al. drew the conclusion that in countries with educational systems closely related to work, unemployment is the lowest among young labor market entrants.

Most information on continuing education and training derives from individual-level survey data. However, research on enterprises confirms the stratified nature of training participation. Hughes et al. (2004) showed that enterprises are more engaged in training of their employees when they experience labor and skill shortages. However, although the vacancy rate among professional and technical workers is associated with an increase in training, vacancies among low-skilled workers have no impact on enterprises' training activities. In general, research on firms suggests that both the incidence and the intensity of training is higher in firms characterized by relatively advantaged workforces – in organizations where average wages are higher and greater proportions of the workforce are in higher-level occupations or possess higher skills (Lynch, 1994; Booth & Zoega, 2000; O'Connell, 2002b). The nature of the firm plays an important role. Small enterprises are more likely to use initial qualification as a substitute for on-the-job-training (Bellmann & Düll, 1999). Firm internal labor markets are of prime importance for the structure of qualifications and wages in the economy (Gerlach & Stephan, 1999).

The previous discussion suggests that institutions are important in the labor market and, consequently, may influence training. Trade unions represent one important dimension of such institutional factors. Unions may affect training either directly, through training agreements, or indirectly, through wage bargaining. The empirical results on the impact of unions of training are mixed. Numerous studies have found a positive impact of union membership or presence on training, for example, in the United States (Lynch, 1992), the UK (Booth et al., 2003), and Germany (Dustmann & Schönberg, 2004). In contrast, however, Mincer (1983) and Barron et al. (1987) find negative effects for the United States, and Bassanini et al. (2005) find no significant effect of unions across the thirteen countries covered by the European Community Household Panel Survey.

For most workers in advanced industrial societies the employment contract entails an ongoing and relatively long-term relationship that may differ in important respects from the competitive labor market assumed in the Becker model (Barrett & O'Connell, 2001). The workplace is an important site for human capital formation, and workplace characteristics may vie for importance with the personal attributes of individual employees in determining allocation and nature of training at work. Indeed, coinciding with the resurgence of interest in human capital discussed previously, there is also growing interest in the impact of workplace change on performance of organizations and enterprises (e.g., flexibility, new technology, new working arrangements). This turns our attention to the demand side of the labor market and to the social organization of work. The segmented labor market approach focuses more on the characteristics of jobs rather than individuals, and argues that different labor market sectors impose structural limitations both on the returns to education and experience and on the career prospects of workers (Doeringer & Piore, 1971; Gordon et al., 1982). At their simplest, labor market segments can be dichotomized, with the primary market consisting of well-paid and secure employment as opposed to jobs in the secondary market that are poorly paid and are of a precarious nature with few or no prospects for upward mobility. From this perspective, workers in the secondary labor market are less likely to participate in job-related training, and the returns to such training are lower. Workers in the primary segment(s) are more likely to receive training, the returns are higher, and such training is likely to be associated with upward mobility, perhaps in an internal labor market.

In their classical study of educational policies and industrial organizations comparing Germany and France, Maurice et al. (1982) showed that the education and training system is closely related to the structure of the internal labor market of the firm. They argued that the education and training system can only be compared in light of the social space situating work organization, human relations, and social mobility. The qualification space in Germany is characterized by an external labor market with professional qualifications in the dual apprenticeship system. In France, the authors discovered a strong hierarchical ranking of positions in the firms related to general education and a devaluation of professional training. However, more recent developments in the French economy, including the advent of new working arrangements and the need for flexibility, have led to a decline in the importance of the internal labor market, and an increase in intercompany mobility has called for new organizational concepts (Lichtenberger & Méhaut, 2001). This has given rise to a shift in training participation in which professionals engaged in the core activities of firms are the more likely to participate in continuing training, whereas professionals in outsourced services to firms are more likely to rely on their initial educational qualifications. Those with the lowest educational attainments are excluded from continuing training in this structural shift (Lichtenberger & Méhaut, 2001).

One issue that does not appear, as yet, to have received much attention in the literature on participation in training is the extent to which these highly stratified patterns of access to continuing vocational training relate to the characteristics of individuals (e.g., education) or to the characteristics of their jobs and workplaces (e.g., nature of contract, sector, size of firm, workplace practices). This relates to the debate between human capital and labor market segmentation approaches: Do workers with lower skills receive less employer-sponsored training because of their low educational attainment, or because their lower skills increase their probability of working in the secondary labor market, a segment in which less training is undertaken? The answer to this question has obvious policy implications for how public intervention might alter the distribution of access to training.

O'Connell (2004) showed that the presence of participation arrangements for deciding how work is actually carried out is associated with a higher probability of training. Similarly, employees reporting extensive consultation relating to their jobs are also more likely to have participated in training. Employees in workplaces that have adopted family-friendly working arrangements

are also more likely to participate in training. These three workplace practices are also associated with increased likelihood of participation in general
rather than firm-specific training.

EFFECTS OF TRAINING

The wealth of empirical research on the labor market effects of initial education (see, e.g., De la Fuente & Ciccone, 2002) stands in stark contrast to the
paucity of research on the effects of continuing vocational training, which
can still be characterized as a developing field of inquiry. Most empirical work
suggests that there are positive wage returns to training. Blundell et al. (1996)
found positive wage returns to training in the UK. Schömann and Becker
(2002) found similar effects in Germany. However, wage returns to training
appear to be low in France, at least in the short-term perspective (Goux &
Maurin, 1998; Gonzales-Demichel & Nauze-Fichet, 2002). However, it should
be acknowledged that when selection effects are controlled for, the returns
are frequently found to be small or even nonsignificant.

In an analysis of European Community Household Panel Survey data for
thirteen European countries, Brunello (2001) found that training, both on
the job and off the job, increases current earnings growth, although likely
only temporarily. Earnings growth is somewhat higher for those with upper
secondary education than those with tertiary education, and among the latter,
the returns to training decline with labor market experience, perhaps because
educational qualifications become outdated over an extensive period of time.

One of the interesting findings from the literature on the impact of training
is that the wage returns may be higher among those with low propensity to
participate in training (e.g., Bartell, 1995, in the United States; Booth, 1991,
and Blundell et al., 1996, in the UK; Pischke, 1996, in Germany). Higher
returns to training among groups with low rates of training participation
(e.g., those with low educational attainment) could be due to selection effects
as well as higher returns to training among those with poor qualifications
who nevertheless work in the primary segment of the labor market, or, in the
formulation of Booth and Zoega (2000), in "good" firms, where the average
stock of human capital is high.

With regard to the returns to training, human capital theory anticipates
that the returns, in the form of wages, are positive and "smooth," so that
additional periods of continuing vocational training should have, on average, positive and linear effects on wages. Again, however, institutional factors,
including wage compression and differential labor mobility may alter the
returns to training in differing institutional contexts, for example, across

countries. However, recent literature again challenges the human capital approach, and the key issue is the departure from a perfectly competitive labor market. Although human capital theory assumes a competitive labor market in which trained employees receive their marginal product and thus the full fruits of their labor enhanced by training, workers in a noncompetitive labor market may not receive their full marginal product, and the benefits of training may be shared between employer and employee. There is some evidence that the benefits of training are shared between employer and employee. Barron et al. (1989) found that the benefits of training are split more or less equally between productivity gains reaped by employers and wage increases to employees in the United States. In a panel study of British industries, Dearden et al. (2000) showed that the effect of training on productivity was twice as large as that on wages. Other studies that have looked at the impact of training on corporate performance also suggest that employers do appropriate at least some of the returns to training investments. These outcomes are consistent with the contracting model advanced by Loewenstein and Spletzer (1999), in which training is determined within long-term contracts, including minimum wage guarantees. This would also be supported by the finding that general training increases company turnover or sales (Barrett & O'Connell, 2001).

Some of the returns to training are captured by workers either with a time lag or when they change employers. Loewenstein and Spletzer (1999) found that the estimated effect of general training in a previous job is three times higher than in the current job. Booth and Bryan (2002) found that employer-provided training increases wages in both current and future firms and that the impact is larger in future firms. These effects suggest that employers have some monopsony power over their own trained workers; trained workers may not receive their marginal product; and training, including general training paid for by employers, may be transferable across jobs. These effects are not consistent with the implications of the human capital approach and the assumption of a competitive labor market. Of interest here is that the empirical research on the incidence and effects of training may be of interest in not only in its own right, but may also have important implications for the dominant theoretical framework informing our understanding of the relationship between human capital formation and labor market behavior.

Research on the longer-term impact of training appears to be particularly scarce. Schömann and Becker (2002) showed that further training of employed workers in East Germany reduces the risk of becoming unemployed over the long term. Blundell et al. (1996) showed that training increases the likelihood of promotion and has a positive effect on job tenure in the UK.

The long-term effects of training on both earnings and career development should be regarded as an important and fruitful area for new research, to take advantage of the improved availability of longitudinal data sets.

Empirical evidence of the impact of training at the level of the enterprise is less developed than the evidence relating to individuals, although there is a growing literature that suggests that training increases the productivity of firms and leads to higher earnings for trained personnel. Quantitative analysis of enterprise-level data has tended to focus more on the effects of training on company performance (e.g., Bartell, 1989; Holzer et al., 1993; Barrett & O'Connell, 2001), although several studies have found evidence of positive effects of training on wages (Booth, 1991; Bartell, 1995; Goux & Maurin, 1997; Loewenstein & Spletzer, 1997). Moreover, numerous studies have found that training enhances both company performance and workers' wages (Bishop, 1994; Groot & Osterbeek, 1995).

The lack of development of research on training at the level of the enterprise is understandable given data constraints, but unfortunate. The workplace is an important site of human capital formation, as we have argued from the outset of this chapter. Moreover, our brief review of the literature on both participation in and effects of training suggests that workplace characteristics are important. We have seen that enterprise size and sector influence training, as do the corporate structure and contractual relations. These findings also point to the potential importance of workplace social relations in influencing both the incidence and the effects of training. Indeed, coinciding with the resurgence of interest in human capital discussed previously, there is also growing interest in the impact of workplace change on performance of organizations and enterprises (including flexibility, new technology, and new working arrangements). Ichniowski et al. (1997) showed that the impact of training on enterprise performance is contingent on complementary human resource practices in a longitudinal study of training in U.S. steel plants. Black and Lynch (1996), however, did not find strong evidence of such interaction in their data. Although the U.S. evidence is thus inconclusive, it does suggest that a focus on the workplace – in particular, on aspects of social relations and human resource practices in the workplace – is a useful area for further sociological work on training.

DISCUSSION

Although stratification in access to training participation may be universal, further research is needed on variations in inequality in access to continuing vocational training. Institutional characteristics of national labor markets, including wage setting institutions as well as national labor market regulations, offer promising potential. Acemoglu and Pischke (1999) argued that national wage setting arrangements that give rise to compressed wage structures may increase the level of training, particularly general training. Where compressed wage structures coincide with strong employment protection legislation, giving rise to lower labor mobility, the incidence of training may be higher while the returns to training are lower. Analysis of the incidence and effects of training in the context of institutional differences in wage compression and labor regulation could contribute to explanations for why earnings have become more dispersed in some countries than others (e.g., the United States vs. many European countries). More generally, if indeed most employer-sponsored training is general, then this raises questions about the assumption underlying the human capital approach. So the focus on training may be of interest not only in its own right, but may also have important implications for our assessment of the human capital approach to the relationship between human capital formation and labor market behavior. Although the human capital approach is based on the expectation that workers who have received general training may be more mobile, workers in organizations that invest in general training may have lower attrition rates if they interpret the provision of general training as part of a long-term contract within which their employable (and therefore transferable) skills are likely to be upgraded (Barrett & O'Connell, 2001). This may have particular relevance in the knowledge economy: "training firms" may be more attractive to employees than nontraining firms and thus use training provision as a recruitment or retention strategy. If this were the case, we might expect that firms would pay for general training of highly skilled workers, where skills are in short supply as part of a retention strategy within an internal labor market.

Research into the effects of training of employed workers is, at best, a developing field. Crucial questions remain to be addressed, particularly with regard to longer-term effects of training on employment security and career progression. Again, obvious areas for investigation include national labor market institutions and other contextual factors. An additional area of work of particular interest for sociology is the relationship between workplace practices and the impact of training for both individuals and organizations.

References

Acemoglu, D., & Pischke, J.-S. (1999). Beyond Becker: Training in imperfect labour markets. *The Economic Journal*, 109, F112–F142.

Arulampalam, W., & Booth, A. L. (1998). Training and labour market flexibility: Is there a trade-off? *British Journal of Industrial Relations*, 36(4), 521–536.

Barrett, A., & O'Connell, P. J. (2001). Does training generally work? The returns to in-company training. *Industrial and Labour Relations Review*, 54, 647–662.

Barron, J., Black, D., & Loewenstein, M. (1987). Employer size: The implications for search, training, capital investment, starting wages, and wage growth. *Journal of Labour Economics*, 5(1), 76–89.

Barron, J., Black, D., Loewenstein, M. (1989). Job matching and on-the-job training. *Journal of Labour Economics*, 7(1), 1–19.

Bartell, A. (1989). *Formal Employee Training Programme and Their Impact on Labour Productivity: Evidence from a Human Resources Survey*. Working Paper No. 3026, National Bureau of Economic Research, Cambridge, MA.

Bartell, A. (1995). Training, wage growth, and job performance: Evidence from a company database. *Journal of Labor Economics*, 3, 401–425.

Bassanini, A., Booth, A., Brunello, G., DaPaola, M., & Leuven, E. (2005). *Workplace Training in Europe*. Conference paper, Fondazione Rodolfo de Benedetti, Venice, July.

Bassanini, G., & Brunello, G. (2003). *Is Training More Frequent When Wage Compression is Higher? Evidence from the European Household Community Panel*. IZA Discussion Paper No. 830.

Becker, G. (1975). *Human Capital* (2nd ed.). New York: Columbia University.

Becker, R. (1999). Berufliche Weiterbildung und Arbeitsmarktchancen im gesellschaftlichen Umbruch. In F. Büchel, M. Diewald, P. Krause, A. Mertens, & H. Solga (Eds.), *Zwischen drinnen und draußen – Soziale Ausgrenzung am deutschen Arbeitsmarkt* (pp. 95–106). Opladen, Germany: Leske + Budrich.

Bellmann, L., & Düll, H. (1999). Die Bedeutung des beruflichen Bildungsabschlusses in der betrieblichen Weiterbildung. Eine Analyse auf der Basis des IAB Betriebspanels 1997 für West- und Ostdeutschland. In L. Bellmann & V. Steiner (Eds.), *Panelanalysen zur Lohnstruktur, Qualifikation und Beschäftigungsdynamik* (pp. 317–352). Nürnberg, Germany: Institut für Arbeitsmarkt- und Berufsforschung, Beiträge zur Arbeitsmarkt- und Berufsforschung Nr. 229.

Bellmann, L., & Düll, H. (2001). Die zeitliche Lage und Kostenaufteilung von Weiterbildungsmaßnahmen – Empirische Ergebnisse auf der Grundlage des IAB Betriebspanels. In R. Dobischat & H. Seifert (Eds.), *Lernzeiten neu organisieren* (pp. 81–128). Berlin: Edition Sigma.

Bishop, J. (1994). The impact of previous training on productivity and wages. In L. Lynch (Ed.), *Training and the Private Sector* (pp. 161–199). Chicago: The University of Chicago Press.

Bishop, J. H. (1996). *What We Know about Employer-Provided Training: A Review of Literature*. Studies Working Paper No. 96–09, Center for Advanced Human Resource, New York.

Black, S., & Lynch, L. (1996). Human capital investments and productivity. *American Economic Review*, 86(2), 263–267

Blundell, R., Dearden, L., & Meghir, C. (1996). *The Determinants and Effects of Work-Related in Britain*. London: Institute for Fiscal Studies.

Booth, A. (1991). Job-related formal training: Who receives it and what is it worth? *Oxford Bulletin of Economics and Statistics*, August, 281–294.

Booth A., & Bryan, M. (2002). *Who Pays for General Training? New Evidence for British Men and Women*. IZA Discussion Paper No. 486.

Booth, A., Francesconi, M., & Zoega, G. (2003). Unions, work-related training and wages: Evidence for British men. *Industrial and Labour Relations Review*, 57(1), 68–91.

Booth, A., & Zoega, G. (2000). *Why Do Firms Invest in General Training? 'Good' Firms and 'Bad' Firms as a Source of Monopsony Power*. CEPR Discussion Paper No. 2536.

Brunello, G. (2001). *On the Complementarity between Education and Training in Europe*. IZA Discussion Paper No. 309.

Checcaglini, A. (2000). Former pour éviter la marginalisation. *Formation Emploi*, 69, 53–63.

De la Fuente, A., & Ciccone, A. (2002). *Human Capital and Growth in a Global and Knowledge-Based Economy*. Report for the European Commission, DG for Employment and Social Affairs.

Dearden, L., Reed, H., & van Reenen, J. M. (2000). *Who Gains When Workers Train? Training and Corporate Productivity in a Panel of British Industries*. CEPR Discussion Paper No. 2486.

Doeringer, P. B., & Piore, M. J. (1971). *Internal Labor Markets and Manpower Analysis*. Lexington, MA: D.C. Heath and Company.

Dustmann, C., & Schönberg, U. (2004). *Training and Union Wages*. IZA Discussion Paper No. 1435.

Evertsson, M. (2004). Formal on-the-job training: A gender-typed experience and wage-related advantage? *European Sociological Review*, 20(1), 79–94.

Fay, R. (1996). *Enhancing the Effectiveness of Active Labour Market Policies: Evidence from Programme Evaluation in OECD Countries*. Labour Market and Social Policy Occasional Paper 18, OECD, Paris.

Fournier, C. (2001). Hommes et femmes salariés face à la formation continue. *Bref-Céreq*, 179(1), 1–4.

Fournier, C. (2003). Développer la formation des "séniors"? Deux questions préliminaires. *Formation Emploi*, 81, 37–49.

Friedlander, D., Greenberg, D. H., & Robins, P. K. (1997). Evaluating government training programmes for the economically disadvantaged. *Journal of Economic Literature*, 35, 1809–1855.

Gelderblom, A., & de Koning, J. (2002). Exclusion of older workers, productivity and training. In K. Schömann & P. O'Connell (Eds.), *Education, Training and Employment Dynamics* (pp. 243–259). Cheltenham, UK: Edward Elgar.

Gerlach, K., & Stephan, G. (1999). Betriebsinterne Arbeitsmärkte und die qualifikatorische Lohn- und Beschäftigungsstruktur. Zum Stand der Diskussion. *Jahrbücher für Nationalökonomie und Statistik*, 219(1/2), 32–48.

Germe, J.-F., & Pottier, F. (1996). *Les formations continues à l'initiative des individus en France: déclin ou renouveau?* Revue Européenne "Formation Professionnelle" No. 8/9.

Gonzales-Demichel, C., & Nauze-Fichet, E. (2002). *Les Déterminants des réussites professionelles*. Rennes, France: Céreq.

Gordon, D., Edwards, R., & Reich, M. (1982). *Segmented Work, Divided Workers: The Historical Transformation of Labour in the United States*. Cambridge, UK: Cambridge University Press.

Goux, D., & Maurin, E. (1997). *Returns to Continuous Training: Evidence from French Worker-Firm Matched Data*. Mimeograph, CREST, Paris.

Goux, D., & Maurin, E. (1998). From education to first job: The French case. In Y. Shavit & W. Müller (Eds.), *From School to Work: A Comparative Study of Educational Qualifications and Occupational Attainment* (pp. 103–142). Oxford, UK: Clarendon Press.

Groot, W., & Osterbeek, H. (1995). *Determinants and Wages Effects of Different Components of Participation in On- and Off-the-Job Training*. Research Memorandum, Tinbergen Institute, Rotterdam, The Netherlands.

Heckman, J. J., Lalonde, R. J., & Smith, J. A. (1999). The economics and econometrics of active labor market programs. In O. C. Ashenfelter & D. Card (Eds.), *Handbook of Labor Economics* (Vol. 3A, pp. 1865–2097). Amsterdam: North-Holland Elsevier.

Holzer, H., Block, R., Cheathem, M., & Knott, J. (1993). Are training subsidies for firms effective? The Michigan experience. *Industrial and Labour Relations Review*, 46, 625–636.

Hughes, G., O'Connell, P., & Williams, J. (2004). Company training and low-skill consumer-service jobs in Ireland. *International Journal of Manpower*, 25(1), 17–35.

Ichniowski, C., Shaw, K., & Prennushi, G. (1997). The effects of human resource management practices on productivity. *American Economic Review*, 87, 291–313.

Lichtenberger, Y., & Méhaut, P. (2001). Les enjeux d'une refonte de la formation professionnelle continue – Bilan pour un futur. *Liaisons Sociales*, 723, 1–11.

Loewenstein, M. A., & Spletzer, J. R. (1997). *Belted Training: The Relationship Between Training, Tenure and Wages*. Mimeograph, U.S. Bureau of Labor Statistics.

Loewenstein, M. A., & Spletzer, J. R. (1999). General and specific training: Evidence and implications. *Journal of Human Resources*, 34(4), 710–733.

Lynch, L. (1992). Private sector training and its impact on the earnings of young workers. *American Economic Review*, 82(1), 299–312.

Lynch, L. (Ed.). (1994). *Training and the Private Sector: International Comparisons*. Chicago: The University of Chicago Press.

Maurice, M., Sellier, F., & Silvestre, J.-J. (1982). *Politique d'éducation et organisation industrielle en France et en Allemagne*. Paris: PUF.

Méhaut, P. (Ed.). (2003). Repenser la formation continue. *Formation Emploi*, 81, 27–37.

Mincer, J. (1983). Union effects on wages, turnover, and job training. *Research in Labour Economics*, 2, 217–252.

Müller, W., Gangl, M., & Scherer, S. (2002). Übergangsstrukturen zwischen Bildung und Beschäftigung. In M. Wingens & R. Sackmann (Eds.), *Bildung und Beruf: Ausbildung und berufsstruktureller Wandel in der Wissensgesellschaft* (pp. 39–64). Weinheim/München, Germany: Juventa.

O'Connell, P. J. (1999). *Adults in Training: An International Comparison of Continuing Education and Training*. Paris: OECD.

O'Connell, P. J. (2002a). Are they working? Market orientation and the effectiveness of active labour market programmes in Ireland. *European Sociological Review*, 18, 65–83.

O'Connell, P. J. (2002b). Does enterprise-sponsored training aggravate or alleviate existing inequalities? Evidence from Ireland. In K. Schömann & P. J. O'Connell (Eds.), *Education, Training and Employment Dynamics* (pp. 285–302). Cheltenham, UK: Edward Elgar.

O'Connell, P. J. (2004). *Who Generally Trains? The Effects of Personal and Workplace Characteristics on Training at Work*. Paper presented to TLM.net conference, Amsterdam, November 25–26.

OECD, (2005). *Education at a Glance.* Paris: Organisation for Economic Cooperation and Development (OECD).

Pischke, J.-S. (1996). *Continuous Training in Germany.* Working Paper No. 5829. National Bureau of Economic Research, Cambridge, MA.

Pischke, J.-S. (2000). *Continuous Training in Germany.* IZA Discussion Paper No. 137.

Schömann, K. (1998). *The Interface between Organizational Learning and Life-Long Learning.* Social Science Research Center (WZB), Berlin: Mimeograph.

Schömann, K., & Becker, R. (2002). A long-term perspective on the effects of training in Germany. In K. Schömann & P. J. O'Connell (Eds.), *Education, Training and Employment Dynamics: Transitional Labour Markets in the European Union* (pp. 152–185). Cheltenham, UK: Edward Elgar.

Schömann, K., & O'Connell, P. (Eds.). (2003). *Education, Training and Employment Dynamics.* Cheltenham, UK: Edward Elgar.

Trautmann, J. (2002). Retours en formation. In Céreq (Ed.), *Formation tout au long de la vie et carrières en Europe.* 9es Journées d'études Céreq – Lasmas-IdL, Rennes, France, May 15–16.

Wingens, M., Sackmann, R., & Grotheer, M. (2000). Berufliche Qualifizierung für Arbeitslose. Zur Effektivität AFG-finanzierter Weiterbildung im Transformationsprozess. *Kölner Zeitschrift für Soziologie und Sozialpsychologie,* 21(1), 60–80.

6 Qualifications and the Returns to Training Across the Life Course

Walter Müller and Marita Jacob

SOCIOLOGICAL PERSPECTIVE ON SKILLS AND QUALIFICATIONS

There are many ways in which the process of skill formation can be socially organized; this process differs substantially even in advanced economies at similar levels of technological development. Many abilities and skills necessary and useful for life are learned from early childhood onward in daily interaction with parents, other adults, and peers, or through the exposition to and use of communication media. In this chapter, however, we are mainly interested in the formation of abilities and skills required to perform work tasks in jobs, and we examine the returns of qualifications in work contexts.

Whereas in psychology and education science, skills and competences are often understood as specific cognitive or other capabilities of individuals to solve particular problems and/or perform particular tasks, sociology usually has a much broader understanding of them. The sociologist's understanding is probably best captured in the concept of *qualification*. The latter refers to sets of skills needed to perform more or less homogeneous sets of tasks, for instance, for a particular job or profession. In most research, the conceptualization of qualifications and their measurement then refers to the successful completion of particular programs in institutions of (general) education and vocational training in a society. Thus, the sociological understanding of skills or competences in the sense of qualifications is to a large degree institutionally shaped and socially and culturally constructed. This includes the institutionally shaped processes of the teaching, learning, testing, and certifying of skills in specific education and training institutions, as well as the recognition, use, and valuation of obtained qualifications in recruitment processes by social actors such as firms or other work organizations.[1]

With the emphasis on the qualifications obtained in the education and training system, the sociological view captures the means and channels through which societies provide these qualification packages to their populations. These packages – highly differentiated from each other as they are – to a large extent shape individuals' future life prospects, especially their opportunities on the labor market. Sociology's interest then is to investigate and understand why and how they do this. Which individuals and social groups (e.g., constituted by gender, class, or ethnicity) have access to the more or less advantageous qualifications? Which dimensions and characteristics of qualifications have what kind of consequences for specific working life and other life course outcomes, and what are the implications for the social structure and stratification of societies? Beyond the more narrow working life and stratification consequences, sociology investigates many other implications of qualifications such as for social attitudes, civic and political engagement, social behavior (e.g., mating or fertility patterns), social cohesion, and social conflicts.

Sociological inquiry of the acquisition and use of qualifications refers to both the individual perspective (i.e., the perspective of actors who invest in the acquisition of skills and collect the returns they provide) and the institutional perspective, focusing on the conditions, in particular, in terms of opportunities, costs, and benefits of skill acquisition and their returns. In many respects, sociology in this area shares the interests and approaches of economists. In contrast to the latter, however, sociologists emphasize a broad variety of social conditions of skill acquisition, examine social inequalities that are intergenerationally transmitted by differential access to education and training, and consider a plurality of outcome dimensions (e.g., employment [security], class, status, income). Moreover, they are usually also more concerned with the institutional arrangements and their variation across time and between societies, as well as with the distributions of occupations or economic sectors, their change over time, and the implications they have on skill requirement.

In this chapter, we review sociological research on qualification attainment and on qualification returns on the labor market, discussing general theoretical perspectives and mechanisms used in sociology to understand the basic characteristics and patterns in the respective processes, as well as the impacts of differences in the institutional and structural conditions that may lead to cross-country variation in the features of qualification attainment and their labor market consequences. Qualification attainment and skill formation and their returns extend over large parts of the life course. We therefore pursue a life course perspective through a special section on the timing of the acquisition of qualifications in the life course, and through differentiating between returns to education and training at labor market entry and in the later work career. Furthermore, in this discussion, we include sociological focus on the social inequalities generated by processes of qualification attainment and returns. Finally, we explore possible responses to the challenges for education and training resulting from recent changes in the world of work and summarize the need for future research.

ACQUISITION OF QUALIFICATIONS OVER THE LIFE COURSE

Human capital theory provides a parsimonious set of assumptions about the mechanisms generating education and training that are quite powerful in accounting for a number of general findings concerning skill formation and skill returns over the life course. According to the basic premise of this microeconomic theory, skill formation is essentially a process of making investments and collecting returns on investments. Economic hypotheses derived from this understanding of investment behavior help elucidate pervasive regularities in the investments made for different kinds of skills by both workers and employers. A core assumption is that investments in human capital actually increase productivity and that higher productivity is the cause for higher returns. The relationship between the costs of investment and the resulting returns determine the amount of investments. However, this assumption is questioned by other theories. The controversy still continues about the extent to which the skills, competences, and productivity acquired through education and training indeed govern the allocation of workers to work tasks and rewards, or whether diplomas and qualifications just signal (more or less correctly) potential productivity (Arrow, 1973; Spence, 1973). In this view, the individuals primarily aim at obtaining recognized signals that are valuable in the competition for more or less rewarding jobs in the labor market. (We return to this point later in this chapter.)

Regardless of the actual reasons for different returns to qualifications in the labor market, several hypotheses concerning investments in education and training can be derived:

1. Individuals whose expectations and/or rates of successful skill acquisition are higher and whose associated costs are lower will obtain more education and training than individuals in less favorable conditions. Individuals who learn easily and quickly should obtain higher levels of education and training than those with lesser learning capacities. This is – according to the microeconomic theory – the basic mechanism that generates the highly unequal distribution of individuals to levels of education and training that can be observed for all advanced societies.

2. The basic investment mechanism of timing encourages individuals to invest in skill formation early in life in order to accumulate returns over longer periods.

3. General hypotheses on who will pay for skill formation have been proposed by Becker (1964) and are based on his distinction between general and specific qualifications. General qualifications are of value for different jobs, and most important, portable between different employers, whereas specific qualifications are tied to jobs with a particular employer. As a consequence, workers should be ready to pay for the acquisition of general qualifications, but not for specific ones. Employers, in contrast, should be ready to pay for investments in specific qualifications, but only if they can expect returns through higher productivity of the worker.

How are these general assumptions and hypotheses specified and revised by sociological research? By introducing the sociological perspective on inequalities in skill acquisition and how these are mediated by institutional variations, we show how sociological research has extended these general assumptions, both theoretically and empirically. We now discuss (1) a general theoretical model for explaining inequality in initial qualification acquisition, (2) historical change in inequality and its dependence on institutional conditions, and (3) the timing of the acquisition of qualifications in the life course.

Inequality in Qualification Acquisition – A General Theoretical Model

The distribution of skills and qualifications obtained through education and training among individuals is highly unequal. The amount, level, and kind of skills and qualifications individuals obtain are clearly associated with their learning capacities, as indicated by correlations with measured IQ or other measures of ability (Kirsch et al., 1993; Desjardins et al., 2005). However, instead of taking this as given, sociological inquiry is interested in understanding how such differences in abilities and learning capacities emerge and how, furthermore, investments in skill formation not only depend on learning capacities, but also on specific social conditions and opportunity structures shaped by education and training systems. Herewith sociological inquiry emphasizes the social and cultural conditions into which individuals are born and in which they grow up. Taking up the distinction between primary and secondary effects of social stratification first introduced by Boudon (1974), a lot of sociological research has established intricate social processes and mechanisms that lead to unequal educational attainment (for a detailed review, see Erikson & Jonsson, 1996a, 1996b). Following Mare (1980), educational attainment and skill acquisition is now generally analyzed as a process of successive educational transitions structured by educational systems in which primary and secondary effects of social origin conditions are interrelated.

Primary effects derive from the different environments for learning and intellectual stimulation caused by different class backgrounds that strengthen cognitive abilities and learning motivation in children, as well as influence performance at school. Different performance at school also derives from differences in parental encouragement and support for schoolwork, or class differences in nutrition and health. Given the nature of primary effects, they are chiefly studied in the education sciences investigating how individual abilities; various economic, social, and cultural conditions of the home environment; school and school class characteristics; tracking and curriculum arrangements; and teacher/teaching characteristics interact in leading to different performance at school. However, this is not reviewed any further here.[2]

Secondary effects refer to class differences in the choices individuals make in their educational careers, given the same performance in schools. Far from just resulting from ability or school performance differences, class-related disparities in these choices typically occur at institutionalized points in the educational careers, when decisions have to be made about whether to leave or continue education and which of the available track or level options to take in continuing education. In rational action models developed to understand such class-dependent choices, there are three components typically seen to be responsible for why middle or upper class students are more likely than working class students to continue to higher levels or more advantageous tracks of education. Students from middle or upper class families can more easily bear the costs of higher education, they expect higher rates of success in education, and they have the incentive to continue to higher education in order to avoid downward mobility (Erikson & Jonsson, 1996a; Breen & Goldthorpe, 1997; Esser, 1999; Breen & Yaish, 2006).

Both primary and secondary mechanisms usually operate at all transitions and levels of educational careers. As effects accumulate over successive transitions, disparities between children from different social backgrounds are more pronounced the higher the attained level of education is, even though – conditional on previous attainment – secondary effects tend to be largest at transition points early in the educational career. The disparities in educational progression and attainment produced by the combined primary and secondary effects can be substantial. In their comparative study of European countries, Breen et al. (2006) found that – depending on country and historical period – at each successive step, the odds of children from a higher salaried background successfully rising to the next level of education rather than leaving at the previously attained level are between 20 and more than 100 times larger than the respective odds of children from unskilled working class families. Studies from Sweden and the UK indicate that primary effects account for about half or somewhat more than half of social class disparities (Erikson & Jonsson, 1996b; Jackson et al., 2006). For an illustration of the extent of secondary disparities, consider the transition from secondary education to university studies in Germany. Among Abitur graduates with the best grades (top 20%), 80% enter a university study program if their father achieved at least upper secondary education and has an upper service class job, while only 40% of similarly high-performing students do so when they come from working class homes and have fathers with less than upper secondary education (Reimer & Pollak, 2005). Being largely independent of ability and demonstrated performance at school, disparities of this size can be seen as an indicator of an undeniably large waste of talent related to the social conditions affecting educational choices.

Although class disparities in qualification attainment are still high in all countries, the once large gender disparities in educational attainment have become fairly equalized.[3] Men and women, however, still differ to a large extent in the choice of subject areas in which they acquire qualifications. The reason for this gender disparity and its implications in terms of labor market prospects is a growing area of sociological stratification research that cannot be discussed here in detail,[4] ditto for the often observed lower level of skill acquisition of ethnic minorities or immigrant groups compared to the ethnic majority or the native population. A consistent finding is that the disparities are usually caused less by characteristics of a specific ethnicity or minority per se than by lower class position and poorer language proficiency of these groups (Alba et al., 1994; Vallet & Caille, 1995; Kalter & Granato, 2002; Esser, 2006; Heath & Cheung, 2007; Kalter et al., 2007).

Historical Change and Institutional Variation in Educational Inequality

The described mechanisms and processes generating social disparities may produce different results in different contexts. To test the impact of social, structural, and institutional factors, sociological research has intensively studied both variations across times and countries in the pattern and extent of social inequalities in educational attainment. A finding of these studies to be noted first, however, is a large degree of commonality in the resulting *patterns* of inequality, even though the *amount* of resulting inequalities may vary across time and between countries. For example, across time and countries, the rank order of social classes according to the level of qualifications reached by children born into different classes is usually very similar. Also, social inequalities are usually largest at the very first transition in the educational career, and then decline at later transitions (Müller & Karle, 1993; Shavit & Blossfeld, 1993). It is often assumed, even though rarely proven, that this occurs because at each higher level of education the survivors from earlier transitions become increasingly homogenous between the social classes in terms of ability and other education relevant resources, and that this leads to declining social disparities in the successive transitions on the educational ladder (Mare, 1981, 1993). The extent of inequalities, however, also varies.

On the grounds of the theoretical model described previously, variation essentially should derive from two major sources: (1) from variation and change in the social, economic, and cultural conditions that different classes face and that affect class-related achievement in schools and/or expectations concerning costs, success, and returns of education; and (2) from variation in the setup of the educational system that affects school performance of children of different classes, or lets them follow different educational routes and reach different levels or kinds of qualifications. These can also be expressed in terms of variation in the costs of education, for instance, length of compulsory schooling, the structure and timing of track differentiation, promotion and track transfer regulations, or the relative availability and rules of access to general versus vocational courses of study (for detailed discussion, see Erikson & Jonsson, 1996a; Breen et al., 2006).

A milestone study examining the development and variation of educational inequality was conducted by Shavit and Blossfeld (1993). It particularly focused on the role of educational reforms and massive educational expansion in the second half of the twentieth century. The key result was that – except for Sweden and the Netherlands – in the thirteen countries studied, neither the massive increase in study places (educational expansion) nor educational reforms "led to a reduction in the association between social origins and *any* of the educational transitions" (Shavit & Blossfeld, 1993, p. 19, our italics). Recent studies, based on more powerful samples, however, found that besides Sweden and the Netherlands, class-related inequalities in educational attainment are found to have declined for successive twentieth-century birth cohorts in various other countries (e.g., Germany, France, the UK, Poland, and [for women] Italy; Breen et al., 2006). Even though in some countries the declining trend has leveled off and in all countries we are still far from a situation of equal educational opportunities, much recent evidence indicates that in many countries inequalities are clearly smaller than in the prewar or immediate post–World War II decades. This evidence is mainly descriptive, and we have not determined which of the various potential social, structural, or institutional conditions are indeed responsible for the decline in inequalities. In an exemplary study for Sweden, Erikson (1996) identified several conditions to be systematically related to declining inequality of educational opportunity, including declining income inequality and high levels of economic security, financial aid to students, and educational reforms (especially postponing educational decisions implemented with the introduction of the comprehensive school system). What can be generalized to other countries is an open question. But the study makes clear that it is likely not a single determinant, but a number of factors that may jointly lead to lower socially based disparities.[5] In particular, in earlier studies for Sweden and other countries, the massive educational expansion was found not to be primarily responsible for the socially more equal participation in education.[6] However, in more recent research, the role of educational expansion is reinterpreted. Although in "persistent inequality" educational expansion was seen to "facilitate(s) to a large extent the persistence of inequalities in educational opportunity" (Shavit & Blossfeld, 1993, p. 22), it is seen now as a mechanism of "inclusion" (Arum et al., 2007).

Shavit and Blossfeld (1993) analyzed changes over time within systems. The study of institutional and structural effects through comparisons between systems is often even more difficult, both because of the inherent epistemological difficulty of drawing conclusions from comparing systems that usually differ in various respects and due to the lack of validly comparable data. Still, it is well established that the extent of inequalities clearly varies between systems. Evidence is based on essentially two sources of data. The first source of data is the various international student assessment projects on competences mastered by students, which indicate huge differences between countries in the social class gradients already at early stages of the school career. Class disparities or social gradients in these studies overwhelmingly – although not exclusively – relate to primary effects, especially in countries in which at the time of measurement students are still in compulsory education and not yet segregated in different tracks or courses of studies. In some countries, however, student segregation occurs earlier – either because tracking starts early or because of choices between different kinds of public or private schools, with the result that competence differences between social groups likely result from a mixture of primary and secondary effects, difficult to disentangle in cross-sectional data. The second source of data, most often used in sociology, derives from population surveys providing information on social background and on the highest qualification obtained by respondents. With some courageous assumptions, the typical school career that has likely been followed to reach the qualification is then reconstructed, and sometimes taken as a problematic base for transition studies (cf. Hillmert & Jacob, 2005a).[7] Still, many revealing analyses can be performed with these surveys, the main advantage – compared to the Programme for International Student Assessment (PISA) or Progress in International Reading Literacy Study (PIRLS) kind of data – is that they allow the assessment of social disparities in the (highest) qualification level obtained and not just disparities in competences at an early stage of the school career. Given the differences in the dimensions of education measured, the two types of studies may order countries differently in terms of educational inequality.[8]

The educational system characteristics that channel the school career of children of different class backgrounds are an important source of difference between countries with regard to social disparities in the highest qualification level obtained. We explore three characteristics: (1) stratification, (2) relocation of stratifying transitions, and (3) the role of vocational education and training systems. Research on these topics produces tentative results because different studies do not always come to the same conclusion. As to stratification, educational inequality based on social background appears to depend on the level in the educational hierarchy to which large proportions of students (including those from low social backgrounds) are induced and enabled to progress. The higher the proportion of students who continues in education beyond the highly selective early transitions, the smaller the class inequalities are in the final qualification outcomes (Müller & Karle, 1993; Arum et al., 2007). A decline in class inequalities in a country is usually achieved by a process with – in the first instance – reduced inequalities in the first crucial transitions, and, as a consequence, reduced inequalities in the highest qualification level obtained as well (Müller & Haun, 1994; Vallet & Selz, 2006; Mayer et al., 2007). When relatively more offspring of low class origin "survive" at the first hurdle, they tend to increase their relative participation in successively higher levels of education.

These findings seem to contradict the hypothesis of relocation of stratifying transitions, which posits that social disparities in transitions at higher levels of the educational pathway increase when social selectivity at earlier transitions declines. Following Mare (1981, 1993), social background effects should become more pronounced at higher-level transitions, when larger proportions of students, including students of low class background, survive lower-level transitions, and the pool of those eligible for transitions at the higher level becomes more heterogeneous in terms of characteristics that make students go on to higher-level studies. This can best be discussed for the transition to postsecondary and tertiary qualifications because of several recent studies addressing this issue. With a large-scale database covering much of the twentieth century, Vallet and Selz (2006) convincingly showed that in France, inequalities in the transition to tertiary education substantially increased when class selectivity in the pool of those eligible for tertiary education declined. However, because the decline of inequality in secondary education participation was larger and affected larger segments of the population than the increase in inequality in the transition to tertiary studies, inequalities in tertiary education attainment and in qualification outcomes at large declined. Similar results are found for Germany (Mayer et al., 2007). Thus, relocation of stratifying transitions can indeed occur, but it must not and often does not completely offset equality gains by reduced inequalities in early transitions or similar gains that can be expected when educational reforms eliminate early educational decisions. In the "Stratification in Higher Education" study, Arum et al. (2007) confirmed this point, where for a large number of countries they find that social disparities in (unconditional) tertiary education attendance are reduced when disparities in tertiary education eligibility decline. However, contrary to the observations for Germany and France, they even find that inequality in (conditional) transitions to tertiary studies declines when inequality in tertiary education eligibility declines. In line with their assumption that educational expansion is the driving force of reducing inequality, Arum et al. (2007, p. 21) suggested that the latter unexpected finding is due to the fact that "higher education expanded somewhat faster, during the period of observation, than did eligibility."

The third system characteristic relates to the types of qualifications offered in a country's vocational education and training system and its consequent inequalities. The guiding hypothesis is that even with similar abilities and performance at school, working class families more likely than middle class families opt for vocational qualification tracks and forgo the better opportunities associated with general tracks of study to reach a higher qualification level with more advantageous returns. Vocational qualifications can often be obtained with lower costs and are less risky than the usually longer and more demanding academic tracks. At the same time, they fit well to the "strategy from below" (Goldthorpe, 2000) pursued in working class families to secure parental status and protect against downward mobility. In contrast, for the middle class families' "strategy from above," the choice of the academic route leading to tertiary qualifications is more rational because they more likely lead to middle class jobs and protect against downward mobility of children. In countries in which well-recognized vocational tracks are available, they thus likely detract working class children from more ambitious general and academically oriented courses of study. This diversion hypothesis was initially formulated for secondary-level vocational tracks (Murray, 1988; Kerckhoff, 1995), but similar mechanisms also operate in higher-level education in countries in which postsecondary vocational tracks or second tier (often vocationally oriented) tertiary-level qualifications are offered (for a simulation study comparing educational systems with and without a vocational track, cf. Hillmert & Jacob, 2003).

Because of its contrafactual nature, the hypothesis is difficult to prove directly, but indirect evidence speaks for its validity. In the 1970s, Sweden introduced vocational courses of study as a section of upper secondary education; children from working class backgrounds opted for these tracks (Murray, 1988). At least in part, it is also likely due to diversion that countries with well-developed secondary-level opportunities for vocational training (e.g., Germany, Switzerland, Austria) have low proportions of students who graduate at the full secondary level and obtain eligibility for tertiary studies.

Also from the CASMIN project data, we know that in all European countries studied, children from working class families choose vocational qualifications at the expense of general qualifications to a much larger extent than children from service class families (Müller & Karle, 1993).[9] From the more recent Arum et al. (2007) study, one learns that in countries with more vocational training in secondary education, tertiary education eligibility depends more on social background conditions than in countries with mainly general subjects of study. The difference in the degree of inequality at the secondary level then transfers to similar differences between systems at the tertiary level. Reimer and Pollak (2005) make this point very strongly for Germany when they showed that – even controlling for academic ability (as indicated by grade point average at secondary education graduation) – among secondary education graduates who are eligible for tertiary studies, those from working class homes are substantially more likely than those from service class homes to obtain a vocational or lower tertiary (Fachhochschule) qualification rather than a university degree.

What can be summarized about the state of research on social inequalities of educational attainment and skill formation, and what future research is especially needed in this area? We have abundant evidence of large disparities in educational attainment and their dependence on family social position. Family, social, economic, educational, and cultural resources impact learning in schools and the educational aspirations and choices for their children. We also have indication that countries differ in the extent of social disparities in the acquisition of qualifications and that this is related to institutional arrangements in the provision of various courses of study. But it is also evident from the review that we face huge challenges for further research. The distinction between primary and secondary mechanisms is certainly highly useful in disentangling the various processes through which the disparities are generated. However, due to the lack of appropriate longitudinal data – especially the lack of measures of ability or acquired competences at crucial transition points in the educational career – we are unable to precisely identify the relative weight and the interplay of both primary and secondary kinds of effects over the whole educational pathway. At different stages of the educational career, the relative weight of primary and secondary mechanisms may vary, depending, for example, on the extent of selection by ability in preceding stages or the cost–benefit balance expected for the next significant step of education. We also know little about how the relative weight of primary and secondary mechanisms varies between countries with different educational pathways.

All this indicates that further research should better identify and quantify the mechanisms through which the huge class-related inequalities and the waste of talent are generated and by which measures they may be reduced most efficiently. The international student assessment studies (e.g., PISA, Trends in International Mathematics and Science Study, PIRLS) focus on the conditions and primary mechanisms affecting learning, competence acquisition, and school performance of children. These efforts need longitudinal designs to better grasp the interplay with secondary mechanisms in educational choices along the school career.[10] At the same time, further research appears especially urgent to identify the role of the various elements in the secondary mechanisms (information and resource constraints, success expectation, anticipation, and valuation in different classes of costs and benefits). Recent studies by Need and de Jong (2000), Becker (2003), Becker and Hecken (2006), Breen and Yaish (2006), and Stocké (2006) are promising examples. Research along these lines is also essential in order to learn at which point in educational careers and with which interventions various obstacles could be counteracted best. Given the different nature of primary and secondary effects, different interventions will be needed to influence their outcomes. This links to the important educational policy issue addressed by Jackson et al. (2006), whether progress in reducing social inequality can be achieved more efficiently and more quickly by interventions to reduce primary disparities or secondary ones, the latter being designed specially to prevent able children growing up in lower class families from dropping out early, despite having already shown in school performance that they possess the abilities and competences for successful further steps.

Timing of the Acquisition of Qualifications in the Life Course

Our discussion of qualifications has referred so far to the institutionalized educational transitions and the highest qualification reached, irrespective of the time in the individual life course at which the transition or qualification eventuates. We now turn to the timing issue, which is pertinent because increasingly the ordering of education and work in the life course becomes blurred. Following human capital theory, there are strong incentives for initial skill formation (before entering into working life) and much less for further education and training. The shorter the time left for accumulation of returns, the less likely investments in further education and training will be made. Also, the opportunity costs for education and further training change over an individual's lifetime. In particular, when individuals have started to work, the opportunity costs rise sharply, and individuals will be much less prepared to spend time on formal education and training.

Empirical research shows that the acquisition of qualifications is concentrated in initial education before entry into working life. Even in the countries with the highest intensity of lifelong learning, continuing education and training represent only a tiny part of total investments in education and training in life. In almost all countries, the massive educational expansion of recent decades was to a large extent due to growth in initial education and training. Although since World War II in most European countries the average duration of initial education and training has increased by about 2 years or more, individuals – once they have started working life – on average spend at most 1 year in further education and training throughout the rest of their lives. Also consistent with the investment–returns argument is the common finding that participation rates in continuing education systematically decline with age (Wolbers, 2003).

The persistent dominance of initial general education and, in some countries, vocational training notwithstanding, participation rates in continuing education and training have increased, and the forms of such training over the life course have multiplied. Three main forms of further education and training and lifelong learning can be usefully distinguished.

First, in recent years, more people return to full-time education and training to obtain complementary or higher qualifications after a period of work, or they combine working and studying. Often such successive work/study careers, however, take place in very early stages of working life, and they usually serve to acquire qualifications corresponding to traditional courses of study offered before entering the labor market. Therefore, they can be understood as alternative forms of (extended) initial education and training. Individuals may pursue such alternative routes for different reasons. Extending initial training and education or returning to education after an initial work episode partly occurs to adapt to labor market conditions and the business cycle (e.g., avoiding unemployment; Walters, 1984; Jacob, 2003, p. 161), or to react to high competition in their labor market segment. Other reasons include risk aversion and security strategies – individuals build a basic security level for labor market prospects with less demanding types of qualifications, and once this is successfully established, they may go on with more demanding courses of study. In as far as such alternative routes are taken close to initial education and early in life, the driving social mechanisms and implications for the further work career of respective forms of skill acquisition are largely similar to those in a traditional course of study. We therefore do not discuss them any further.

Second, for many workers the most important form of further skill formation throughout the life course is possibly informal learning at the workplace. In the human capital framework, this aspect is conventionally included as "experience," usually only crudely and indirectly measured by years of labor force participation. Even with such a crude measure, one usually finds robust significant (wage) returns to it. Another admittedly rough indicator of the significance of informal learning is how workers themselves perceive what the most important means are for learning the daily tasks of their jobs. According to recent German data (Kuwan et al., 2003, p. 302), the most important means are perceived to be *self-learning in the workplace* and experiences from former workplaces. Other important means are *instructions by and learning from colleagues and supervisors* at the workplace. *Formal further training* provided in the firm or by outside suppliers only ranks at third place. The rest is *private self-learning*. Thus, at least according to the judgment of those concerned, informal lifelong learning occurs to a substantial extent, even though in practice it occurs in unspectacular ways as learning inherent in the practice of daily work.

Third, the most tangible form of explicit and intended further skill formation over the life course is work-related further training following initial education. It includes all forms of training offered by firms or outside agencies, and includes short training episodes as well as extended studies or training for additional or new qualifications in the more advanced work career. If counted as single training episodes or as training participation rates over a year – as is usually done in statistical sources – incidence of further education and training can appear to be quite high. For instance, in the countries of central and northern Europe, according to various sources (Labour Force Survey [LFS]; Continuing Vocational Training Survey [CVTS]) each year, from 30% to more than 50% of workers participate at least once in further education. It is such figures and their growth over the years that nurture the assumptions of a steadily increased significance of lifelong learning compared to initial education and training. However, many of the counted training episodes are usually of short duration and of limited training intensity; therefore, in most countries further formal training following initial education is still very limited, but its extent varies a lot between countries.

In the following discussion, we address three questions: (1) Does further education contribute to weaken the strong impact of social origin conditions on skill acquisition in initial education and training?, (2) Why is there – on average – little formal further education and training?, and (3) How can we explain the considerable variation in the extent of further education among countries? Summarizing, we finally indicate priorities for further research.

Social Inequality in Education and Training Beyond Initial Education

For all three forms of further education and training, the answer to the first question is essentially negative. It has been shown that it is the privileged offspring of middle or upper classes who are most likely to pursue alternative routes of education and training in the early life course (Lucas, 2001; Jacob, 2003; Hillmert & Jacob, 2005a, 2005b). Concerning informal learning through work experience, human capital models usually assume homogeneous effects of experience for all workers. However, sociological research consistently finds significant class differences in patterns of earnings growth over the life course. Workers in service class jobs have clearly stronger earnings growth that extends over longer periods of experience than workers in working class jobs (Goldthorpe & McKnight, 2006). Opportunities of informal learning appear to be distributed unequally, depending on the class location of jobs. This hypothesis is confirmed by results such as those from the German Socioeconomic Panel, which indicate strong class differences in the prevalence to learn something new on the job.[11] The accumulation of additional skills, or their adaptation to new demands over the life course through informal learning, magnify the shortcomings of offspring of working or other disadvantaged classes rather than compensating for them. Essentially, the same holds for participation in more formal ways of further education and training in adult life. Many studies repeatedly confirm that those who have more initial education and training receive and use more opportunities to add to it in later life.

Why Is There Little Further (Formal) Education and Training During the Active Working Life?

To answer this question, it is worth considering who pays for and who collects returns for education and training. This leads us to the third general human capital hypothesis mentioned at the beginning, according to which general, portable qualifications should be paid by the worker, while firm-specific qualifications should be paid by the firm (Becker, 1964). This hypothesis does not consistently hold (see Chapter 5). However, basic schooling, advanced general secondary education, and even most of tertiary education (overwhelmingly oriented toward the acquisition of portable general qualifications) are usually paid by the individual student and/or provided or heavily subsidized by the state. In view of the skills and abilities needed for practical work and specific jobs, countries differ widely in the institutional organization of vocational training and employers' involvement in it. For instance, they differ in the extent to which workers are expected to have obtained skills and qualifications before they enter a particular job or whether workers gradually obtain skills while already working for an employer. Formally structured vocational training seems to presuppose that either the state takes responsibility for such training and provides opportunities in state-administered and state-financed training institutions (e.g., in France and most of the Scandinavian countries) or that the state cooperates in special arrangements with employers (and partly also with worker organizations) in providing such training (e.g., in the dual system in Austria, Germany, or Switzerland). Without state involvement or specific institutional arrangements to secure a high training equilibrium (Marsden, 1990; Soskice, 1994; Culpepper, 1999; also see Chapters 2 and 4), one tends to find rather little initial vocationally oriented skill formation (e.g., see the countries for southern Europe). Thus, for initial education and training, Becker's hypothesis generally seems to hold.

Concerning further training, it is useful to consider the logic of action of firms and workers in turn.[12] Data from many countries show that *firms* invest little in further education and training of their personnel. Even in countries with the highest training intensity in Europe, they use – on average – at most 1.5% of working time for the further training of their staff. Over a life course of some 40 working years, on average, workers will have received only about half a year of further training in total.[13] Compared to the extent of initial education and training, and its growth during the educational expansion of recent decades, time devoted by firms to further education and training is thus still very low. Most firms only invest in training when it is really needed at the workplace. In most industries, the most frequent instances of training occur by far when new machines or new versions of computer programs are introduced, changes in work organization occur (Kuwan et al., 2003), and selling strategies for new products are developed. One exception is employees with management responsibilities who participate in so called "competence-enhancing learning." The most frequent answers from firms to the question of why they do not train or do little training are that there is no need because the staff has the qualifications required to do the job or because staff with relevant qualifications can be recruited on the market (Nester & Kailis, 2002).

With regard to *workers*, research findings indicate an ambiguous position toward further education and training. Although most workers show high interest in further training and are motivated to participate, they are reluctant to train at their own cost (Kuwan et al., 2003). In fact, work-related training is paid overwhelmingly by employers and occurs during working hours.[14] Although workers acknowledge that the training received is useful for the work they do, they assume that it mainly profits the employer.[15] According to the Organisation for Economic Co-operation and Development (OECD; 2003, p. 239), training indeed increases the productivity of firms, while "employees cannot fully reap the benefits from training." The evidence concerning *wage growth* tied to further training participation is mixed.[16] The main asset of further training for workers seems to consist of positive *employment effects* of further training, in particular for older and poorly educated workers. Workers who have received training subsequently face lower risks of unemployment, and, if unemployed, they have better chances of finding new employment. If – except for cases of heavy investments to acquire a significantly higher level of qualification – sustaining employment prospects and thus mainly defensive aims are seen as the main rewards, this may not provide sufficiently strong motives for workers to invest heavily in further training. Economists see the emergence of this constellation as market failure due to labor market rigidities, constraints on borrowing for training, and "lack of contractibility of training content and quality" (OECD, 2003, p. 239). A likely result then is underinvestment[17] in human capital formation through further training in adult life, similar to the underinvestment one would have to expect for initial education and training if it was not made compulsory or heavily subsidized by state resources.

On average, there is rather little lifelong learning so far because it encounters barriers that are not easily overcome. For individual workers, the (opportunity) costs are high,[18] while immediate returns appear to be limited. Workers mainly see that employers profit from their further training, and therefore, they expect them to pay for it. Employers indeed induce and finance most further education and training, but they clearly have an economical approach to it and only invest when they really see needs for it.

Cross-Country Variation in Further Education and Training

As discussed in detail in Chapter 5, there are huge differences between countries in further education and training participation. Participation in continuing vocational training is highest in the Scandinavian countries, the UK, Ireland, or the Netherlands, where up to 60% of all employees participate in such training in a given year. It is lower in most other countries in the West and in the center of Europe. With participation rates of 10% to 20%, it is still lower in most countries in the south of Europe and in the new member or candidate countries in Eastern Europe. According to Bassanini et al. (2005), differences in training intensity between countries are due to the composition in a country's economy of firms with varying training needs. Innovative firms and firms with a technology- or knowledge-driven production profile train more than other firms. Training involvement also varies by firm size. Small firms train less than large firms, and countries with large proportions of small firms (e.g., in southern Europe) train less than countries with larger firms. In addition to such compositional effects, Bassanini et al. (2005) found several conditions in a country's institutional framework that significantly affect training involvement of firms. Although no clear relationship can be found between union density and the extent of training, institutions that foster competition in product markets lead to further investment in training. The diffusion of temporary contracts reduces training investments because workers with temporary contracts receive less training than workers with unlimited contracts. At the same time and somewhat unexpectedly, another element of labor market flexibility, such as lower degrees of employment protection for regular workers, increases the provision of training (Bassanini et al., 2005, p. 115). Training incidence decreases with age, but the age gradient is related to a country's generosity with the pension system for early retirement: with less early retirement in a country, training provision and participation declines less with age and remains at a higher level in older age groups. Country differences in a firm's demand for continuing vocational training may also result from differences between countries in initial training. Training needs in the UK or Ireland may be particularly large because in these countries study programs are short, and young people enter the labor market very early and often without specific vocational qualifications. In countries with extended initial vocational training, the need for further training may be smaller because workers with high-quality initial training may adapt more easily to new task requirements. The need for formal training should also be decreased when the organization of work and cooperation among workers allows for more informal learning on the job. Finally, differences between countries in training intensity can also result from varying provisions of publicly supported training opportunities.[19] The high public resources conferred to further education and training in Scandinavian countries may explain the generally high participation rates – independent of firm and sector characteristics – and minimize the underinvestment problem in these countries.

In summary, both initial and further education and training have expanded in recent decades. However, it is initial education rather than further education that has seen most of the increased investment in education and training. For large parts of the population, explicit and formal further education and training is not yet spread over wide parts of the life course. Its increase in recent decades is probably less the result of behavioral change of workers or employers, but rather results from compositional change in the labor force. More lifelong learning occurs because of labor force expansion in learning intensive occupational segments, while employment has contracted in areas with little training. Also, larger proportions of workers have higher levels of initial education, and this induces more lifelong learning.

Because much of further work-related learning is informal, an appealing strategy to advance skill formation over the life course would be to foster informal learning. Sociological research, so far, has concentrated mostly on institutions of formal learning that lead to formal qualifications; thus, there is, unfortunately, little research about the social and institutional conditions of informal learning and its consequences. Therefore, informal learning at the workplace is among the areas in which further research is needed.

Although research exploring the huge differences between countries in the extent of further training participation and lifelong learning is growing, more work is needed on the systematic explanation of these differences, and – because there is much uncertainty about various possible returns of further education and training – also on how different combinations of initial and further education and training existing in different countries impact career development.

RETURNS TO EDUCATION AND TRAINING AT LABOR MARKET
ENTRY AND IN FURTHER WORK CAREERS

Our concern so far has been with the social inequalities of skill acquisition and its location in the life course. We now turn to the returns of education and training and to the institutions and structural conditions in the education and training system and in the labor market, which shape the links between acquired skills and labor market outcomes. As to education and training, sociological research has mainly concentrated on the organization, the broad (general or vocational) curricular contents, and the social selectivity of the various education and training tracks established in the educational system. With respect to labor market institutions, issues of labor market segmentation and (more recently) of labor market regulation and worker protection have been studied. The main macrostructural conditions of interest are those of the supply of specific qualifications (delivered from the educational system) and the demand for these qualifications resulting from long-term trends in the occupational structure and cyclical variation in the labor market.

We begin with brief remarks on the theoretical understanding of such institutional and structural effects on the returns of education. We then summarize recent findings of related empirical research, both concerning the core dimensions of institutional variation and their effect on the interplay between qualifications and labor market outcomes. As we focus on institutions and macrostructural conditions, we rely heavily on cross-national comparative work because this approach can best capture effects of variation at the system level. In the empirical part, we first focus on the transition from school to work because at this stage of working life the skills and qualifications acquired through education and training are most directly linked to labor market opportunities. The study of the transition from school to work is also crucial because the consecutive work career very much depends on the positions individuals obtain at the beginning of their working life. After that, research on the returns of education in the later work career is reviewed.

Theoretical Background and Core Dimensions of Institutional Variation

One of the crucial problems of the human capital assumptions is the huge difficulty in recognizing productivity and the incomplete information employers have on it. Firms are also subject to constraints of organizational rationality and – even if known – cannot simply organize and reward work according to productivity of individual workers when designing their job structures and hierarchies. Taking this into account, matching models (Kalleberg & Sørensen, 1979; Logan, 1996) are probably the most useful starting point to understand the allocation of individuals to jobs, the effect of institutions, and why similar skills acquired through education and training may have different labor market outcomes across educational systems and countries. Matching models explain the outcome of decisions of two contracting actors – in our case, workers with their certified qualifications and employers with specific jobs. Employers try to recruit those applicants that they perceive to be both most productive and least costly to train for the kind of work the job requires (Thurow, 1976). They use qualifications as signals to assess actual and/or potential productivity and costs. Workers with given preferences strive to obtain the jobs that promise the best possible returns for their educational investments – monetary and nonpecuniary rewards, status, security, or other aspects of job quality.[20]

Employers' choices, for instance, are affected by expected costs and productivity of competing candidates. Thereby the expectations for costs not only depend on salary, but also on expected expenses for additional training the worker will need to undergo. Other costs derive from the uncertainty that is associated with the selection. For both the training costs and the costs associated with the screening under insecurity, the setup of the education and training system is crucial. Training costs will depend on the extent to which educational systems provide qualifications that prepare workers to perform more or less immediately without any further training. The costs associated with insecurity will depend on the signaling capacity of credentials and on the reliability of these signals. They also depend on labor protection regulations insofar as the latter determine how easy, or how costly, it is for an employer to dismiss workers who are not needed or who do not perform as expected. Other labor market institutions relevant in personnel selection include arrangements for wage setting or prescriptions requiring particular diplomas for specific jobs. Both the institutional characteristics of educational systems – how education and training are organized and what students learn – and labor market institutions vary considerably among countries.

Besides the institutional settings, the matching will also depend on the demand for specific qualifications and the qualifications job applicants command in comparison to the level of qualifications acquired by competitors. Both affect the conditions of competition among different groups of workers in a given country at a given point in time. There is not a fixed level of skills for a given job. The varying institutional and structural conditions under which decisions are made and that define the terms of competition can thus lead to different outcomes in different contexts even if the matching mechanism formally operates in similar ways.

What are important variants of institutional settings, and how can they be expected to work? Concerning the education and training system, several general characteristics have been shown to systematically affect matching personnel to jobs. Allmendinger (1989) developed a typology of educational systems based on two dimensions: the degree of standardization of educational provisions and the stratification of educational opportunity. Müller and Shavit (1998) added the degree of occupational specificity. Standardization refers to the degree to which the quality of education meets the same standards nationwide. The concept of stratification refers to the extent and form of tracking in the educational system. It measures whether there are clearly distinct tracks in the educational system, with different levels and kinds of requirements and training. Occupational specificity relates to the extent to which training fosters specific occupational competences rather than more general knowledge or cognitive abilities. How can these characteristics be assumed to affect personnel selection and job allocation? The more training is organized in recognizably separate institutions, or visibly in tracks with specific training curricula, and the more standardized training is, the stronger the signaling capacity of qualifications. The more occupationally specific (rather than general) the training, the more qualifications should be of direct use in specific jobs and require less training investments by employers. Although in their comparative study Müller and Shavit (1998) did find clear evidence of the relevance of stratification and occupational specificity for various early labor market outcomes, standardization had no effect once the other dimensions were controlled. In reality, stratification and occupational specificity of educational systems tend to be related to different arrangements of labor market segmentation. Educational systems with a high degree of occupational specificity support the prevalence of occupationally segmented labor markets, while firm internal labor market structures prevail in countries with little occupation-related training in the educational system (Maurice et al., 1982; Blossfeld & Mayer, 1988; Allmendinger, 1989; Marsden, 1990; Shavit & Müller, 1998).

A further crucial distinction refers to different organizational forms of training, that is, whether vocational training is mainly school based or consists of a systematic combination of training and working, such as in apprenticeships (Allmendinger, 1989; Kerckhoff, 1995; Shavit & Müller, 1998, 2000; OECD, 2000; Ryan, 2001; see also Chapter 4). At least two big issues nurture the debate about this distinction. One concerns the question of how skills and competencies are most efficiently learned – in schools or by doing at the workplace, or at least in combination with practical application. This skill formation problem is posed not just in view of learning a given skill for a specific task, but also in view of the transfer of skills and competencies to solve related or new tasks. This issue is essentially a problem for psychological or education learning research and cannot be addressed here (but see Chapter 8).

The other issue relates to the matching and personnel selection problem and to the distinction between general and specific qualifications. It can be assumed that even if vocational education in an apprenticeship trains transferable skills – as is required in the German dual system – apprenticeship training in firms will still include firm-specific elements. Firms also use the training periods for screening future workers. School leavers who have received such training, when recruited into regular jobs, will not incur costs for further training or for information or insecurity. This can make apprenticeship training profitable for firms and explain why firms engage in it (Franz & Soskice, 1994; see Chapter 4). At the same time, these circumstances facilitate a smooth transition of former apprentices into regular employment.

With regard to labor market institutions, employment protection regulations are of particular importance.[21] Economists argue that employment protection makes employers think twice before they hire additional staff because it implies costs to dismiss workers who do not perform according to expectations or when for some reason the firm has to reduce personnel. Employment protection also enhances the disadvantages of outsiders as compared to insiders (Flanagan, 1988; Lindbeck & Snower, 1988). It tends to reduce the dynamics of the labor market and, in consequence, the chances of finding a job (Bertola & Rogerson, 1997; Gregg & Manning, 1997; Gangl, 2004). Protection of employed workers may make it particularly difficult for school leavers to become integrated into stable employment because they are in a weak competitive position against experienced workers. However, it would be too short sighted to see only the negative side of employment protection. Employment protection provides security and prevents against easy hiring and firing at the employer's will (see Chapter 7). Other employment regulations such as in apprenticeship-based training systems, if set up in cooperative relationships between corporate partners as, for example, in the Austrian, German, and Swiss dual training systems, can introduce economically viable institutional structures of youth integration into the labor market.

Qualifications and Labor Market Integration of School Leavers: Evidence from Recent Comparative Research

Even if we want to stress the implications of these different institutional arrangements and related differences between countries in the use and valuation of qualifications, it would be misleading not to mention findings that are widely common for many countries. Thus, we begin with these commonalities and then describe a number of important cross-national differences. Empirical illustrations will be mainly based on European countries. These countries vary to a large extent in their educational and labor market institutions, and thus provide a good testing ground to study commonality and variation.

Commonalities Across Countries

One of the most stable findings is that the higher the level of education achieved, the more favorable the life prospects are. There are clear positive, often substantial, effects of educational achievement on class position, status and prestige of job, income, autonomy, stability of employment, job security, unemployment risk, finding a new job on unemployment, health, and even life expectancy. Tertiary qualifications provide the strongest differential in advantage. Graduates with tertiary education (International Standards Classification of Education [ISCED] 5–6) find employment much quicker than education leavers with only secondary education or less. Once unemployed, those with higher qualifications have better chances of reemployment (Shavit & Müller, 1998; Ryan, 2001; Kogan & Müller, 2003; Kogan & Schubert, 2003; Müller & Gangl, 2003).[22] Better employment prospects are a long-term life course asset of education (Blossfeld et al., 2006). The quality of jobs obtained by tertiary education leavers is also much more advantageous than that of workers with less education. About 70% of the former obtain professional or managerial first jobs, whereas almost none of those with the lowest level of education do so.[23]

In most dimensions, the level of education is a more powerful predictor of outcomes than the distinction between general-academic education or vocationally oriented education or training and has a higher impact on the quality of future jobs than differences between different fields of study (Lucas, 2001; van de Werfhorst & Kraaykamp, 2001). For the secondary level, however, Gangl (2003a, p. 177) showed that returns in different dimensions depend on the kind of vocational education obtained: in terms of class position, status, or income, returns to general/academic qualifications often tend to be higher than those to vocational qualifications. However, school leavers with an apprenticeship initially seem to be better protected against low-skilled employment than school leavers from vocational or general upper secondary education, but within a few years of working life those who stayed at schools do as well or even better than apprentices.

As expected from the matching model discussed previously, vocational qualifications tend to ease access into jobs and are associated with lower risks of unemployment than general qualifications (Gangl, 2003a, p. 177). The relatively smooth integration into the labor market thus appears to be one of the clear assets of vocationally oriented forms of skill formation.

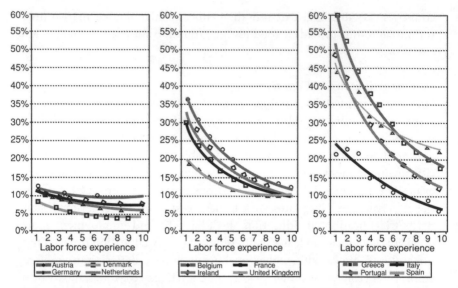

Figure 6.1. Unemployment rates by country and years of labor force experience, leavers from upper secondary education (ISCED 3). *Source:* Gangl (2003a: 116), based on EU-LPS 1992–7.

Variation Among Countries

Regardless of the quite consistent and substantial basis of commonality, institutional variation among countries has important implications for education–labor market linkages. Probably most marked are the differences among European countries in the unemployment risks experienced by school leavers in the first years of their working life. Figure 6.1 illustrates this for the case of labor market entrants with upper secondary education (ISCED 3; i.e., upper secondary education of whatever kind). Huge differences exist between countries in the extent of unemployment and its evolution in the first 10 years after labor market entry. In Austria, Denmark, Germany, and the Netherlands, levels of unemployment tend to be relatively low, and risks of unemployment do not differ much among labor market entrants and more senior workers (i.e., workers who have already 10 years' work experience). In all other countries, unemployment risks are much higher for labor market entrants and only slowly converge toward the level of unemployment characteristics for more senior workers. In the south of Europe – except Portugal – young people face the highest difficulties in integrating into the labor market.

An explanation for these patterns can be found in the interaction of certain educational system characteristics with labor market regulations, in particular, employment protection legislation. As Breen (2005) in coherence with the matching model introduced previously shows, employment protection (which makes it difficult and costly to dismiss a nonfitting worker) impedes employment chances of new entrants mainly under conditions in which entrants lack specific qualifications for the job and/or in which employers cannot easily and reliably guess from credentials the training costs and the workers' potential productivity. In countries with well-signaled vocational and occupation-specific training, high employment protection hardly has any negative effects on youth integration because costs for additional training, as well as costs resulting from incomplete information, are low. Breen's model quite convincingly accounts for the high variation in the unemployment rate among labor market entrants in the groups of countries in Figure 6.1. Unemployment in the countries of southern Europe is extremely high because these countries have high employment protection and at the same time lack ready-to-use and reliably signaled vocational qualifications. In Germany and other countries with similar training systems, unemployment is low despite a high level of employment protection. In several countries in the middle group of Figure 6.1, there is less employment protection – in particular, in the UK and Ireland – and therefore the signaling capacity of education is not so important in an employer's decision to hire someone because contracts can easily be dissolved.

Countries also differ – although to a lesser extent – in the degree to which education shapes the status of jobs school leavers obtain in the early working life. Education plays a particularly strong role in Eastern Europe. The Eastern European countries operated manpower planning and manpower allocation in highly credentialist ways during the state-socialist period. In these countries, education continues to strongly affect the status of the jobs school leavers are able to obtain. To understand differences between Western European countries, we can draw on the findings of the From School to Work Study (Müller & Shavit, 1998), which shows that the more stratified and the more occupationally specific education is, the stronger the association between a particular kind and level of education and the social status or class position individuals obtain in the labor market. In countries with more stratified and occupationally specific education and training systems, there is also less hopping around in the early work career until a fitting match is reached (Allmendinger, 1989). In Europe, Germany, Austria, Switzerland, Denmark, and the Netherlands are prime examples of both high stratification and vocational specificity, while the UK is probably at the other extreme.

Many studies on the labor market returns to education and training are flawed (and often contradict each other) because they do not properly take account of aggregate structural conditions. Such conditions can strongly vary among countries and points in time and can significantly alter the premium paid for skills and qualifications on the markets. For example, the returns to specific educational and vocational qualifications vary with macrostructural conditions, such as the ups and downs in business cycles, the speed of educational expansion, and the change in demand for qualifications resulting from changes in occupational structures. Gangl (2003b) showed that business cycles strongly influence unemployment risks for labor market entrants, but not the quality of the job attained (in terms of status or class). *Ceteris paribus*, educational expansion, is associated with lower net returns to education in terms of occupational status and class. Within a given occupational level, better-qualified school leavers tend to substitute for less qualified ones. However, these changes in the effect of education on labor market outcomes depend on the structural balance of supply and demand, and this balance can develop differently among countries. Germany, for instance, had a rather balanced development of expansion of educational participation and upgrading of occupational demand. In the UK and Spain, expansion of tertiary qualifications has grown faster than the demand for such qualifications, thus displacement has been stronger. Furthermore, if change takes place, it is generally not change that affects returns to all qualifications alike; returns to some specific qualifications may decline or increase. All three aggregate structural conditions – business cycles, educational expansion, and occupational upgrading – tend to have the most severe effects on school leavers with low qualifications, in particular those with neither general education nor vocational training beyond the lower secondary level.

All in all, it should be noted, however, that the cross-national differences in labor market outcomes are, to a large extent, compositional. This means that given levels or types of education and qualifications have broadly similar labor market consequences (in Europe). Their effects are similar, but the educational systems of different countries differ to a large extent in the composition by level and type of the qualifications they offer. Countries vary to a large extent in their institutional provision of the various educational tracks and programs; hence, different proportions of their students find places in different programs and leave the educational system with different qualifications and skills. It can be shown that cross-national differences in the aggregate outcomes are mainly (although not exclusively) due to these different compositional structures (Gangl et al., 2003). An important part of cross-national differences is thus institutionally based, in the sense that national systems of education provide different educational opportunities, which are then associated with systematically varying labor market prospects.

Qualifications and Work Careers in Comparative Perspective

Research and knowledge on consequences of skill formation and qualifications on later work careers and on the implications of different systems of education and training is much less advanced than is the case for entry into working life. The more advanced life is, the more various circumstances and events in the sphere of work and in other life domains may have affected the course of life and the outcomes attained at a given stage. These factors may be related more or less directly to education, but their causal relationship to education is not always clear. This makes it difficult to disentangle the real consequences of education and qualifications from consequences of other factors, be it individual characteristics, individual life course decisions and experiences, or societal institutional or structural conditions. Take cognitive abilities as an example. Educational attainment is clearly related to such abilities, and independent of their effect through education, they also affect the progression of work careers. Not controlling for ability must then lead to overestimating the effects of education. The role of cognitive abilities is likely overstressed and partly misrepresented among adherents of genetic explanations of individual achievements. However, Hauser (2002) is certainly right in his claim that much more attention must be given to individual abilities and other individual characteristics that affect work careers and labor market outcomes in order to properly assess effects of education and qualifications. Solid knowledge on this is very scarce so far, not least because we lack adequate longitudinal data that include measures (e.g., of ability) or that show how particular skills and competences are gained or lost during working life and how this is related to education.[24] Furthermore, only little comparative research so far has studied how different types of qualifications obtained in different education and training systems affect individual performance in successive jobs and influence – under varying institutional and structural conditions – work career outcomes in different countries. Also, data are often not available or not sufficiently comparable among countries.

We therefore only briefly summarize a few general observations that we believe can be made from available research on how work career attainment is related to qualifications in different countries.

First, for practically all countries with advanced economies, initial education and training has lasting effects on advantageous career development and career outcomes for almost all dimensions that have been studied. Advantages that school leavers with higher qualifications have on labor market entry are conserved during their working life. The most recent national case studies, collected by Blossfeld et al. (2006) and Blossfeld and Hofmeister (2006), consistently indicate lower risks of unemployment during working life, better chances of re-employment, enhanced chances of upward job mobility, and lower risks of downward mobility. There is also no doubt that education has consistently high returns on status, class position, or wages and income. In the course of the career, income differences between workers with different levels of qualifications tend to diverge. Workers with higher education are usually also more satisfied with their jobs and work conditions than workers with less education.

However, as mentioned, only few studies show how these effects of education change over the life course and are mediated through intervening processes. So far, the best information comes from the Wisconsin Longitudinal Study and the British Cohort Studies. Both data sets assess the effects of education and of ability (measured at young ages) on outcomes for different job characteristics at successive ages of cohort members (see Warren et al., 2002, for U.S. results and Iannelli, 2006, for British results). In both cases, gross effects of education[25] on job outcomes decline with advancing age of the cohort. The effects of ability on work career outcomes are mediated to a considerable extent though education, but in contrast to education, they appear to affect job characteristics to a similar extent throughout the work career. According to the Wisconsin data, ability does "exert an independent – albeit small – influence at each stage of the occupational career" (Warren et al., 2002, p. 450), even when education and earlier stages of the work career are controlled. A similar conclusion is drawn by Levy and Murnane (2001) summarizing the results of several American studies that use both measures of literacy and formal educational attainment and their effects on income. Although educational attainment explains most of the variation of incomes, taking present literacy measures into account explains further differences within the same level of educational attainment. When earlier stages of the work career are controlled, education effects on later career outcomes differ for the United States and Britain. In the United States, education matters a great deal at labor market entry but does not directly affect any later job (cf. also Green & Riddell, 2002, for Canada). In the UK, direct effects of education remain. According to the Warren et al. (2002) analysis, in the United States, qualifications seem to be widely used to allocate individuals to initial work positions. However, when working life proceeds, job performance, intervening events (e.g., unemployment), ability or other individual characteristics, and situational circumstances seem to be decisive for career development.[26] In the UK, in contrast, qualifications obtained seem to affect work careers in more enduring ways beyond initial job placements.[27]

Iannelli (2006) also examined effects on work career outcomes of qualitative aspects of the course of education pursued, such as the school type attended (e.g., private, comprehensive, grammar) or the menu of subjects studied. Although these specific elements of the educational career and curriculum clearly matter in the sense of gross effects for later work career outcomes, to a large extent they are mediated through the final level obtained in the hierarchical ladder of qualifications.

Reviewing the previous findings on school-to-work transitions, we found substantial differences between countries in the extent to which education and training qualifications affect initial labor market placement. We can also draw a second general conclusion – initial labor market placement strongly predicts later work career outcomes. As a consequence, differences among countries in the effects of education on early outcomes tend to persist along the life course (i.e., countries in which – compared to other countries – education generates larger differences among workers with different levels and kinds of education at the beginning of working life tend to show stronger effects of education on outcomes at later stages of the life course). According to findings from labor force surveys for Germany, France, the UK, and Hungary, these countries differ widely in the effects specific qualifications have on labor market outcomes at different stages of the work career. As this finding is replicated for different cohorts who moved through working life in different historical periods, much speaks for the conclusion that country differences in education effects persist throughout the life course (see König & Müller, 1986; Brauns et al., 1997; Müller et al., 2002). Again, this conclusion must be handled cautiously because it is based on empirical evidence for only a few countries and essentially draws on cross-sectional data.

Third, differences between countries in education effects persist even though countries vary in the prevalence of between-firm and between-job mobility. In countries with a highly stratified and occupationally specific education and training system, good matches between individual qualifications and job demands and characteristics appear to be achieved to a large extent at the transition from education to work. In countries in which educational qualifications have a less distinct signaling capacity and/or in which labor markets are less segmented along occupational lines, more moves between jobs or firms during a longer period appear to be required. The early stabilization of work careers may be an advantage for some workers, but it has clearly negative implications for low qualified workers. In countries with strict qualification regimes (Maurice et al., 1982), initially unqualified workers have clearly less favorable opportunities for later career development than their counterparts in countries with less strict regimes (König & Müller, 1986; Büchtemann et al., 1993; Scherer, 2004).

CONCLUSION

Both the processes of qualification attainment and their returns on the labor market share many similarities in modern economies, but they are also shaped by particular institutional and structural conditions prevailing in different countries. The institutional setup of a country's education and training system forms the structure of qualifications the workforce holds, the huge disparities between social groups, and the potential waste of talents in the acquisition of skills, not to mention the integration of school leavers into the labor market and their further work career.

As to learning over the life course, despite much public debate on the urgent need of it, most investments in qualifications and skill acquisition are made during adolescence before labor market entry. Skill acquisition by extended periods of intensive study during working life is still rare. Considering this, the most crucial question appears to be whether there is in fact little need for a more even distribution for skill formation over the life course – a conclusion one could draw from the fact that employers and employees do not invest in it much. We also need to consider whether there is underinvestment in further education and training along the life course, and if so, how this could be changed.

In light of the findings discussed in this chapter, we look at the following aspects in more detail: (1) the structural balance of educational expansion and occupational change and how developments in both spheres influence each other, and (2) the implications for the education and training system and for educational policies. This leads us to (3) the questions for further research that should be addressed.

Occupational Upgrading and New Skill Requirements

The most prominent aspect in the current debates on the profound changes in the world of work is the massive technological progress and the overall upgrading of the occupational structure. Although for some jobs skill requirements may have declined or continue to decline, job growth over the last fifty years mainly occurred in occupational fields with higher skill requirements.[28] Also, in the future, the changes in the world of work in the advanced economies will have a significant effect on the structure of skill requirements and qualifications, due to the growth of knowledge-intensive work and the concentration of unskilled work in cheap labor countries. Therefore, it is assumed that large parts of the workforce have to be trained more intensively and more continuously over their lifetime. The structural changes in the world of work can be counterbalanced by essentially two main mechanisms through which new skills are brought into the labor market: (1) the substitution of a less-qualified generation of workers by better-qualified labor market entrants, and (2) a steady participation in education and training over the life course of all employees. The first mechanism seems to have been most important in the past because investments before entering the labor market were high and increasing over time. However, if skill demand changes more quickly than the substitution of differently skilled generations of workers, adaptation is also required among the active working population. The expected lengthening of working life and the expected increasing speed of change point in this direction. Knowledge is developing quickly, production chains are restructured in shorter periods, and innovations in technology appear rapidly but can hardly be predicted. Therefore, it remains unclear which skills and competencies will be required in future working life. All this evokes the general questions about how individuals can be prepared to best cope with the uncertain demands of the future.

Implications for Skill Formation and Educational Policies

There is certainly no single strategy to respond to the rapid development of knowledge and changes in skill demands. Rather we can think of various ways to foster the adaptability to new skill demands. First, to be able to teach up-to-date skills, the educational system faces the challenge of implementing the rapid development of skill requirements into the training system without delay (e.g., by more training for teachers and trainers and stronger connections and links between the training system and technology-innovative sectors, and a continuous examination and reform of curricula content). The second strategy is based on the assumption that future requirements are unknown and the variety of specific skills that can be taught is limited. The conclusion from this is that in order to satisfy the increasing demand of flexibility, workers must be empowered in initial education with more general analytic skills, allowing readjustments and a flexible updating of skills in later working life. Extending that argument, a third strategy to increase flexibility and to enable employees to perform new and challenging tasks involves increasing education and training during the life course.

Sociology can hardly give answers to the long-running pedagogical question of how to best achieve trainability and the capability to transfer and adapt skills to new tasks. However, sociology can provide answers by referring to existing knowledge on the types of qualifications and institutional conditions that have been "successful" for labor market entry and further career development.

Previous research has shown that initial education not only structures successful labor market entry and further career development, but also participation in further education. Thus, one key to promote further education lies in initial education. One of the utmost measures to foster the propensity for lifelong learning is to remedy the respective deficits in the structure of initial education. To invest early in the educational career to combat entry into working life with low qualifications thus seems one of the most productive and efficient ways to enhance lifelong learning. Besides, it also helps reduce the waste of talent and moderate social inequalities in educational opportunities.[29]

In almost all Western societies, graduates of tertiary education have better labor market chances than those who enter the labor market after secondary education. This might be due to credentialist allocation mechanisms or signaling advantages for those with the highest qualification, but the actual skills that graduates of higher education possess might also better satisfy the (changing) demands from the labor market. Assuming at least a partial role by the latter, the characteristics of higher education that may be responsible for its long-term success should be seriously explored. One feature of higher education compared to secondary education in almost all countries is the broader emphasis on generic skills; for example, individuals are supposed to work and learn on their own, and this is also one reason for their stronger involvement in lifelong learning. The good labor market prospects of tertiary education graduates may also be due to changes in the occupational structure providing new (qualification-adequate) employment opportunities for the growing number of tertiary graduates (cf. Gangl, 2003b). Analyzing occupational change in the UK labor market, Elias and Purcell (2003) showed that the share of jobs appropriate for graduates grew and largely absorbed the increasing number of graduates in recent decades. Although today's graduates work in a much wider range of (new) occupations that require their higher qualifications, some substitution has occurred, and graduates more frequently start working life in "nongraduate jobs." However, graduates move out of nongraduate jobs rather quickly, and from the perspective of individual labor market careers, overqualification is often a transitory state (Büchel & Pollmann-Schult, 2004). The extent to which the observations made in the UK can be generalized to other contexts is an open question. Still, strengthening tertiary education seems to be a means to build a workforce well prepared for the future. Even acknowledging that tertiary-level qualifications are provided in secondary-level vocational training institutions in some countries, it must be recognized that these countries (with strong vocational traditions) need big efforts to catch up with other leading countries in extending and developing the tertiary education sector.

With regard to secondary education and the country-specific institutional settings that differently emphasize and combine generic or vocational elements, the conclusions are less straightforward. Different systems need different adaptations. More vocationally oriented systems should certainly care to safeguard their assets, including, among others, the smooth transitions into the labor market. However, long-term skill requirements could be strengthened by enhancing training of generic competences and providing better opportunities to enter tertiary education in further steps.[30] Measures should also aim to reduce diversion losses. In countries where secondary education includes little vocational specialization and school leavers face high unemployment risks, the education and training system may profit from the introduction or strengthening of a curricular option in which vocational/occupational qualifications can be acquired. They tend to be accepted as (signals of) useful acquired skills improving the competitive position of labor market entrants against experienced workers and serve to facilitate integration into the labor market.

When it comes to fostering further education during working life, one should recognize that one of the likely reasons for the strong growth in initial education is that to a large extent it is provided by the state as a public good and that access to it has been facilitated by providing more places for higher education and making such places easier to reach. If there is significant underinvestment in further education and training because it does not appear sufficiently profitable for the individual workers or firms (even though it is socially productive), then this is a strong argument for more public involvement and investments. Significant growth in lifelong learning and, in particular, substantial investment in education and training in later stages of life may necessitate more public opportunities and more than marginal supports to this aim. Another strategy is to reshape the institutional conditions and incentives for lifelong learning. We should ask whether the labor markets and the institutions of the welfare state are sufficiently supportive of extended formalized training during the life course and sufficiently gratify (full-time) education at later stages in life. Also, how can firms be led to allow their employees to interrupt work for participation in further training, even if in the short-term employees are still productive enough, and in spite of (short-term) forgone profits? Is there sufficient compensation for forgone earnings and sufficient support in the case of borrowing constraints on the market?

If the acquisition of further qualifications along the life course should depend less on firms willing to pay for it and build more on an individual's own initiatives and individual investments, then individuals must be able to collect reliable benefits from it. One possibility to promote individual investments in education at later stages in the life course could involve structuring the education and training system in ways to create multiple and easily accessible points of entry for the acquisition of (portioned) further qualifications. These have to be well connected to earlier learning, they must become portable (e.g., through formal recognition), and they must provide positive expectations of returns to those who acquire them. To reach a more even participation in further training, respective opportunities must be broad and ensure that employees of different initial qualification levels profit from and find suitable extensions of their already acquired skills. One incentive for further learning among persons with little initial qualifications might be to recognize skill acquisition through informal learning. Providing these different, easily accessible (re-)entry possibilities to gain further qualifications are the promise of the so-called qualification frameworks, the development of which is spreading.[31]

Open Questions and Further Research

In the previous sections, we pointed out some of the open questions that we now summarize, beginning with the macrolevel and moving to the meso- and microlevel.

Although there is wide public debate on the changes in the world of work – as indicated by the high currency of the "knowledge society" catchword – the relationship of the concomitant developments in education and the occupational structure and how their counterbalance occurs are still unclear. Most research studies the allocation and placement of holders of particular qualifications – be it school leavers or experienced workers – into an assumed given occupational structure. Little work exists on the demand side evolution of changing skill and qualification requirements resulting from technological or organizational innovation or changes in product or service markets. We know even less on the dynamic interdependence and mutual relationship between supply and demand, and on how the occupational structure and the organization of work is changing as a result of higher education expansion.

A related problem concerns the balance in the distribution of qualifications and jobs along the life course of a cohort (e.g., the changing distribution of a cohort's qualifications during the life course and the labor market changes that a cohort is exposed to and that shape the social positions that individuals can occupy). Further research in these areas can profit from improving longitudinal data and especially from the creation of longitudinal linked employer–employee databases.

On the mesolevel, firms are a crucial context that individuals are exposed to, thus the different strategies and involvement of firms with regard to formal or informal training structure the individual's skill formation during employment and therefore later labor market chances. Although education science studies learning processes at school and in classrooms in depth, comparable research on learning in firms and at the workplace is largely missing (see Chapter 9). The translation of usually measured "work experience" into actual skills and qualifications that individuals somehow and somewhere attained during employment is not yet accomplished. Besides firm- or sector-specific participation rates in formal further training, we know little about learning processes within firms (e.g., how skills are acquired at the workplace, how they are maintained and continuously established, what are favorable contexts for formal and especially informal learning). We also lack knowledge on the impact of other situations on the skill profile of individuals, such as promotion and change of job, employer, or occupation.

With this, we have moved to the individual level, the acquisition of skills and qualifications during the life course and their payoffs. We have seen that several black boxes need to be opened, both concerning the specific mechanisms that produce the huge social disparities in the acquisition of skills and qualifications and those that generate their long-term career returns. As to the socially structured process of qualification attainment, further research should concentrate on the cumulative interplay of the discussed primary and secondary mechanisms, and especially concerning the latter, identify the various elements that lead to the marked class disparities in educational choices among the high-performing students. As to the payoffs, further research is particularly needed on the long-term consequences of qualification attainment. What is their impact on later career development beyond the initial labor market placement in the school-to-work transition stage? Are education effects essentially mediated through the initial placement, or how, why, and under which labor market circumstances do they continue to influence the later career independently of initial placement and independently of other individual characteristics, such as ability or social class background? How do different combinations of initial and further education shape the life course of different social groups? Which combinations are not only economically efficient but also contribute to reduce social inequalities? To pinpoint the relevant qualifications, skills, and competences – generic or specific – that empower individuals to successfully respond to unknown requirements in the distant future, research needs not only long-term longitudinal observations, but also more specific measures (e.g., the general or vocational character or the curricula, field of study, or attributes of the educational institution). We need better knowledge along these lines to decide on firm grounds how to reform education and training in ways that both let individuals successfully face the challenges of a changing world of work and add to the welfare of societies at large.

Notes

1. In addition to qualifications that are acquired and certified in institutions of the education and training system, the concept of qualifications can also be extended to any form of references and certificates referring to acquired qualifications that are socially acknowledged if they fulfill the same function of easy recognition and relevance in the labor market.
2. For an exemplary study, see, e.g., Baumert et al. (2006).
3. Hout and DiPrete (2004, p. 14) even summarized the international evidence with the empirical generalization "trends in educational stratification favour women."
4. See Davies & Guppy, 1997; Lucas, 2001; van de Werfhorst & Kraaykamp, 2001; van de Werfhorst et al., 2001; Finnie & Frenette, 2003; van de Werfhorst et al., 2003.
5. Treiman (1970), Treiman and Yip (1989), Ganzeboom and Treiman (1993), and Rijken (1999), among others, have claimed educational inequality to decline with various aspects of modernization.
6. In some countries, inequalities declined before the massive expansion took off, whereas in others, such as in the UK, the decline in inequalities leveled off in periods in which the expansion was strongest. In Sweden, "equalization coincided with periods of rapid increase and decline in overall transition probabilities" (Jonsson, 1993, p. 120).
7. Longitudinal cohort or panel studies or surveys in which information on the school career is collected retrospectively would be a better base, but such surveys are often not available in comparable ways for comparative purposes.
8. In both types of studies, the Scandinavian countries and the Netherlands are identified as countries with relatively smaller class inequalities, whereas in Germany, and, for recent cohorts, also in Poland and other countries of Eastern Europe, class inequalities are larger. Countries for which results differ between the dimensions studied include the UK, where the class gradient in reading competence at age 15 is high and class inequalities in final outcomes are relatively small. In contrast, in France and Italy, the class gradients in competences at age 15 are relatively small and inequalities in final outcomes are large (compare Müller & Karle, 1993; Jonnson et al., 1996; Baumert et al., 2001, p. 391; PISA-Konsortium Deutschland, 2004, p. 249; Breen et al., 2006).

9. Class disparities in obtaining secondary-level vocational qualifications are found consistently smaller than in obtaining secondary-level general qualifications.

10. See Köller and Baumert (2001) for an exemplary study.

11. Although 60% of higher managers and professionals strongly agree to the question "Do you often learn something new on the job?", only 41% of respondents in routine nonmanual occupations, 33% of skilled manual workers, and 17% of routine manual workers do so (calculations of Jean-Marie Jungblut, based on the German Socio-Economic Panel 2002, respondents employed in jobs of respective EGP classes).

12. The issue is reviewed more thoroughly in Chapter 5.

13. Course hours per 1,000 working hours, as measured through the CVTS survey of Eurostat (see Nester & Kailis, 2003). For another telling comparison, one can refer to the working days firms lose due to illness of employees. For Germany, this figure is currently 14 working days per year and employee, and thus is incomparably greater than 1 day per year and employee. German employers on average are presently investing in further training of their staff.

14. As found in SOEP, BSW, IAB firm-panel data for Germany, and for other countries by CVTS and other sources.

15. This, however, contrasts with the perception of workers that further training helps advance their career (e.g., Kuwan et al., 2003, pp. 295, 300). Thus, at the current workplace, the individual's returns of further training are seen to be marginal, but workers assume that participation in further training may pay off in the long run.

16. Although some studies find positive effects of further training on wages, others find – if selectivity into training and third factors explaining wage are adequately controlled – no effects (Pischke, 1996) or effects only for specific groups of workers such as younger or highly educated employees (OECD, 2004, p. 185).

17. For some groups of workers (low-educated and older workers), such underinvestment is found to result from lack of demand for training from workers. For other groups (notably, women, immigrants, involuntary part-time and temporary workers, and workers in small firms), it results from the fact that employers provide less training than workers would like (OECD, 2003, Chapter 5).

18. Perhaps, not surprisingly, a large portion of adult time used for further education and studies occurs outside the rationality of skill formation for working life among elderly citizens once they have retired from working.

19. Interestingly, countries that rank high in continuing vocational training reach this position through a high level of training involvement in all sectors and kinds of firms. In countries with lower overall training, in contrast, differences among sectors, among large and small firms, and among innovative and noninnovative firms are much more pronounced.

20. Evidently, on both sides, it is not just education and training that count. Other crucial factors are work experience or, for particular groups of workers (e.g., gender), preferences they may have for specific kinds of jobs. Employers may have specific expectations, or prejudices, about the suitability or ability of gender, ethnic, or other groups of workers for particular jobs. Even if not considered here, such factors can be integrated into the model.

21. Particular diploma regulations that are often highly idiosyncratic for specific countries especially exist for many jobs in the civil service, various professions

or semiprofessions, and, in some countries, also for various craft occupations. Specifics cannot be discussed here, but differences between countries in the kind of education required (e.g., for the various teaching or nursing occupations) can be quite crucial to understand cross-national differences in education–job linkages.

22. See also Smyth & McCoy, 2000; Müller et al., 2002; Brauns et al., 2003; Kogan & Schubert, 2003. Some of the countries of southern Europe do not seem to fit into these patterns. Here, graduates with different levels of education differ less from each other in length of search for first job and unemployment in early careers than in other countries (Gangl, 2003b, Iannelli, 2003; Ianelli & Soro Bonmatí, 2003; Scherer, 2004).

23. These findings clearly contradict assertions sometimes made by adherents of postmodernism or individualization theory who claim that – due to increased global competition, mass unemployment, and rapid structural change – education and other structuring forces (e.g., social class) have lost significance in shaping the life course of individuals. For some instances, even the contrary appears to be true. According to results of the GLOBALIFE project (Blossfeld & Hofmeister, 2006; Blossfeld et al., 2006), for some countries education has become even more important in shaping men's and women's work careers.

24. Although there are some recent studies that added measurements of literacy and numeracy of adults (e.g., the International Adult Literacy Study and the Adult Literacy and Lifeskills Survey) in large-scale surveys, these studies are cross-sectional so far, thus dealing only partly with the previously mentioned questions about the impact of education, ability, and other factors during an individual's working life.

25. That is, education effects in reduced form models when no information on earlier jobs is controlled.

26. Desjardins et al. (2005) examined the congruence of formal educational attainment and literacy that is negatively influenced by age – the older persons are, the higher the divergence. Thus, the decreasing impact of formal education on working careers might in part be due to their decreasing validity for present ability and actual skills in recruitment processes or for promotion.

27. The differences between the results for the United States and Britain should not be overstated. They could be due to differences in the methodological approach. Although Ianelli uses logistic regression models, Hauser uses a path analytic structural equation modeling approach, controlling for measurement error and using data for sibling pairs more extensively than Iannelli controls for family background characteristics. Iannelli's finding of lasting qualification effects on work career progression are essentially in line with the findings of most of the country studies in the Blossfeld and Hofmeister (2006) and Blossfeld et al. (2006) volumes, even though the latter studies again address a slightly different issue. They study how qualifications affect further upward or downward class or status mobility, controlling for the class of status of the job that so far has been obtained with one's qualification.

28. Still, the notion of an overall upgrading of the job structure ignores that it is still an (empirically) open question if at the same time – at least some – jobs are deskilled. Growing cognitive requirements in some parts of the economy will not affect all workers similarly. Tyler (2004) illustrated the thesis of changing rather than upgrading skills with a receptionist, who nowadays needs to make fewer calculations than to exhibit friendliness, empathy, and intuitiveness (cf. also Autor

et al., 2002). Thus, the increase in skill requirements might also be accompanied by a decrease in cognitive skills (e.g., within a growing sector of [low-skilled] personal services). Empirical evidence with regard to the two theses of either increasing complexity or decreasing importance of cognitive skills in certain occupational areas has been scarce to date.

29. Because of the strong relationship between initial education and further education and training, recommendations sometimes made to increase lifelong learning to the expense of initial education appear to be contraproductive.

30. The Swiss and Austrian models of combining vocational and general training to reach the "Berufsmaturs" (vocational matriculation certificate) are promising examples. Simply enhancing the possibilities and pathways to enter higher education is not sufficient because, in consequence, the number of dropouts may rise accordingly. Furthermore, with regard to social inequality, it is often only the socially privileged who profit most from more open access to higher education as discussed previously.

31. For discussions of qualifications frameworks, see the respective OECD reports (OECD, 2004, n.d.) and EU Kommission (2003).

References

Alba, R., Handl, J., & Müller, W. (1994). Ethnische Ungleichheit im deutschen Bildungssystem. *Kölner Zeitschrift für Soziologie und Sozialpsychologie*, 46, 209–237.

Allmendinger, J. (1989). Educational systems and labor market outcomes. *European Sociological Review*, 54, 231–250.

Arrow, K. J. (1973). Higher education as a filter. *Journal of Public Economics*, 2, 193–216.

Arum, R., Gamoran, A., & Shavit, Y. (2007). More inclusion than diversion: Expansion, differentiation, and the market structure in higher education. In Y. Shavit, R. Arum, & A. Gamoran (Eds.), with G. Menahem, *Stratification in Higher Education: A Comparative Study* (pp. 1–61). Stanford, CA: Stanford University Press.

Autor, D. H., Levy, F., & Murnane, R. J. (2002). Upstairs, downstairs: Computers and skills on two floors of a large bank. *Industrial and Labor Relations Review*, 55(3), 432–447.

Bassanini, A., Booth, A., Brunello, G., de Paola, M., & Leuven, E. (2005). *Workplace Training in Europe*. IZA Discussion Paper No. 1640. Bonn: Forschungsinstitut zur Zukunft der Arbeit.

Baumert, J., Klieme, E., Neubrand, M., Prenzel, M., Schiefele, U., Schneider, W., Stanat, P., Tillmann, K.-J., & Weiß, M., (Eds.). (2001). *PISA 2000: Basiskompetenzen von Schülerinnen und Schülern im internationalen Vergleich*. Opladen, Germany: Leske + Budrich

Baumert, J., Stanat, P., & Watermann, R. (2006). Schulstruktur und die Enstehung differenzieller Lern- und Entwicklungsmilieus. In J. Baumert, P. Stanat, & R. Watermann (Eds.), *Herkunftsbedingte Disparitäten im Bildungswesen: Differentielle Bildungsprozesse und Probleme der Verteilungsgerechtigkeit. Vertiefende Analysen im Rahmen von PISA 2000* (pp. 95–188). Wiesbaden, Germany: VS Verlag für Sozialwissenschaften.

Becker, G. S. (1964). *Human Capital: A Theoretical and Empirical Analysis, with Special Reference to Education*. New York: Columbia University Press.

Becker, R. (2003). Educational expansion and persistent inequalities of education: Utilizing the subjective expected utility theory to explain the increasing participation rates in upper secondary school in the Federal Republic of Germany. *European Sociological Review*, 19(1), 1–24.

Becker, R., & Hecken, A. E. (2006). *Warum werden Arbeiterkinder vom Studium an Universitäten abgelenkt? Eine empirische Überprüfung der "Ablenkungsthese" von Müller und Pollak (2007) un ihre Erweiterung durch Hilmert und Jacob (2003)*. Unpublished manuscript, Universität Bern, Switzerland.

Bertola, G., & Rogerson, R. (1997). Institutions and labour reallocation. *European Economic Review*, 41, 1147–1171.

Blossfeld, H.-P., & Hofmeister, H. (2006). *Globaliziation, Uncertainty and Women's Careers*. Cheltenham, UK: Edward Elgar.

Blossfeld, H.-P., & Mayer, K. U. (1988). Arbeitsmarktsegmentation in der Bundesrepublik Deutschland. *Kölner Zeitschrift für Soziologie und Sozialpsychologie*, 40(2), 262–283.

Blossfeld, H.-P., Mills, M., & Bernard, F. (2006).*Globalization, Uncertainty and Men's Careers*. Cheltenham, UK: Edward Elgar.

Boudon, R. (1974). *Education, Opportunity, and Social Inequality*. New York: Wiley.

Brauns, H., Gangl, M., & Scherer, S. (2003). Education and unemployment risks among market entrants: A comparison of France, the United Kingdom and West Germany. In J. H. P. Hoffmeyer-Zlotnik & C. Wolf (Eds.), *Advances in Cross-National Comparison: A European Working Book for Demographic and Socio-Economic Variables* (pp. 328–345). New York: Kluwer Academic/Plenum.

Brauns, H., Müller, W., & Steinmann, S. (1997). Educational expansion and returns to education: A comparative study on Germany, France, the UK, and Hungary. *Arbeitspapiere Arbeitsbereich I*, 23.

Breen, R. (2005). Explaining cross-national variation in youth unemployment: market and institutional factors. *European Sociological Review*, 21(2), 125–134.

Breen, R., & Goldthorpe, J. H. (1997). Explaining educational differentials: Towards a formal rational action theory. *Rationality and Society*, 9(3), 275–305.

Breen, R., & Goldthorpe, J. H. (2001). Class, mobility and merit: The experience of two British birth cohorts. *European Sociological Review*, 17(2), 81–101.

Breen, R., Luijkx, R., Müller, W., & Pollak, R. (2006). *Non-persistent inequality in educational attainment: Evidence from eight European countries*. Manuscript, Nuffield College, Oxford, UK.

Breen, R., & Yaish, M. (2006). Testing the Breen-Goldthorpe model of educational decision making. In S. L. Morgan, D. B. Grusky, & G. S. Fields (Eds.), *Frontiers in Social and Economic Mobility* (pp. 232–258). Stanford, CA: Stanford University Press.

Büchel, F., & Pollmann-Schult, M. (2004). Career prospects of overeducated workers in West Germany. *European Sociological Review*, 20(4), 321–331.

Büchtemann, C., Schupp, J., & Soloff, D. (1993). From school to work: Patterns in Germany and the United States. In J. Schwarze, F. Buttler, & G. G. Wagner (Eds.), *Labor Market Dynamics in Present Day Germany* (pp. 507–520). Frankfurt: Campus.

Culpepper, P. D. (Ed.). (1999). *The German Skills Machine: Sustaining Comparative Advantage in a Global Economy*. New York: Berghahn Books.

Davies, S., & Guppy, N. (1997). Fields of study, college selectivity and student inequalities in higher education. *Social Forces*, 75(4), 1417–1438.

Desjardins, R., Werquin, P., & Dong, L. (2005). Skills and economic outcomes. In Statistics Canada & OECD (Eds.), *Learning a Living: First Results of the Adult Literacy and Life Skills Survey* (pp. 163–178). Paris: OECD.

Elias, P., & Purcell, K. (2003). *Measuring Change in the Graduate Labor Market: A Study of the Changing Nature of the Labor Market for Graduates and High Level Skills.* Research Paper, University of the West of England, Warwick Institute for Employment Research.

Erikson, R. (1996). Explaining change in educational inequality: Economic security and school reforms. In R. Erikson & J. O. Jonsson (Eds.), *Can Education Be Equalized? The Swedish Case in Comparative Perspective* (pp. 95–112). Boulder, CO: Westview Press.

Erikson, R., & Jonsson, J. O. (1996a). Explaining class inequality in education: The Swedish test case. In R. Erikson & J. O. Jonsson (Eds.), *Can Education Be Equalized? The Swedish Case in Comparative Perspective* (pp. 1–63). Boulder, CO: Westview Press.

Erikson, R., & Jonsson, J. O. (1996b). The Swedish context: Educational reform and long-term change in educational inequality. In R. Erikson & J. O. Jonsson (Eds.), *Education Be Equalized? The Swedish Case in Comparative Perspective* (pp. 65–93). Boulder, CO: Westview Press.

Esser, H. (1999). *Soziologie. Spezielle Grundlagen Band 1: Situationslogik und Handeln.* Frankfurt: Campus.

Esser, H. (2006). *Sprache und Integration: Die sozialen Bedingungen und Folgen des Spracherwerbs von Migranten.* Frankfurt: Campus.

EU Kommission. (Ed.). (2003). *Allgemeine und berufliche Bildung 2010 – die Dringlichkeit von Reformen fuer den Erfolg der Lissabon-Strategie.* Available at: http://ec.europa.eu/education/policies/2010/doc/com_2003_685-a1_23013_de.pdf.

Finnie, R., & Frenette, M. (2003). Earning differences by major field of study: Evidence from three cohorts of recent Canadian graduates. *Economics of Education Review*, 22(2), 179–192.

Flanagan, R. J. (1988). Unemployment as a hiring problem. *OECD Economic Studies*, 11, 123–154.

Franz, W., & Soskice, D. (1994). *The German Apprenticeship System.* Discussion Paper FS I, Wissenschaftszentrum Berlin.

Gangl, M. (2003a). Returns to education in context: individual education and transition outcomes in European labor markets. In W. Müller & M. Gangl (Eds.), *Transitions from Education to Work in Europe: The Integration of Youth into EU Labor Markets* (pp. 156–185). Oxford, UK: Oxford University Press.

Gangl, M. (2003b). Explaining change in early career outcomes: Labour market conditions, educational expansion, and youth cohort sizes. In W. Müller & M. Gangl (Eds.), *Transitions from Education to Work in Europe: The Integration of Youth into EU Labor Markets* (pp. 251–276). Oxford, UK: Oxford University Press.

Gangl, M. (2004). Institutions and the structure of labor market matching in the United States and West Germany. *European Sociological Review*, 20(3), 171–187.

Gangl, M., Müller, W., & Raffe, D. (2003). Conclusions: Explaining cross-national differences in school-to-work transitions. In W. Müller & M. Gangl (Eds.), *Transitions from Education to Work in Europe: The Integration of Youth into EU Labor Markets* (pp. 277–305). Oxford, UK: Oxford University Press.

Ganzeboom, H. B. G., & Treiman, D. J. (1993). Preliminary results of educational expansion and educational attainment in comparative perspective. In H. A. Becker & P. L. J. Hermkens (Eds.), *Solidarity of Generations: Demographic, Economic and Social Change, and Its Consequences* (Vol. I, pp. 467–506). Amsterdam: Thesis.

Goldthorpe, J. H. (2000). *On Sociology: Numbers, Narratives, and the Integration of Research and Theory*. Oxford, UK: Oxford University Press.

Goldthorpe, J. H., & McKnight, A. (2006). The economic basis of social class. In S. L. Morgan, D. B. Grusky, & G. S. Fields (Eds.), *Frontiers in Social and Economic Mobility* (pp. 109–136). Stanford, CA: Stanford University Press.

Green, D., & Riddell, W. C. (2002). *Literacy and Earnings: An Investigation of the Interaction of Cognitive and Non-Cognitive Attributes in Earnings Generation*. Ottawa, Ontario, Canada: Statistics Canada.

Gregg, P., & Manning, A. (1997). Labour market regulation and unemployment. In D. J. Snower & G. de la Dehesa (Eds.), *Unemployment Policy: Government Options for the Labour Market* (pp. 395–429). Cambridge, UK: Cambridge University Press.

Hauser, R. M. (2002). *Meritocracy, Cognitive Ability, and the Sources of Occupational Success*. Unpublished manuscript, The University of Wisconsin–Madison, Department of Sociology.

Heath, A., & Cheung, S. Y. (Eds.). (2007). *Unequal Chances: Ethnic Minorities in Western Labour Markets*. Oxford, UK: Oxford University Press for the British Academy.

Hillmert, S., & Jacob, M. (2003). Social inequality in higher education: Is vocational training a pathway leading to or away from university? *European Sociological Review*, 19, 319–334.

Hillmert, S., & Jacob, M. (2005a). Institutionelle Strukturierung und inter-individuelle Variation: Die Entwicklung herkunftsbezogener Ungleichheiten im Bildungsverlauf. *Kölner Zeitschrift für Soziologie und Sozialpsychologie*, 57, 414–442.

Hillmert, S., & Jacob, M. (2005b). Zweite Chance im Schulsystem? Zur sozialen Selektivität bei späteren' Bildungsentscheidungen. In P. Berger & H. Kahlert (Eds.), *Institutionalisierte Ungleichheiten* (pp. 155–178). Weinheim, Germany: Juventa-Verlag.

Hout, M., & DiPrete, T. (2004). *What Have We Learned: RC28's Contribution to Knowledge about Social Stratification. Research in Social Stratification and Mobility*. Working Paper, University of California, Berkley, Survey Research Center.

Iannelli, C. (2003). Young people's social origin, educational attainment and labour market outcomes in Europe: Youth transitions from education to working life in Europe (Part III). In Eurostat (Ed.), *Statistics in Focus. Theme: Population and Social Conditions* (pp. 1–8). Luxembourg: Eurostat.

Iannelli, C. (2006). *Educational and Occupational Pathways: A Longitudinal Perspective in the Study of Social Mobility*. Unpublished manuscript, University of Edinburgh, Centre for Educational Sociology.

Iannelli, C., & Soro Bonmatí, A. (2003). Transition pathways in Italy and Spain: Different patterns, similar vulnerability? In W. Müller & M. Gangl (Eds.), *Transitions from Education to Work in Europe: The Integration of Youth into EU Labor Markets* (pp. 212–250). Oxford, UK: Oxford University Press.

Jackson, M., Erikson, R., Goldthorpe, J. H., & Yaish, M. (2006). *Primary and Secondary Effects in Class Differentials in Educational Attainment: The Transition to A-Level Courses in England and Wales*. Manuscript, Nuffield College, Oxford, UK.

Jacob, M. (2003). *Mehrfachausbildungen in Deutschland. Karriere, Collage, Kompensation.* Wiesbaden, Germany: VS Verlag für Sozialwissenschaften.

Jonsson, J. O. (1993). Persisting inequalities in Sweden. In Y. Shavit & H.-P. Blossfeld (Eds.), *Persistent Inequality: Changing Educational Attainment in Thirteen Countries* (pp. 101–132). Boulder, CO: Westview Press.

Jonsson, J. O., Mills, C., & Müller, W. (1996). Half a century of increasing educational openness? Social class, gender and educational attainment in Sweden, Germany and Britain. In R. Erikson & J. O. Jonsson (Eds.), *Can Education Be Equalized? The Swedish Case in Comparative Perspective* (pp. 183–206). Boulder, CO: Westview Press.

Kalleberg, A. L., & Sørensen, Å. B. (1979). The sociology of labour markets. *Annual Review of Sociology*, 5, 351–379.

Kalter, F., & Granato, N. (2002). Demographic change, educational expansion, and structural assimilation of immigrants: The case of Germany. *European Sociological Review*, 18, 199–226.

Kalter, F., Granato, N., & C. Kristen (2007). Disentangling recent trends of the second generation's structural assimilation in Germany. In S. Scherer, R. Pollak, G. Otte, & M. Gangl (Eds.), *From Origin to Destination: Trends and Mechanisms in Social Stratification Research* (pp. 220–251). Frankfurt: Campus.

Kerckhoff, A. C. (1995). Institutional arrangements and stratification processes in industrial societies. *Annual Review of Sociology*, 15, 323–347.

Kirsch, I. S., Jungeblut, A., Jenkins, L., & Kolstad, A. (1993). *Adult Literacy in America: A First Look at the Results of the National Adult Literacy Study.* Princeton, NJ: Educational Testing Service.

Kogan, I., & Müller, W. (Eds.). (2003). *School-to-Work Transitions in Europe: Analyses of the EU LFS 2000 Ad Hoc Module.* Mannheim, Germany: Mannheim Centre for European Social Research.

Kogan, I., & Schubert, F. (2003). *General Indicators on Transition from School to Work – Youth Transitions from Education to Working Life in Europe, Part I.* Statistics in Focus: Population and Social Conditions. Luxembourg: Eurostat.

Köller, O., & Baumert, J. (2001). Leistungsgruppierungen in der Sekundarstufe I und ihre Konsequenzen für die Mathematikleistung und das mathematische Selbstkonzept der Begabung. *Zeitschrift für pädagogische Psychologie*, 15(2), 99–110.

König, W., & Müller, W. (1986). Educational systems and labour markets as determinants of worklife mobility in France and West Germany: A comparison of men's career mobility, 1965–1970. *European Sociological Review*, 2, 73–96.

Kuwan, H., Thebis, F., Gnahs, D., Sandau, E., & Seidel, S. (2003). *Berichtssystem Weiterbildung. Integrierter Gesamtbericht zur Weiterbildungssituation in Deutschland.* Bonn, Germany: Bundesministerium für Bildung und Forschung.

Levy, F., & Murnane, R. J. (2001). Key competencies critical to economic success. In D. S. Rychen & L. H. Salganik (Eds.), *Defining and Selecting Key Competencies* (pp. 151–173). Seattle, WA: Hogrefe & Huber.

Lindbeck, A., & Snower, D. J. (1988). *The Insider-Outsider Theory of Employment and Unemployment.* Cambridge, MA: MIT Press.

Logan, J. A. (1996). Opportunity and choice in socially structured labour markets. *American Journal of Sociology*, 102, 114–160.

Lucas, S. R. (2001). Effectively maintained inequality: Education transitions, track mobility, and social background effects. *American Journal of Sociology*, 106, 1642–1690.

Mare, R. D. (1980). Social background and school continuation decisions. *Journal of the American Statistical Association, 75*, 295–305.

Mare, R. D. (1981). Change and stability in educational stratification. *American Sociological Review, 46*, 73–87.

Mare, R. D. (1993). Educational stratification on observed and unobserved components of family background. In Y. Shavit & P. Blossfeld (Eds.), *Persistent Inequality: Changing Educational Attainment in Thirteen Countries* (pp. 351–376). Boulder, CO: Westview Press.

Marsden, D. (1990). Institutions and labor mobility: Occupational and internal labour markets in Britain, France, Italy, and West Germany. In R. Brunetta & C. Dell'Aringa (Eds.), *Labour Relations and Economic Performance* (pp. 414–438). London: Macmillan.

Maurice, M., Sellier, F., & Silvestre, J.-J. (1982). *Politique d'éducation et d'organisation industrielle en France et en Allemagne. Essai d'analyse sociétal.* Paris: Presses Universitaires de France.

Mayer, K. U., Müller, W., & Pollak, R. (2007). Institutional change and inequalities of access in German higher education. In Y. Shavit, R. Arum, & A. Gamoran (Eds.), *Stratification in Higher Education* (pp. 240–265). Stanford, CA: Stanford University Press.

Müller, W., Brauns, H., & Steinmann, S. (2002). Expansion und Erträge tertiärer Bildung in Deutschland, Frankreich und im Vereinigten Königreich. *Berliner Journal für Soziologie, 12*(1), 37–62.

Müller, W., & Gangl, M. (Eds.). (2003). *Transitions from Education to Work in Europe: The Integration of Youth into EU Labour Markets.* Oxford, UK: Oxford University Press.

Müller, W., & Haun, D. (1994). Bildungsungleichheit im sozialen Wandel. *Kölner Zeitschrift fur Soziologie und Sozialpsychologie, 46*, 1–42.

Müller, W., & Karle, W. (1993). Social selection in educational systems in Europe. *European Sociological Review, 9*(1), 1–22.

Müller, W., & Shavit, Y. (1998). The institutional embeddedness of the stratification process: A comparative study of qualifications and occupations in thirteen countries. In Y. Shavit & W. Müller (Eds.), *From School to Work: A Comparative Study of Educational Qualifications and Occupational Destinations* (pp. 1–48). Oxford, UK: Clarendon Press.

Murray, M. (1988). Educational expansion, policies of diversion, and equality: The case of Sweden 1935–85. *European Journal of Education, 23*, 141–149.

Need, A., & de Jong, U. (2000). Educational differentials in the Netherlands. *Rationality and Society, 13*, 71–98.

Nester, K., & Kailis, E. (2002). *Continuing Vocational Training in Enterprises in the European Union and Norway* (CVTS2). Eurostat Statistics in Focus: Population and Social Conditions. Theme 3-3/2002.

Nester, K., & Kailis, E. (2003). *Working Time Spent on Continuing Vocational Training in Enterprises in Europe.* Eurostat Statistics in Focus: Population and Social Conditions. Theme 3-1/2003.

Organisation for Economic Co-operation and Development (OECD). (2000). *From Initial Education to Working Life: Making Transitions Work.* Paris: Author.

Organisation for Economic Co-operation and Development (OECD). (2003). *OECD Employment Outlook: Towards More and Better Jobs*. Paris: Author.

Organisation for Economic Co-operation and Development (OECD). (2004). *Report from Thematic Group 1: The Development and Use of 'Qualification Frameworks' as a Means of Reforming and Managing Qualification Systems*. Paris: Author.

Organisation for Economic Co-operation and Development (OECD). (n.d.). *Australia's Qualification System and Lifelong Learning: A Country Background Report Prepared for the OECD Project "The Role of National Qualification Systems in Promoting Lifelong Learning."* Paris: Author.

PISA-Konsortium Deutschland. (Ed.). (2004). *PISA 2003 – Der Bildungsstand der Jugendlichen in Deutschland – Ergebnisse des zweiten internationalen Vergleichs*. Münster, Germany: Waxmann-Verlag.

Pischke, J.-S. (1996). *Continuous Training in Germany*. Working Paper No. 5828 of NBER Working Paper Series, National Bureau of Economic Research, Cambridge, MA.

Reimer, D., & Pollak, R. (2005). The impact of social origin on the transition to tertiary education in West Germany 1983 and 1999. *Arbeitspapiere – Mannheimer Zentrum für Europäische Sozialforschung*, 85.

Rijken, S. (1999). *Educational Expansion and Status Attainment: A Cross-National and Over-Time Comparison*. Amsterdam: Thela Thesis (ICS dissertation).

Ryan, P. (2001). The school-to-work transition: A cross-national perspective. *Journal of Economic Literature*, 39, 34–92.

Scherer, S. (2004). *Erwerbseintritt und Berufsverlauf: Westdeutschland, Italien und Großbritannien im Vergleich*. Frankfurt: Lang.

Shavit, Y., & Blossfeld, P. (Eds.). (1993). *Persistent Inequality: Changing Educational Attainment in Thirteen Countries*. Boulder, CO: Westview Press.

Shavit, Y., & Müller, W. (Eds.). (1998). *From School to Work: A Comparative Study of Educational Qualifications and Occupational Destinations*. Oxford, UK: Clarendon Press.

Shavit, Y., & Müller, W. (2000). Vocational secondary education: Where diversion and where safety net? *European Societies*, 2(1), 29–50.

Smyth, E., & McCoy, S. (2000). Differentiation among school leavers in the transition process: A comparative analysis. In T. Hammer (Ed.), *Transitions and Mobility in the Labour Market* (Proceedings of the workshop on European network on transitions in youth, Oslo, September 2–5, 1999). Oslo: NOVA.

Soskice, D. (1994). Reconciling markets and institutions: The German apprenticeship system. In L. Lynch (Ed.), *Training and the Private Sector: International Comparisons* (pp. 25–60). Chicago: The University of Chicago Press.

Spence, M. (1973). Job market signaling. *Quarterly Journal of Economics*, 87(3), 355–374.

Stocké, V. (2006). *Explaining Secondary Effects of Families. Social Class Position. An Empirical Test of the Breen-Goldthorpe Model of Educational Attainment*. Discussion paper 06–07, Universität Mannheim, SFB 504.

Thurow, L. C. (1976). *Generating Inequality: Mechanisms of Distribution in the US Economy*. London: Macmillan.

Treiman, D. J. (1970). Industrialization and social stratification. In E. O. Laumann (Ed.), *Social Stratification: Research and Theory for the 1970s* (pp. 207–34). Indianapolis: Bobbs-Merrill.

Treiman, D. J., & Yip, K.-B. (1989). Educational and occupational attainment in 21 countries. In M. L. Kohn (Ed.), *Cross-National Research in Sociology* (pp. 373–394). Newbury Park, CA: Sage.

Tyler, J. H. (2004). Basic skills and the earnings of dropouts. *Economics of Education Review*, 23(3), 221–235.

Vallet, L.-A., & Caille J.-P. (1995). Les carrières scolaires au collège des élèves étrangers ou issus de l'immigration. *Éducation et Formations*, 40, 5–14.

Vallet, L.-A., & Selz, M. (2006). La démocratisation de l'enseignement et son paradoxe apparent. In Institut National de la Statistique et des Études Économiques (Eds.), *Données Sociales – La société francaise* (pp. 101–107). Paris: Institut National de la Statistique et des Etudes Economiques.

van de Werfhorst, H. G., de Graaf, N. D., & Kraaykamp, G. (2001). Intergenerational resemblance in field of study in the Netherlands. *European Sociological Review*, 17(3), 275–293.

van de Werfhorst, H. G., & Kraaykamp, G. (2001). Four field-related educational resources and their impact on labor, consumption, and sociopolitical orientation. *Sociology of Education*, 74(4), 296–317.

van de Werfhorst, H. G., Sullivan, A., & Cheung, S. Y. (2003). Social class, ability and choice of subject in secondary and tertiary education in Britain. *British Educational Research Journal*, 29(1), 41–62.

Walters, P. B. (1984). Occupational and labor market effects on secondary and postsecondary educational expansion in the United States 1922–1979. *American Sociological Review*, 19, 659–671.

Warren, J. R., Hauser, R. M., & Sheridan, J. T. (2002). Occupational stratification across the life course: Evidence from the Wisconsin Longitudinal Study. *American Sociological Review*, 67, 432–455.

Wolbers, M. H. J. (2003). Learning and working: Double statuses in youth transitions. In W. Müller & M. Gangl (Eds.), *Transitions from Education to Work in Europe* (pp. 131–155). Oxford, UK: Oxford University Press.

7 Lack of Training

Employment Opportunities for Low-Skilled Persons from a Sociological and Microeconomic Perspective

Heike Solga

Over the past three decades, low-skilled persons[1] have received increasing attention by researchers on skill formation and labor markets across disciplines as well as by politicians. "In many OECD [Organisation for Economic Co-operation and Development] countries, discussions of the transition between education and employment are dominated by the problem of how to help a small minority of young people with severe and often multiple problems: who are doing badly at school; who experienced prolonged and regular unemployment; and who are extremely likely to experience a lifetime of low income, insecure employment, and relatively poor health" (OECD, 1999a: 26f). In all Western societies, we find an increasing labor market vulnerability of low-skilled persons over the past twenty-five years, although at different levels.

Disadvantages that low-skilled persons have in labor markets are studied in both microeconomics and sociology. Here, sociologists have quickly adopted microeconomic explanations. In doing so, however, they have ignored valuable sociology contributions toward explaining changes in the relationship between low education and labor market opportunities. This chapter delivers not competing but complementary sociological *and* microeconomic explanations for the increasing labor market vulnerability of low-skilled persons over the past three decades. These accounts are then used to explain variation in the vulnerability of low-skilled workers in developed countries.

This chapter starts with a portrayal of the dominant microeconomic explanation for the increase in labor market problems of low-skilled persons – the displacement argument – followed by a discussion of its shortcomings. From those, I derive three additional social mechanisms that contribute to explaining the rise of educational disadvantage. After this theoretical discussion, I formulate empirical expectations for the international variations in the explanatory power of the different mechanisms and conduct empirical

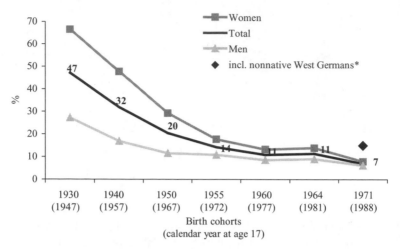

Figure 7.1. Proportions of persons *without* completed vocational education at age 25 (in percent, only West German origin). Persons in vocational education at age 25 are not counted as "without" completed vocational education. *Persons ages 25 to 29 (birth cohorts 1968–72; Survey of the BIBB, Governmental Institute for Vocational Education). *Source:* German Life History Study, Max Planck Institute for Human Development (Berlin).

analyses using OECD aggregated data. I finish with some concluding remarks on the benefit of a multidisciplinary perspective.

THE SUPPLY–DEMAND STORY FOR THE INCREASING LABOR MARKET VULNERABILITY OF LOW-SKILLED PERSONS

What do we mean by the increasing labor market vulnerability of the low skilled? Educational expansion has supplied our labor markets with a high availability of qualified and highly qualified young persons since the mid-1960s. The other side of the coin is a remarkable decrease in the share of low-skilled youth. This is displayed for West Germany in Figure 7.1. The share of people without completed vocational or tertiary education decreased from 47% of the birth cohort 1929–31 to only 7% of the birth cohort 1971.[2] Including immigrant youth, it decreased to about 15%. Such a relative reduction in the share of low-skilled youth can be observed in most Western countries, although resulting in different absolute levels.

Looking at the employment opportunities for the same time period, low-skilled persons face an increasingly higher risk of unemployment, especially

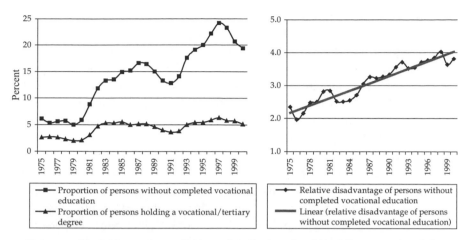

Figure 7.2. Unemployment rate by (vocational) educational level (in percent) and the relative unemployment risk of the low skilled (ratio), West Germany 1975–2000. Population = 15–64 years old. *Source:* Reinberg & Hummel (2002).

long-term unemployment. For West Germany, Figure 7.2 shows that already in the 1970s, their unemployment rate was twice as high as the unemployment rate of persons with completed vocational or tertiary education. Today, however, that rate has grown to four times as high. Moreover, one-half of the long-term unemployed are low skilled.

In labor market research, this increasingly deprived labor market situation of low-skilled persons is seen as a result of the following:

- A decreasing demand for low-skilled labor (due to a loss of low-skill jobs)
- An oversupply of trained persons (due to the educational expansion)
- A general shortage of jobs (caused by a declining demand of labor due to recessions and an increasing labor supply by women and immigrants)[3]

Taking these three developments on the supply and demand side into account, decreasing labor market opportunities of low-skilled persons are explained dominantly by the so-called *displacement argument*: in situations of increased job competition, higher-educated persons outqualify low-skilled persons. The displacement argument is derived from multiple microeconomic theories – such as human capital theory (Becker, 1964; Bowman, 1966), signaling (Spence, 1974; Stiglitz, 1975), and job competition/vacancy chains (Thurow, 1975, 1979; Sørensen, 1977; Sørensen & Kalleberg, 1981) – which together deliver the following matching argument for explaining individuals' labor market opportunities. Given that educational attainment is taken as an indicator of an individual's future productivity and trainability, and given a fixed number of vacant jobs, then the matching of persons to jobs is based on the following recruitment rule: the lower an individual's educational degree, the lower is her rank in the labor queue, thus her probability to be hired declines because vacant positions will be filled with available persons with higher educational attainment (e.g., Boudon, 1974; Thurow, 1975; Hirsch, 1977; Blossfeld, 1985, 1990; Kalleberg, 1996).

Based on this matching argument, the *displacement mechanism* explains the increasing labor market vulnerability of low-skilled persons as follows: in times of high unemployment and an oversupply of higher-educated persons, more and more higher-educated persons have had to enter into jobs that were previously carried out by low-skilled persons. Higher-educated persons, thereby, increasingly *displace* low-skilled persons from "their" previously available jobs. As a consequence, low-skilled persons end up in poorer job placements compared to the past – if they are not pushed out of the labor market entirely.

The theoretical merit of the displacement argument is that decreasing employment opportunities of low-skilled persons are primarily due to "lack of opportunity" and only secondarily, if at all, due to "lack of absolute skills." Education is conceptualized as *relative* skills and, therefore, the employment opportunities of low-skilled persons depend on labor supply–demand relationship. Moreover, displacement shows that hiring standards are not fixed. They do change, and they do so not only in response to technological requirements, but also in response to shifts in the distribution of labor supply. With respect to educational expansion, the rising educational participation has resulted in an "upgrading" of recruitment criteria or job requirements.

The displacement argument's implicit assumption, however, is that increasing labor market difficulties of the low skilled are solely due to a (labor supply–demand) capacity problem. Applying this assumption *not* to a situation with an oversupply, but to a situation of supply *shortage* of qualified labor (a situation that could well develop in the future in some developed countries, given the huge decline in their fertility rates), we would have to expect that employers should increasingly consider hiring low-skilled persons again. However, in contradiction to the displacement mechanism, they may not do so – as I show in this chapter.

Displacement is certainly a compelling explanation, but it is far from being sufficient; it is only part of the story. Empirical analyses by the German labor economist Wolfgang Franz (1999) showed that in Germany only 20% to 30% of the increase in the relative unemployment risk of the low-skilled group can be attributed to processes of labor supply–demand imbalances (either due to a loss of low-skill jobs or their "displacement" by higher-qualified persons). Thus, 70% to 80% of their increasing unemployment risk remains unexplained. Can sociology help fill this explanatory gap with complementary mechanisms?

SHORTCOMINGS OF THE DISPLACEMENT STORY

The starting points in answering this question are the shortcomings of the displacement argument. It ignores the following:

- Changes in the *group size* of educational groups and resulting changes in social majority–minority definitions
- Changes in the *social composition* of the low-skilled group due to a stratified outflow from the low-skilled group and resulting changes in the group's available social resources
- Changes in the *educational and biographical experiences* of low-skilled youth

Moreover, the displacement argument only tells a *recruitment* story. It ignores the job search and application side. Possible changes in the application behavior of low-skilled youth during the course of educational expansion are missed. Before developing further explanations, it is helpful to consider these shortcomings in more detail.

Changes in the low-skilled group size: The displacement argument employs Spence's (1973) signaling idea – namely, that employers use educational degrees as an indicator of *trainability* – and takes into account that employers' perceptions and expectations about the productivity of low-skilled persons are crucial for hiring decisions. It does *not*, however, account for *changes in these perceptions*. Yet, the signal "low skilled" is certainly perceived differently in a time period when this characteristic constitutes a minority "deviating" from the educational norm. This may well add an additional source of changes in recruitment behavior of employers due to which employers – even under conditions of labor–supply shortage – might *not* be willing to hire low-skilled youth (cf. Solga, 2002a).

Changes in the low-skilled group's social composition: Suppose that during educational expansion, the "remaining" low-skilled persons are a "negative selection" in terms of social background because children and youth with more advantageous family resources will have increasing probabilities to attend higher schools or school tracks and to acquire higher educational certificates. If that is true, low-skilled youth will have less and less social and cultural resources in their networks of classmates, friends, and friends' parents. Thus, their increasing labor market vulnerability could be well caused by changes in the group's social resources for job search, as well as in the group's environmental contexts in terms of experiences, aspirations, and expectations.[4]

Changes in the educational experiences of low-skilled youth: We have to take into account that "low educational attainment" is not a single event, but the result of an institutionalized process of "failure" in school and vocational education. Given that in the younger cohorts most of the cohort members were "successful" in school and vocational education, this increased rate of successful experiences also means that those remaining persons increasingly experienced "failure" during their educational careers on the path to becoming low skilled. Thus, the development of the low-skilled group into a social minority may contribute to unfavorable alterations of low-skilled persons' social identity formation and occupational expectations.

ADDITIONAL SOCIAL MECHANISMS RESPONSIBLE FOR THE INCREASING LABOR MARKET VULNERABILITY OF LOW-SKILLED PERSONS

In response to these shortcomings of the displacement mechanism, three additional social mechanisms must be taken into account for explaining the declining employment opportunities of low-skilled persons in the course of educational expansions. These three additional mechanisms are not counterarguments to the displacement argument. Economic processes related to supply and demand of labor, of course, considerably shape low-educated persons' employment opportunities. The three additional mechanisms, therefore, constitute *complementary* explanations (contributing to fill the explanatory gap mentioned previously).

The three complementary mechanisms are as follows:

• Discredit
• Impoverished network resources (or in German, *soziale Verarmung*)
• Stigmatization

The two latter changes are connected to the application behavior of low-skilled youth – taking into account the processes of "becoming low skilled": given a loss of social resources and institutionalized "damage" to their self-efficacy beliefs, in younger cohorts, low-skilled youth may not apply to jobs to the same extent as they did in the past, and they may not apply for the same kind of jobs.

What are the theoretical background of these three additional social mechanisms and their lines of reasoning? The *discredit* argument is based on the same microeconomic theories as the displacement argument (cf. Solga, 2005: 59–111). Based on these, one can derive that employers are not only interested in hiring the best applicant available, but also in avoiding the hire of applicants whom they believe are incapable of mastering a given job. Or, as Lester Thurow (1975: 174) formulated, "An individual who belongs to a group that has ... a higher probability of having an undesired characteristic is not paid less, he is completely excluded from the job in question." Empirically, this has been shown in many organizational studies in which employers were interviewed (e.g., Bills, 1988; Baron & Pfeffer, 1994; Rosenbaum & Binder, 1997; Bennett & Weiss, 1998).

Given this line of reasoning, what is the response of employers to the rapid and enormous reduction in the group size of low-skilled youth? Especially for the lowest educational category – school dropouts or, in Germany, persons without any completed vocational training – studies have shown that employers increasingly complain about the low or even nonemployability of the low skilled (see Murnane & Levy, 1996; Rosenbaum & Binder, 1997; Giloth, 1998; Sehringer, 1989). Today, low-skilled youth are hardly considered to be "employable." This indicates that educational expansion has exacerbated the negative *signaling value* of a missing educational credential. The growth of the higher-educated population has changed the character of those remaining low skilled; it has transformed the meaning of "not having completed higher or vocational education" into "failure" (see Parsons, 1959: 317; Trow, 1977: 112f.).

From these considerations, the following discredit mechanism can be derived: the increasingly negative valuation of low-skilled persons' human capital by employers – indicating a significant change in the signaling value of "being low skilled" – has increased the risk for low-skilled persons of being excluded from applicants' queues. For them, the ranking of individuals in an applicants' queue has turned into a *sorting-out* process.[5]

So far, we have ignored the *constitution* of pools from which employers select competing candidates. Applicants' pools are the result of processes by which individuals select *themselves* into or out of such pools. Entry pools and eligibility pools, therefore, are not random (Blalock, 1991). The two sociological mechanisms allow us to take into account such socially stratified processes of self-selection and their changes during educational expansion.

The mechanism of *impoverished network resources* is based on compositional changes of educational categories as a product of socially stratified shifts in educational participation. Applying Boudon's (1974) idea that primary and secondary effects of social stratification are responsible for class differentials in educational attainment, outflow mobility from the lower educational group was and is *not* random in terms of social background. Children from families with advantageous socioeconomic/cultural resources should have shown more ambition to complete higher educational degrees than those with poorer socioeconomic/cultural resources. As a consequence, the remaining individuals in the lowest educational group are a "negative selection" in terms of social background (cf. Solga, 2002a). The consequence of this decreasing social heterogeneity of the low-skilled group is an increase in the homogeneity of their employment opportunities (cf. Mare, 1980; Leschinsky & Mayer, 1999). Why? Network theorists (e.g., Granovetter, 1973, 1974; Burt, 1992, 1997; Elliott & Smith, 2004) have shown that individuals' job search patterns are crucially determined by socially stratified recruitment and supply networks, for example, because they provide information on vacant job positions, they give secondhand accounts of experiences of job requirements, or because they deliver a good reputation through having employed persons in one's network (in terms of *borrowed social capital*).

To introduce "education" and educational categories into network analysis, we can employ Charles Tilly's (1998) concept of opportunity hoarding. Tilly's basic idea is that organizations – such as firms – match organizationally external categories to internal categories in order to lower transaction costs for organizational tasks – such as hiring – and to increase stability (Tilly, 1998: 8of). The internal and external categories are *social groups* – so that here the matching processes are conceptualized as social relationships between the organizational outsiders and insiders belonging to social categories. Such categorical matching processes of persons to persons via network connections would channel low-skilled persons' job search into low-skill jobs far more often than those of more highly educated persons, especially because of the higher share of low-skilled persons in their network who are already employed in low-skill jobs. Such categorical matching processes would also contribute to a higher unemployment risk of low-skilled persons because in their networks there is a higher share of unemployed (because low-educated) persons. The underlying mechanism is that educational groups define categorical boundaries that entail structural differences in available contacts, one's base of experiences as well as assistance or resistance from others.

Given an increasingly selective social composition of the low-skilled group during educational expansion, the decreasing labor market opportunities of low-skilled persons are also caused by having fewer connections to *employed* family members and friends than in the past and, if connected, by having fewer connections to qualified jobs. As a result, these individuals know less and less about "where, when, and how to apply" (Wial, 1991: 412). In addition, networks are important for low-skilled persons' recruitment because their missing credentials and low school achievement signal only what they *cannot* do, whereas they fail to signal what these persons *are* able to do (nonetheless).[6] That is the *"impoverished network resources" mechanism.*[7]

Finally, we come to the *stigmatization mechanism*. Applying Goffman's (1963) stigma definition, we can hypothesize that during educational expansion the risk of disengagement and social isolation of low-skilled youth has increased, resulting in unfavorable "cooling-out" processes (Clark, 1960). Given the success of most of their cohort members, their experiences of "failure" during their educational career have increased. In addition, "low education" has become more and more a discrediting, stigmatizing attribute of individuals because of

- Its increasing visibility
- The increasing belief that educational attainment and failure are under the control of the individuals themselves ("individual failure")
- Because of the increasing importance accorded to educational attainment in modern societies

These factors make it difficult for low-skilled people to hide their low educational attainment in many life domains, and, according to Goffman (1963), "low education" thus becomes a "master status" in their life. As a result, many of today's low-skilled youth may give up any hope of a recognized career and "disidentify" with educational and employment goals for fear of possible humiliation and further negative reaction (Jones et al., 1984: 111). On the one hand, self-stigmatization may be touched off or learned by others' marginalization, whereas on the other hand, these same youth may "protect" themselves by using self-exclusion (e.g., by dropping out of schools and educational programs as well as self-exclusion from job applicants' pools) in order to avoid further stigmatization by others (cf. Pfahl, 2003; Solga, 2004): "The marked person may still be able to improve his life in society by reducing the mark's saliency (e.g., not applying for certain jobs)" (Jones et al., 1984: 34).

Based on their experiences in school, low-skilled persons in younger cohorts increasingly have learned and internalized their "inferior status" in society. If they perceive this negative-stereotypic lack of fit to qualified and even to low-skill jobs – also by being aware that other low-skilled persons (in the family or among peers) often experience negative outcomes in the labor market – they may self-select from certain jobs or the labor market in general. Applying symbolic interactionism and sociopsychological research on stigma, stereotypes, and intergroup relations (cf. Brown, 1996; Brewer

& Brown, 1998; Fiske, 1998), the result is that low education has become a "social stigma" in knowledge-based societies. Thus, low-skilled persons may face an increasing risk of withdrawal or self-exclusion from labor markets. This may occur even prior to labor market entry.

To summarize the *stigmatization mechanism*, we can formulate that more and more low-skilled youth may respond to institutionalized processes of "failure," to their status as "outsiders," and to the social stigma of "being low skilled" by withdrawing from qualified labor market segments or the labor market in general. Similar to the displacement mechanism, the discredit mechanism is based on microeconomic theories. Both mechanisms consider "low education" (or "being low skilled") to be an individual characteristic in terms of (relative) skill certification and attribution. The two sociological mechanisms – impoverished network resources and stigmatization – incorporate processes of "becoming low skilled" into explaining labor market vulnerability and thereby consider "low education" to be group membership in terms of resources and social identity.

INTERNATIONAL VARIATION IN LABOR MARKET VULNERABILITY OF LOW-SKILLED PERSONS – EMPIRICAL INSIGHTS

There is certainly widespread consensus that the *displacement argument* is generally applicable to explain the increasing labor market vulnerability of low-skilled persons in Western societies. However, because both labor supply and demand are shaped by (vocational) educational and labor market institutions, we should find cross-national differences in the relative impact of displacement on low-skilled persons' labor market problems (as outlined in this section).

Disagreement in their generality, in contrast, might exist for the *discredit, the impoverished network resources,* and *the stigmatization mechanism.* One might ask whether these three social mechanisms apply only to Germany[8] because of its highly standardized and stratified schooling and vocational training systems, which may make it easier to identify "educational failure" (Allmendinger, 1989; Esping-Andersen et al., 1994: 120). My answer is, however, that they are relevant for other developed countries as well – as I show by a cross-country comparison.

The basic idea behind this comparison is that these mechanisms are not only adequate for explaining historical changes in the labor market opportunities of low-skilled persons (as outlined previously), but also for today's variation in low-skilled persons' opportunities across countries because both historical and cross-national analyses attempt to examine social phenomena under varying institutional and economic conditions. Thus, under "statistical control" for the group size of the low-skilled (in linear regressions), cross-sectional country comparisons do reveal how differences in labor market regimes and educational institutions contribute to differing (relative) relevance of the four mechanisms in these countries.

As background for this statistical cross-country analysis, it is useful to have a brief look at policies and policy statements concerning low-skilled persons/youth. Studies by the OECD, European Centre for the Development of Vocational Training (Cedefop), or Eurydice and therein expressed social perceptions of low-skilled persons, as well as policy agendas concerning them, reveal that in many Western societies, the low skilled are considered as being a "problem group." Two quotations from OECD studies of two very different countries – Denmark and the United States – illustrate this "problem group" definition:

The safety net and the problem of the last 15 per cent (…) – those young people who exit from the education system without having obtained a recognised qualification (…). They may be bright but are more likely to be slow. They are almost certainly bored or frustrated to tears by the usual schools organised in the usual way. Many live in family circumstances that have caused great stress. Quite a few of these young people have given up on themselves and grown dispirited and resentful. (OECD, 1999b: 36)

In many OECD countries, discussions of the transition between education and employment are dominated by the problem of how to help a small minority of young people with severe and often multiple problems: who are doing badly at school; who experience prolonged and regular unemployment; and who are extremely likely to experience a lifetime of low income, insecure employment, and relatively poor health. (OECD, 1999b: 26f)

Accordingly, since the mid-1970s, not only countries with a less than 20% share of low-skilled young adults, but also countries with a rather high share (e.g., the UK, Italy, Spain, or Portugal), first implemented or considerably expanded *special* (pre-)training and labor market measures for low-skilled youth (see Eurydice, 1997: 21f). Since the mid-1970s, most of these measures have also started to include a component of "social education and rehabilitation." Many measures do not provide a recognized full vocational education/training but "only" intend to increase these youth's social skills, motivation, and self-efficacy beliefs (Eurydice, 1997: 14) – with the aim "to get them back into the mainstream of learning" (OECD, 1999b: 37). In addition, more and more of these programs take into account these youth's impoverished social resources (e.g., unstable family situations) and "negative" social relationships or withdrawal tendencies (e.g., membership in drug gangs or

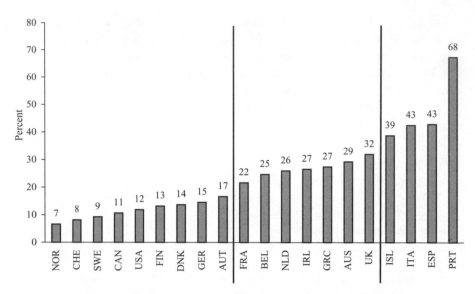

Figure 7.3. Percentage of 25- to 34-year-olds with less than upper secondary education (ISCED 0/1/2), 2001 (in percent). NOR = Norway, CHE = Switzerland, SWE = Sweden, CAN = Canada, FIN = Finland, DNK = Denmark, GER = Germany, AUT = Austria, FRAU = France, BEL = Belgium, NLD = Netherlands, IRL = Ireland, GRC = Greece, AUS = Australia, UK = Great Britain, ISL = Iceland, ITA = Italy, ESP = Spain, PRT = Portugal. *Source:* OECD (www.oecd.org/xls/M00035000/M00035099.xls).

homelessness) (cf. European Union, 2000).[9] These developments indicate that processes of impoverished network resources and stigmatization have gained relevance across countries, and not only in Germany.

Concerning the *visibility* of low-skilled youth (i.e., the identification problem), there are numerous statistics in which this group is defined as "below upper secondary education (International Standards Classification of Education [ISCED] 0/1/2)" (OECD, 2000a: 271; 2000b: 199)[10] as well as international studies dealing explicitly with low-skilled persons (e.g., Eurydice, 1994, 1997; Cedefop, 1999). Only in Spain is the description of "youth without qualification" defined by law (in the educational law, called *LOGSE*). In other Western industrial nations (e.g., in France, the Netherlands, Finland, and Great Britain) there are either official definitions (for statistical purposes or to justify claims on the supply or transfer of benefits) or definitions corresponding to the daily use of language (cf. Eurydice, 1997: 8). Hence, low-skilled persons can be and are identified, and they are considered to be a "social problem."

Figure 7.3 displays the share of low-skilled young adults (ages 25–34) in different Western societies. It is obvious that the low-skilled group is a "minority" in many countries, not only in Germany. In nine out of the twenty countries, its share is less than 20% (i.e., in the Scandinavian countries, Germany, Switzerland, Austria, Canada, and in the United States); in seven of them, the share is still less than one-third (i.e., in France, Belgium, the Netherlands, Ireland, Greece, Australia, and in the UK); and in four of them, they still constitute a rather large group (i.e., in Iceland, Luxemburg, Italy, Spain, and Portugal). A comparison (not displayed here) between the group of low-skilled youth (24–34 years old) and older low-skilled persons (55–64 years old) reveals that in most of these countries, the share of the low educated has diminished considerably (by 20% and more).

These twenty countries are the units of analysis in the following comparison. "Low education" is defined as having completed *less* than upper secondary education (ISCED 0/1/2). This comparison explores the relative explanatory weights of the four mechanisms in different countries and thereby cross-national differences in the sources of disadvantaging low-skilled young adults in labor markets.

Cross-National Differences: Hypotheses and Indicators[11]

The relative disadvantage of low-skilled young adults (as the dependent variable) is measured by their *relative unemployment risk* (i.e., their unemployment rate divided by the rate of persons belonging to the next higher educational group [ISCED 3/4] as their immediate competitors). Values larger than 1 indicate a disadvantaged labor market position of the low skilled. Considering the *relative* magnitude reduces the problem of country differences in measuring unemployment. Moreover, taking the unemployment risks of the 25- to 29-year-olds[12] controls for country differences in the age distribution of educational groups, for variations in the duration of schooling and vocational education as well as for differences in programs combating youth unemployment (because in most of them entitlement stops after age 25).

The relevance of *displacement* should vary with country differences in the labor supply–demand relationship – specified by three indicators. First, displacement could depend on the magnitude of labor oversupply, which is indicated by the *overall unemployment rate of the active population* (ages 25–54, thereby taking into account variations in transition age to retirement). This overall rate reveals, for example, a large oversupply in Germany (8.8%) and France (10.8%), as well as a rather balanced supply and demand in Norway (2.3%) and the Netherlands (1.1%). According to the displacement argument, we would expect that in countries with a higher overall unemployment rate (indicating a higher imbalance between labor supply and demand), low-skilled persons face a higher risk of competition and therefore of displacement processes.

Second, the countries differ in the *share of regular full-time employed persons* ("Normalarbeitsverhältnisse"). More than 60% of the employed persons in the UK, Belgium, Germany, and Italy have full-time contracts, whereas in Greece, Spain, and the Netherlands less than 50% of the employed work full time. A high proportion of such full-time contracts could increase the relative disadvantage of the low skilled because they either have to compete with higher-educated persons for "attractive" jobs or, given "closed" employment relationships, there are fewer vacant jobs.

Third, the employment protection laws vary widely among these countries, although employment relationships became more "flexible" in all Western countries since the 1990s (cf. Blank, 1997).[13] In the late 1990s, Norway and Portugal had the highest OECD regulation indices (for "regular employment" and "difficulty of dismissal"), whereas Great Britain had the lowest.[14] Employment regulations are important for displacement because they define whether employment relationships are "open" or "closed" (Sørensen, 1983; Weber, 1994). Due to a relatively unrestricted hire-and-fire mechanism, open relationships create a larger number of vacant positions but, at the same time, increase the risk of job competition because employees can be more easily replaced when labor supply changes. Closed relationships create an insider–outsider problem (Esping-Andersen, 1999) because they protect job holders; they create less job vacancy but, in contrast, lower the risk of dismissal once employed. In terms of displacement, the impact of employment protection can go in two opposite directions: (1) low-skilled persons might be disadvantaged by high protection because of less job mobility leading to fewer vacant positions, and because employers might be more risk averse in hiring them (given restricted opportunities for dismissal). It is questionable, however, whether low-skilled persons really would profit from "free" job competition. Would they in fact be selected from applicant pools given open employment relationships? On the contrary, therefore, (2) low-skilled persons might benefit from high protection because once employed, they are less exposed to external competition (cf. Nickell, 1997; Ganßmann, 2000).

The relevance of *discrediting* low-skilled youth should be higher in countries in which upper secondary education is strongly occupation specific than in countries with a *general* upper secondary education – because in the former, employers' beliefs of a severe lack of skills by persons without upper secondary education should be stronger (cf. Shavit & Müller, 1998; Russell & O'Connell, 2001: 15f). Occupational specificity of upper secondary education is measured by the OECD classification of institutional arrangements of upper secondary education ("upper secondary education pathways") (Müller, 1994; OECD, 2000b: 31f, 170):

Type 1: *Apprenticeship system* – more than 50% of a birth cohort enter apprenticeships (Germany and Switzerland)

Type 2: *Mixed system* – a significant part of a birth cohort enters apprenticeships and another part attends vocational schools (Denmark, the Netherlands, Norway, and Austria)

Type 3: *School-based vocational system* – upper secondary (vocational) education takes place in vocational schools or general schools (Belgium, Great Britain, Finland, France, Italy, and Sweden)

Type 4: *General education system* – there is no vocational education, only general upper secondary education (Australia, Canada, Greece, Ireland, Portugal, Spain, and the United States)

Thus, the expected direction of the correlation is negative. That is, the more occupation specific secondary education is (i.e., the lower the type number), the higher should be the risk of discredit and, therefore, the higher is the disadvantage caused by the label "low education."

For *impoverished network resources*, equality of educational opportunities is of particular importance. This equality is not given if children from socially disadvantaged families show significantly lower school achievement compared to children from higher-status families. That is, the more unequal learning opportunities and educational achievement in terms of social origin, the higher is the "negative" social selection of the low-skilled group, and the poorer are the group's job search/network resources. The proxy indicator for class differentials in educational opportunities and the social stratification of schooling is class differentials in reading literacy – as revealed by the international PISA study (Baumert & Schümer, 2001: 400). The indicator is the relative risk (odds ratio) of 15-year-olds whose parents belong to the lowest quarter of the social hierarchy (ISEI) of having only achieved competence level I in reading literacy – compared to the risk of children whose parents belong to the highest quarter of the social hierarchy (controlled for parents' education, migration, gender). Empirically, a higher impact of the impoverished network mechanism should be indicated by a positive correlation between social disparities in educational opportunities and the relative unemployment risk of the low skilled – that means, the higher this social origin odds ratio in a country, the higher is the disadvantage of low-skilled persons in terms of network resources, and as a consequence, the higher is their relative unemployment risk.

Stigmatization should be higher in countries in which low-skilled youth face higher institutional risks of overt and recurring educational failure – such as being channeled into lower segregated school types, class retention, and/or delayed school entry – contributing to an increase in their risk of marginalization and stigmatization. These institutionalized failures increasingly convey the (individualizing) interpretation as missed or failed "opportunities," and they increase the risk of concomitant processes of discreditory labeling, both external and self-imposed, and the danger of institutional damages to their social identity and self-schema (cf. Riesman, 1967/1997: 266). Thus, the higher the share of (low-skilled) youth with "deviant" school careers in a country, the higher should be the risk of self-exclusion, withdrawal, and ultimately, marginalization (cf. Stauber & Walther, 2000). The indicators of number of years of comprehensive schooling (*segregation*) and the percentage of 15-year-olds who experienced delayed school entry and/or retention (*retention*) are used. With regard to segregation, the hypothesis is that the earlier segregation starts (or the less the number of years in comprehensive schooling), the higher is the risk of stigmatization and ultimately withdrawal from the labor market or, in other words, a higher risk of non-/unemployment (hence, a negative correlation). For *retention*, we expect the higher the percentage of youths with "deviant" school careers, the higher is the risk of stigmatization resulting in withdrawal (hence, a positive correlation).

An overview of the empirical expectations and their operationalization is displayed in the Table 7.1.

Findings

Figure 7.4 displays the relative unemployment risk of low-skilled young adults in the twenty countries at hand. It reveals that in all countries in which they constitute a "social minority" of less than one-third of their birth cohorts, they face a higher risk of unemployment than in countries such as Iceland, Spain, and Portugal, in which they still exist in larger numbers.

Given these country variations in the relative unemployment risk as well as in the institutional settings and economic conditions, what is the relative importance of the four mechanisms developed previously? This question is answered by calculating OLS regressions in which the variation in the low-skilled group's size is controlled for.

Table 7.2 shows the results. Comparing the empirical expectations (formulated previously) with the empirical findings, we do find support for the displacement expectations: the risk of displacement is larger in countries with lower demand of labor (i.e., a higher percentage of regular full-time employment [RFE]), and it is lower in countries with stronger employment

Table 7.1. Overview of the empirical expectations for the direction of the regression coefficient (controlling for country's proportion of low-skilled population of 25- to 34-year-olds*)

Indicators (independent variables)	Dependent variable: Relative unemployment risk (*Rel-Unempl*) [+ indicates disadvantage, – indicates disadvantage]
Displacement	
Total unemployment rate (*Umempl-total*)	+
Share of regular full-time employment contracts (*RFE*)	+
Employment protection legislation (EPL) (from 1 = low to 6 = strong)	
OECD strictness of EPL – regular employment (*OECD-strict 1*)	(i) + / (ii)–
OECD strictness of EPL – difficulty of dismissal (*OECD-strict 2*)	(i) + / (ii)–
Discredit	
Occupational specificity of upper secondary pathways (*pathway type*; from 1 = strongly occupation specific, apprenticeship system to 4 = general education)	–
Impoverished network resources	
Relative risk of socially disadvantaged children exhibiting poor reading literacy compared to children from families of the highest quarter of the social hierarchy – findings of the international PISA study (*Social origin odds ratio*)	+
Stigmatization	
Number of years of comprehensive schooling (*Segregation*)	–
Percentage of 15-year-olds who experienced delayed school entry and/or retention – findings of the international PISA study (*Retention*)	+

In parenthesis: variable labels.
* Variable label = % low skilled.
i and ii refer to the competing hypotheses mentioned above.
For data sources, see Table A1 (appendix).

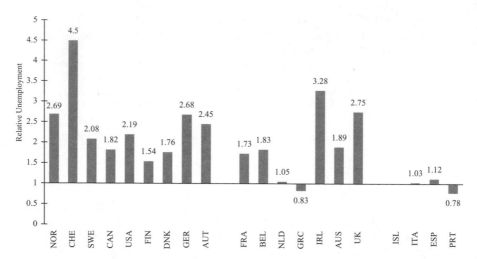

Figure 7.4. Relative unemployment risk of 25- to 29-year-olds with less than upper secondary education (ISCED 0/1/2), 1998. Sorted by country's share of low-skilled youth (Figure 7.3).

protection legislation (expectation 2). The latter might indicate that low-skilled persons – once employed – are protected against hire-and-fire job competition (and that more open employment relationships do not improve employment chances for this group).

In terms of discredit, we find a significant correlation between the relative unemployment risk of low-skilled young adults and occupational specificity of upper secondary education (in the expected direction).

The correlations between the extent of social stratification of educational opportunities and the relative unemployment risk of the low-skilled support country variations in the mechanism of impoverished network resources are as expected: the more socially stratified the educational system (conveyed by a more homogeneous, negative social selection of the low-skilled group), the poorer are the (relative) employment opportunities of low-skilled persons.

Finally, institutional variation in the relative importance of low-skilled youth's stigmatization is – also as expected – signaled by a significantly higher unemployment risk of the low skilled in countries in which they are exposed to the risk of "deviant" school careers due to the possibility of retention, delayed school entry, and/or segregation.

All in all, these results corroborate the conclusion that the magnitude of the relative labor market disadvantage of low-skilled youth is not solely defined by their "individual" lack of (certified) skills, but dependent on the institutional and economic environment to which they are exposed during their educational career and in labor markets. Here, it is also interesting to compare the

Table 7.2. Ordinary least squares (OLS) regression on the relative unemployment risk of low-skilled young adults (ISCED 0/1/2), depending on institutional and economic conditions

| Dependent variable Y | Independent variable X | Control variable/s | Correlation coefficient BETA | Significance level | | R^2 contribution* |
				Two sided	One sided	
Displacement						
Rel.Unempl	Unempl-total	% Low skilled	n.s.			
Rel.Unempl	% RFE	% Low skilled	0,465	0,091	0,045	0,14
Rel.Unempl	OECD-strict 1	% Low skilled & Unempl-total	n.s.			
Rel.Unempl	OECD-strict 2	% Low skilled & Unempl-total	−0,290	0,179	0,090	0,04
Discredit						
Rel.Unempl	Pathway type	% Low skilled	−0,274	0,195	0,097	0,05
Rel.Unempl	Pathway type	% Low skilled & expenditures	−0,397	0,044	0,022	0,14
Impoverished network resources						
Rel.Unempl	Social origin odds ratio	% Low skilled	0,604	0,001	0,001	0,36
Stigmatization						
Rel.Unempl	Segregation	% Low skilled	−0,409	0,040	0,020	0,14
Rel.Unempl	Retention	% Low skilled	0,312	0,165	0,083	0,05

% Low skilled = percentage of low-skilled 25- to-34-year-olds (ISCED 0/1/2).

n.s. = not significant

* Displayed are the differences between the corrected R^2 of the "basic model," which only includes the control variable/s (corrected R^2 = 0,26) and the "full model" including the independent factor X.

For a definition of the variables and data sources, see Table A1 (appendix).

impact of the different institutional settings and, thus, the four social mech-anisms on the variation in the higher-than-average unemployment risk of the low skilled – by means of corrected R^2 (Table 7.2).[15] The highest impact has social inequality in educational attainment or the impoverished network mechanism – measured by odds ratios of social origin and reading literacy – with an R^2 contribution of 0.36, followed by equal R^2 contributions of 0.14 for displacement (indicator: percentage of regular full-time employment), discredit, and stigmatization (indicator: segregation).[16] This might indicate that, at least in terms of unemployment risks, the educational stratification of network resources "dis/connecting" individuals to labor markets is more important than labor market capacity problems due to an oversupply of labor.

Discussion

Based on the findings presented previously, what can we conclude in terms of the relative importance of the four mechanisms for the different countries – indicating the influence of institutional educational and labor market arrangements on the sources of low-skilled labor market vulnerability and the extent of their labor market disadvantage (i.e., the relative unemployment risk)? The basic assumption for deriving such conclusions is that by compar-ing only the countries in which low-skilled youth constitute less than 20% of the population (and thereby doing a quasi-"control" for group size), the regression coefficients tell us something about the relative importance of the different mechanisms in this country group. The same idea can also be applied to the group of countries in which the low-skilled group's share is larger than 20% but smaller than one-third (such that they still constitute a "social minority"). The conclusions – that remain to be corroborated by analyses based on individual data – are visualized in Table 7.3.

Within the first group of countries (i.e., the low-skilled group's share is "less than 20%"), the findings indicate that in Canada and Finland, processes of displacement are more important than discredit, impoverished networks, and stigmatization; in Norway, discredit, and in Sweden, impoverished net-works, are more important compared to the other three mechanisms.[17] In contrast, in Germany, Switzerland, and Austria, all four mechanisms seem to be of distinctive importance. In-between positions with particular impor-tance of two mechanisms are held by Denmark (displacement and discredit) and the United States (displacement and impoverished networks).

Within the second group of countries ("more than 20%, but less than one-third"), in Australia and the UK especially, displacement and impoverished networks operate, and in France, displacement and stigmatization are

Table 7.3. Country comparison on the relative weight of displacement, discredit, impoverished networks, and stigmatization

Country	Displacement	Discredit	Impoverished networks	Stigmatization
Group 1: Share of low-skilled young adults is less than 20%				
CAN	Low OECD-strict 2			
FIN	High% RFE			
NOR		Occupation-specific pathway type (= 2)		
SWE			Large social origin odds ratio	
DNK	High% RFE	Occupation-specific upper secondary education pathway (= 2)		
USA	Low OECD-strict 2		Large social origin odds ratio	Early segregation High retention
CHE	Low OECD-strict 2	Occupation-specific pathway type (= 1)	Large social origin odds ratio	Early segregation High retention
GER	High% RFE	Occupation-specific pathway type (= 1)	Large social origin odds ratio	Early segregation High retention
AUT	High% RFE	Occupation-specific pathway type (= 2)	Large social origin odds ratio	Early segregation High retention
Group 2: Share of low-skilled young adults is larger than 20% but less than one-third				
AUS	Low OECD-strict 2		Large social origin odds ratio	
UK	Low OECD-strict 2		Large social origin odds ratio	
FRA	High % RFE			High retention
BEL	Low OECD-strict 2		Large social origin odds ratio	Early segregation High retention
IRL	Low OECD-strict 2			
GRC	*No relative labor market disadvantage of the low skilled (Figure 7.4)*		Large social origin odds ratio	Early segregation
NLD	*No relative labor market disadvantage of the low skilled (Figure 7.4)*			

For a definition of the variables, see Table A1 (appendix).

paramount. In Belgium and Ireland,[18] the risk of displacement, impoverished networks, and stigmatization is higher than the risk of discredit compared to the other countries.

CONCLUSION: THE SOCIAL EMBEDDEDNESS OF LABOR MARKET VULNERABILITY OF LOW-SKILLED PERSONS

This chapter pursues two goals: (1) to close the explanatory gap left by exclusive reliance on the dominant displacement argument by searching for sociological contributions, and (2) to provide indications for variations in the relevance of the different causes of the low-skilled group's labor market disadvantages.

With respect to the first goal, I show that for an appropriate explanation of the increasing labor market vulnerability of low-skilled persons over the past three decades, it is important to apply a multidimensional concept of education and educational groups. Education and low education represent not only levels of skills and qualifications, but also a social phenomenon that is connected to social meanings and social relationships. Only such a multidimensional (economic-sociological) concept allows us to depict changes in both the "individualized" processes of skill certification and attribution and changes in educational groups' social relationships, available resources, and social identity formation that have consequences for their performance in labor markets.

The four social mechanisms that are connected to these different dimensions of education result in long-term disadvantages of low-skilled persons in labor markets – starting with severe problems at labor market entry, followed by disadvantages in terms of stable employment trajectories and (on-the-job) learning opportunities (cf. Solga, 2005). As laid out in the beginning, the four mechanisms are additive (or compensatory) and not competing explanations. One major advantage of this multidimensional approach is that the heterogeneity of the low-skilled group can be taken into account – in contrast to the "single-cause" economic explanation of displacement (assuming a homogeneous low-skilled group). In this economic-sociological framework, the "magnitude" of the labor market disadvantage of each low-skilled individual is the result of an individual interplay of the four mechanisms. Given the heterogeneity of the low-skilled group in terms of school experiences and educational biographies (i.e., risk of stigmatization) as well as social background and network resources (i.e., risk of impoverished networks), they face different risk of labor market exclusion. Moreover, subdividing the low-skilled group by gender or ethnicity, we find group variation in the threshold of what counts as "deviation from the educational norm" (cf. Solga, 2005, chapters 11 and 12). Thus, the risk of discredit is different for "ascriptive" subgroups.

Given these variations in employers' recruitment and the application behavior of low-skilled persons, the dominant economic explanation attributing the labor market disadvantages of the low skilled only to displacement is incorrect. Here, historical changes in educational groups' size lead only to changes in the educational *distribution*, resulting in so-called compositional effects (or "demographic explanations," cf. Stinchcombe, 1987, or Coleman, 1991). They are the basic idea behind the displacement mechanism: compositional changes in labor supply in relationship to labor demand are the causes of decreasing employment chances of the low skilled. However, changes of employers' recruitment *behavior* and low-skilled persons' job search *behavior* are a concomitant of historical changes in educational groups' size as well – causing discredit and stigmatization of low-skilled persons and a loss of network resources. For explaining their disadvantageous "labor market outcomes," being low skilled has to be expanded into becoming low skilled in a life course perspective – starting with individuals' school careers, followed by their job search processes and, then, by employers' recruitment decisions.

The results of the country comparison presented in this chapter depict and corroborate the idea of "social embeddedness" of the consequences of low education – indicating the impact of institutional conditions on labor market opportunities for low-skilled persons. This comparison based on aggregated data certainly has to be backed up by in-depth country analyses founded on individual data. Classifying the countries by the degree of stratification and standardization of country's upper secondary (vocational) education systems (Allmendinger, 1989) – and thus by crucial institutional dimensions of skill formation processes – we can derive the following typology of countries according to the relative importance of the four mechanisms (Table 7.4). In countries with a low degree of stratification and standardization (e.g., Canada, Finland), labor market institutions have a larger impact on the labor market situation of the low skilled than on the educational system. In contrast, in the "apprenticeship" countries (e.g., Germany, Switzerland, Austria), the labor market system and the educational system equally contribute to their high labor market vulnerability. The impoverished networks mechanism plays a major role in countries with a highly stratified – but less standardized – educational system (e.g., the United States, Sweden), whereas poorer labor market opportunities of the low skilled caused especially by a discrediting of low-skilled youths can be found in countries with rather

Table 7.4. Relative weight of displacement, discredit, impoverished networks, and stigmatization – by type of (vocational) educational system

		Stratification	
		High	Low
Standardization	High	AUT/CHE/GER: All four mechanisms	DNK: Discredit and displacement NOR: Discredit
	Low	USA: Impoverished networks and displacement SWE: Impoverished networks	CAN: Displacement FIN: Displacement

Based on Table 7.3; only countries in which the share of less-educated young adults <20%. Definitions of standardization and stratification by Allmendiger (1989).

standardized educational certificates, but a low stratification (e.g., Denmark, Norway).

In sum, dependent on the prevailing institutional and economic conditions in Western societies, low-skilled young adults are exposed *to different degrees* of displacement, discredit, impoverished network resources, and stigmatization.

Notes

1. The term "low skilled" refers to individuals that hold low or no educational certificates. Thus, "low-skilled" individuals could possess uncertified skills.
2. According to the German educational system with its strong emphasis on vocational training, "low education" or "low skilled" is not defined by a threshold level of general education (e.g., below upper secondary education) but by completed vocational education (including German apprenticeships, full-time vocational schools, and tertiary education). Therefore, persons with upper secondary education (e.g., "Realschulabschluss" or "Abitur") who do *not* hold a vocational education certificate are counted as "low skilled." The vast majority of the low skilled, however, has not completed upper secondary education. In terms of data quality, there are only minor differences between the percentages calculated on the basis of the retrospective data of German Life History Study (displayed in Figure 1) and on the data of the German Microcensus.
3. See, e.g., Nickell (2004).
4. Taking Germany as an example: the share of youth attending the lowest school track (the *Hauptschule*) has decreased from 77% in the mid-1950 to only about 20% today. Due to this development, the *Hauptschule* as the most heterogeneous school type in the 1950s, has become the most homogeneous school type in Germany. Today, about 75% of the youth attending a *Hauptschule* come from families belonging to the lower half of the socioeconomic status hierarchy (Prenzel et al., 2004).

5. Why do I call it "discredit" and not "discrimination"? The common economic concept of discrimination is "statistical discrimination." Here, individuals' potential productivity is judged based on their group membership. Thus, it is a probabilistic belief in the lower trainability and productivity of low-skilled persons. By using the term "discredit" instead, I like to point to a process in which particular social meanings – marking a deviant status – come to be attached to categories of behavior. In this sense, discredit expresses the labeling of low-educated persons as "deviant" in terms of educational behavior and achievement – based on which "statistical discrimination" might occur.

6. A study on recruitment behavior of German firms has revealed that especially for low-skilled persons, "recommendations by family members, neighbors, and friends" play a major role for their hiring. Three-fourths of small and medium business (up to 50 employees) reported that such recommendations are "very important" to take into account hiring low-skilled persons. In larger firms, the percentages are lower but still high: 66% for firms with 51 to 200 employee and 57% for firms with more than 200 employees (Seyfried, 2006: 35).

7. For further details and discussion, cf. Solga (2005, pp. 134–155, 184–188).

8. Analyses for West Germany are published in Solga (2002b, 2005).

9. Examples are the *Job Corps* in the United States (OECD, 1999b: 28), the two projects *Social and Occupational Integration of Young People Who Have Dropped Out of School* and *Education and Training in the fight against the Exclusion of Young People* in France, *Youth Support Centres* in Greece, the projects *Rewarding and Widening Achievement: Personal, Social and Key Skills Accreditation, One Step, Right Track,* and *Wise Start* in the UK, *Integrated Pathways to Integration for the Young Unemployed* in Luxemburg, and *Social Integration of Young People with Risk of Social Exclusion* in Spain (European Union, 2000).

10. OECD *International Standard Classification of Education* (ISCED) (1997) (cf. OECD, 2000b: 371f) defines seven vertical educational levels: 0 = prep school education, 1 = primary education, 2 = lower secondary education, 3 = upper secondary education, 4 = postsecondary, nontertiary education (e.g., technical and vocational training), 5 = tertiary education (5A = full-time studies, 5B = short-time studies), and 6 = higher tertiary education (e.g., doctoral degree).

11. For the country data of the outlined indicators, see Table A1 (appendix).

12. The unemployment rates of 1998 are considered because it is the year with the most complete OECD data on unemployment by education and age. Taking the unemployment data for 25- to 29-year-olds in 1998 allows us to partially observe the same persons classified as low-skilled 25- to 34-year-olds in 2001 (those who were 25 to 29 years old in 1998 are 28 to 32 years old in 2001).

13. In Germany, France, and Belgium, dismissal has become less restricted, Spain and the Netherlands decentralized wage negotiations, and in many western European countries, more flexible rules of terminating work contracts were introduced (especially in terms of their permitted durations).

14. The correlations between share of full-time employed persons and the OECD regulation indices are very low ("regular employment" = -0.344 and "dismissal" = -0.269) and negative. The Netherlands, for example, have a low share of full-time employment but relative high regulation indices.

15. I use (partial) corrected R^2 as indication of the proportion of the total variance in the dependent variable "explained" by the variance in the independent variable

because I have a rather small number of observations and, thus, should avoid an overfitted R^2 by "correcting" for the relatively few degrees of freedom in the data.

16. A stepwise linear regression, including the percentage of low skilled (control variable), the displacement indicator "percentage of full-time employment," and the impoverished network indicator "social origin odds ratio," corroborates the higher impact of the latter (with a R^2 contribution of 0.16 compared to a R^2 contribution for %RFE of 0.06).

17. For Sweden, individual data analyses corroborate this conclusion (see Aberg, 2003: 212).

18. This conclusion is supported by findings presented in the report of the National Economic and Social Forum (2002).

References

Aberg, R. (2003). Unemployment persistency, over-education and the employment chances of the less educated. *European Sociological Review*, 19(2), 199–216.

Allmendinger, J. (1989). *Career Mobility Dynamics* (Studien und Berichte 49). Berlin: Max-Planck-Institut für Bildungsforschung.

Baron, J. N., & Pfeffer, J. (1994). The social psychology of organizations and inequality. *Social Psychological Quarterly*, 57(3), 190–209.

Baumert, J., & Schümer, G. (2001). Familiäre Lebensverhältnisse, Bildungsbeteiligung und Kompetenzerwerb. In Deutsches PISA-Konsortium (Ed.), *PISA 2000* (pp. 323–407). Opladen, Germany: Leske + Budrich.

Becker, G. S. (1964). *Human Capital.* New York: National Bureau of Economic Research.

Bennett, H., & Weiss, M. (1998). Labor market restructuring and workforce development. In R. P. Giloth (Ed.), *Jobs and Economic Development. Strategies and Practice* (pp. 19–41). London: Sage.

Bills, D. B. (1988). Educational credentials and hiring decisions. *Research in Social Stratification and Mobility*, 7, 71–97.

Blalock, H. M., Jr. (1991). *Understanding Social Inequality: Modeling Allocation Processes.* Newbury Park, CA: Sage.

Blank, R. M. (1997). The misdiagnosis of eurosclerosis. *The American Prospect*, 8, 81–85.

Blossfeld, H.-P. (1985). *Bildungsexpansion und Berufschancen: Empirische Analysen zur Lage der Berufsanfänger in der Bundesrepublik.* Frankfurt/Main: Campus.

Blossfeld, H.-P. (1990). Changes in educational careers in the Federal Republic of Germany. *Sociology of Education*, 63(3), 165–177.

Boudon, R. (1974). *Education, Opportunity, and Social Inequality.* New York: John Wiley & Sons.

Bowman, M. J. (1966). The human investment revolution in economic thought. *Sociology of Education*, 39(2), 111–138.

Brewer, M. B., & Brown, R. J. (1998). Intergroup relations. In D. T. Gilbert, S. T. Fiske, & G. Lindzey (Eds.), *The Handbook of Social Psychology* (4th ed., pp. 554–595). Boston: McGraw-Hill.

Brown, R. J. (1996). Intergroup relations. In M. Hewstone, W. Stroebe, & G. M. Stephenson (Eds.), *Introduction to Social Psychology: A European Perspective* (pp. 530–561). Oxford, UK: Basil Blackwell.

Burt, R. S. (1992). *Structural Holes.* Cambridge, MA: Harvard University Press.

Burt, R. S. (1997). The contingent value of social capital. *Administrative Science Quarterly*, 42, 339–365.

Clark, B. R. (1960). The "cooling-out" function of higher education. *American Journal of Sociology*, 65(6), 569–576.

Coleman, J. S. (1991). Matching processes in the labor market. *Acta Sociologica*, 34(1), 3–12.

Elliot, J. R., & Smith, R. A. (2004). Race, gender, and workplace power. *American Sociological Review*, 69, 365–386.

Esping-Andersen, G. (1999). Politics without class: Postindustrial cleavages in Europe and America. In H. Kitschelt, P. Lange, G. Marks, & J. D. Stephens (Eds.), *Continuity and Change in Contemporary Capitalism* (pp. 293–316). Cambridge, UK: Cambridge University Press.

Esping-Andersen, G., Rohwer, G., & Sørensen, S. L. (1994). Institutions and occupational class mobility: Scaling the skill barrier in the Danish labour market. *European Sociological Review*, 10(2), 119–134.

European Centre for the Development of Vocational Training (Cedefop). (Ed.). (1999). *Agora – IV: Gering qualifizierte Personen am Arbeitsmarkt: Ausblick und politische Optionen*. Thessaloniki, Greece: Author.

European Union. (2000). *Integrating All Young People into Society through Education and Training. Volume 2: Compendium of the Projects*. Strasbourg, Luxembourg: Office for Official Publications of the European Communities.

Eurydice. (1994). *Die Bekämpfung des Schulversagens: eine Herausforderung an ein vereintes Europa*. Strasbourg, Luxembourg: Amt für amtliche Veröffentlichungen der europäischen Gemeinschaften.

Eurydice. (1997). *Studie zu den Maßnahmen der Mitgliedsstaaten der Europäischen Union für Jugendliche, die das Bildungssystem ohne Qualifikation verlassen haben*. Brüssels, Belgium: Europäische Eurydice-Informationsstelle (Informationsnetz zum Bildungswesen in Europa).

Fiske, S. T. (1998). Stereotyping, prejudice, and discrimination. In D. T. Gilbert, S. T. Fiske, & G. Lindzey (Eds.), *Handbook of Social Psychology* (4th ed., pp. 357–411). New York: McGraw-Hill.

Franz, W. (1999). *The Role of Skills and Technology*. Paper presented at the Conference of LSE and Centre for Economic Performance on "Employability and Exclusion: What Governments Can Do," Mannheim, Germany.

Ganßmann, H. (2000). Labor market flexibility, social protection and unemployment. *European Societies*, 2(3), 243–269.

Giloth, R. P. (1998). Jobs and economic development. In R. P. Giloth (Ed.), *Jobs & Economic Development: Strategies and Practice* (pp. 1–16). London: Sage.

Goffman, E. (1963). *Stigma: Notes on the Management of Spoiled Identity*. New York: Simon & Schuster.

Granovetter, M. (1973). The strength of weak ties. *American Journal of Sociology*, 78(6), 1360–1380.

Granovetter, M. (1974). *Getting a Job: A Study of Contacts and Careers*. Cambridge, MA: Harvard University Press.

Hirsch, F. (1977). *Social Limits to Growth*. Cambridge, MA: Harvard University Press.

Hoffmann, E., & Walwei, U. (2000). *Strukturwandel der Erwerbsarbeit: Was heißt eigentlich noch "normal"?* IAB-Kurzbericht Nr. 14/25.10.2000. Nürnberg, Germany: Institut für Arbeitsmarkt- und Berufsforschung.

Jones, E. E., Farina, A., Hastorf, A. H., Markus, H., Miller, D. T., & Scott, R. A. (1984). *Social Stigma: The Psychology of Marked Relationships.* New York: W. H. Freeman.

Kalleberg, A. L. (1996). Changing contexts of careers. In A. C. Kerckhoff (Ed.), *Generating Social Stratification* (pp. 343–358). Boulder, CO: Westview Press.

Lenhardt, G. (2002). Die verspätete Entwicklung der deutschen Schule. *Pädagogische Korrespondenz,* 29, 5–22.

Leschinsky, A., & Mayer, K. U. (1999). Comprehensive schools and inequality of opportunity in the Federal Republic of Germany. In A. Leschinsky & K. U. Mayer (Eds.), *The Comprehensive School Experiment Revisited: Evidence from Western Europe* (2nd ed., pp. 13–39). Frankfurt/Main: Peter Lang.

Mare, R. D. (1980). Social background and school continuation decisions. *Journal of the American Statistical Association,* 75(370), 295–305.

Müller, W. (1994). The process and consequences of education differentiation: Summary report. In European Centre for the Development of Vocational Training (Cedefop) (Ed.), *The Determinants of Transitions in Youth* (pp. 207–213). Berlin: Cedefop.

Murnane, R., & Levy, F. (1996). *Teaching the New Basic Skills.* New York: The Free Press.

National Economic and Social Forum. (2002). *Early School Leavers.* Forum Report 24. Dublin: Author. Available at: National Economic and Social Forum

Nickell, S. (1997). Unemployment and labor market rigidities: Europe versus North America. *Journal of Economic Perspectives,* 11(3), 55–74.

Nickell, S. (2004). *Why Are the Unskilled Doing So Badly?* Paper prepared for the EuroConference series "European Society or European Societies?" Granada, Spain, September 18–23.

Organisation for Economic Co-operation and Development (OECD). (1999a). *Thematic Review of the Transition from Initial Education to Working Life: Denmark. Country Notes.* Paris: Author.

Organisation for Economic Co-operation and Development (OECD). (1999b). *Thematic Review of the Transition from Initial Education to Working Life: United States of America.* Paris: Author.

Organisation for Economic Co-operation and Development (OECD). (2000a). *Education at Glance: OECD Indicators.* Paris: Author.

Organisation for Economic Co-operation and Development (OECD). (2000b). *From Initial Education to Working Life: Making Transitions Work.* Paris: Author.

Parsons, T. (1959). The school class as a social system: Some of its functions in American society. *Harvard Educational Review,* 29, 297–318.

Pfahl, L. (2003). *Stigma-Management im Job-Coaching: Berufsorientierungen benachteiligter Jugendlicher.* Master's thesis, Free University, Department of Sociology, Berlin.

Prenzel, M., Baumert, J., Blum, W., Lehmann, R., Leutner, D., Neubrand, M., Pekrun, R., Rolff, H.-G., Rost, J., & Schiefele, U. (Eds.). (2004). *PISA 2003: Ergebnisse des zweiten internationalen Vergleichs. Zusammenfassung.* Available at: http://pisa.ipn.uni-kiel.de/Ergebnisse_PISA_2003.pdf.

Reinberg, A., & Hummel, M. (2002). *Qualifikationsspezifische Arbeitslosenquoten – reale Entwicklung oder statistisches Artefakt?* IAB-Werkstattbericht Nr. 4/23.4.2002. Nürnberg, Germany: Institut für Arbeitsmarkt- und Berufsforschung.

Riesman, D. (1967/1997). Notes on meritocracy. In D. Bell & S. R. Graubard (Eds.), *Toward the Year 2000: Work in Progress* (pp. 265–276). Cambridge, MA: MIT Press.

Rijken, S. (1999). *Educational Expansion and Status Attainment: A Cross-National and Over-Time Comparison*. Amsterdam: Thesis.

Rosenbaum, J. E., & Binder, A. (1997). Do employers really need more educated youth? *Sociology of Education*, 70(1), 68–85.

Russell, H., & O'Connell, P. J. (2001). Getting a job in Europe: The transition from unemployment to work among young people in nine European countries. *Work, Employment & Society*, 15(1), 1–24.

Schümer, G. (2001). Institutionelle Bedingungen schulischen Lernens im internationalen Vergleich. In Deutsches PISA-Konsortium (Ed.), *PISA 2000* (pp. 411–427). Opladen, Germany: Leske + Budrich.

Sehringer, R. (1989). *Betriebliche Strategien der Personalrekrutierung*. Frankfurt/Main: Campus.

Seyfried, B. (2006). *Berufsausbildungsvorbereitung aus betrieblicher Sicht*. Bonn, Germany: Bundesinstitut für Berufsbildung.

Shavit, Y., & Müller, W. (Eds.). (1998). *From School to Work: A Comparative Study of Educational Qualifications and Occupational Destinations*. Oxford, UK: Clarendon Press.

Solga, H. (2002a). "Stigmatization by negative selection": Explaining less-educated persons' decreasing employment opportunities. *European Sociological Review*, 18(2), 159–178.

Solga, H. (2002b). "Ausbildungslosigkeit" als soziales Stigma in Bildungsgesellschaften. Ein soziologischer Erklärungsbeitrag für die wachsenden Arbeitsmarktprobleme von Personen ohne Ausbildungsabschluss. *Kölner Zeitschrift für Soziologie und Sozialpsychologie*, 54(3), 476–505.

Solga, H. (2004). Increasing risks of stigmatization: Changes in school-to-work transitions of less-educated West Germans. *Yale Journal of Sociology*, 4, 99–129. Available at: www.yale.edu/socdept/yjs/YJSFall2004.pdf.

Solga, H. (2005). *Ohne Abschluss in die Bildungsgesellschaft: Die Erwerbschancen gering qualifizierter Personen aus ökonomischer und soziologischer Perspektive*. Opladen, Germany: Verlag Barbara Budrich.

Sørensen, A. B. (1977). The structure of inequality and the process of attainment. *American Sociological Review*, 42(6), 965–978.

Sørensen, A. B. (1983). Processes of open and closed positions in social structure. *Zeitschrift für Soziologie*, 12(3), 203–224.

Sørensen, A. B., & Kalleberg, A. L. (1981). An outline of a theory of matching persons to jobs. In I. Berg (Ed.), *Sociological Perspectives on Labor Markets* (pp. 49–74). New York: Academic Press.

Spence, M. A. (1973). Job market signaling. *Quarterly Journal of Economics*, 87(3), 355–379.

Spence, M. A. (1974). *Market Signaling: Informational Transfer in Hiring and Related Screening Processes*. Cambridge, MA: Harvard University Press.

Stauber, B., & Walther, A. (2000). *Avoiding Misleading Trajectories: Transition Dilemmas of Young Adults in Europe*. Tübingen, Germany: IRIS e.V. Available at: www.nuff.ox.ac.uk/projects/UWWCLUS/Papers/papers.htm.

Stiglitz, J. E. (1975). The theory of "screening," education, and the distribution of income. *American Economic Review*, 65(3), 283–300.

Stinchcombe, A. L. (1987). *Constructing Social Theories*. Chicago: The University of Chicago Press.

Thurow, L. C. (1975). *Generating Inequality*. New York: Basic Books.

Thurow, L. C. (1979). A job competition model. In M. J. Piore (Ed.), *Unemployment and Inflation* (pp. 17–32). New York: M. E. Sharpe.

Tilly, C. (1998). *Durable Inequality*. Berkeley: University of California Press.

Trow, M. (1977). The second transformation of American secondary education. In J. Karabel & A. H. Halsey (Eds.), *Power and Ideology in Education* (pp. 105–118). New York: Oxford University Press.

Weber, M. (1994). Open and closed relationships. In D. B. Grusky (Ed.), *Social Stratification: Class, Race, and Gender in Sociological Perspective* (pp. 126–129). Boulder, CO: Westview Press.

Wial, H. (1991). Getting a good job: Mobility in a segmented labor market. *Industrial Relations*, 30(3), 396–416.

Appendix

Table A1: Country indicators

Country	% low skilled (2001), ages 25–34	Pathway-type	Relative labor market disadvantage of low-skilled 25- to 29-year-olds (1998) Relative Unempl.	Indicators of labor supply and demand (1998) Unempl. (25- to 54-year-olds)	% RFE	Labor force participation of the 25- to 29-year-olds (1998) Empl. ISCED 0/1/2	Empl. ISCED 3/4	Unempl. ISCED 0/1/2	Unempl. ISCED 3/4	Total	Employment protection legislation (late 1990s) – OECD index Regular empl. Strict 1	Dismissal Strict 2	Stratification and segregation of the educational system Number of years of comprehensive schooling	Social origin odds ratio	Retention
1	2	3	4	5	6	7	8	9	10	11	12	13	14	15	16
Group 1: Share of low-skilled young adults is less than 20%															
NOR	7	2	2.69	2.3		75.1	83.4	9.4	3.5	4.0	2.4	4.5	(10)	2.13	0
CHE	8	1	4.50	3.3		71.5	87.2	11.7	2.6	5.1	1.5	1.2	4	2.70	10.3
SWE	9	3	2.08	7.5	58.9	59.0	76.7	21.2	10.2	10.1	2.8	3.8	(9)	2.30	0
CAN	11	4	1.82	7.0		57.5	76.2	17.8	9.8	8.5	0.9	2.0	(12)	2.07	1.15
USA	12	4	2.19	4.1		63.0	77.8	7.0	3.2	3.0	0.2	0.5	(12)	2.29	1.8
FIN	13	3	1.54	9.4	64.3	59.3	70.6	19.4	12.6	12.5	2.1	2.3	(9)	1.79	0
DNK	14	2	1.76	4.6	62.3	73.2	80.2	10.4	5.9	6.4	1.6	2.3	(10)	1.44	0
DEU	15	1	2.68	8.8	62.7	52.7	74.8	20.4	7.6	8.3	2.8	3.5	4	2.45	15.9
AUT	17	2	2.45	4.0	66.8	68.4	82.7	8.1	3.3	4.1	2.6	3.3	4	2.61	5
Group 2: Share of low-skilled persons is larger than 20% but less than one-third															
FRA	22	3	1.73	10.8	63.2	56.9	74.1	26.7	15.4	16.1	2.3	2.8	9	2.19	7.4
BEL	25	3	1.83	8.2	63.5	61.5	78.0	20.9	11.4	11.0	1.5	1.8	6	2.73	5.6
NLD	26	2	1.05	1.1	50.2	70.6	88.8	2.2	2.1	1.5	3.1	3.3	7	2.30	6.1
GRC	27	4	0.83	9.0	48.2	64.6	67.9	14.2	17.1	16.6	2.4	3.0	(9)	1.77	2.5
IRL	27	4	3.28	7.3	60.6	64.7	84.9	15.1	4.6	6.9	1.6	2.0	6	2.55	3.4
AUS	29	4	1.89	6.3		63.0	80.8	12.1	6.4	5.4	1.0	1.5	(10)	2.28	0.1
UK	32	3	2.75	5.0	61.3	48.4	77.9	19.8	7.2	6.9	0.8	0.3	(10)	3.09	0

Table A1: (cont.)

Country	% low skilled (20c1), ages 25–34	Pathway-type	Relative labor market disadvantage of low-skilled 25- to 29-year-olds (1998) — Relative Unempl.	Indicators of labor supply and demand (1998) — Unempl. (25- to 54-year-olds)	% RFE	Labor force participation of the 25- to 29-year-olds (1998) — Empl. ISCED 0/1/2	Empl. ISCED 3/4	Unempl. ISCED 0/1/2	Unempl. ISCED 3/4	Total	Employment protection legislation (late 1990s) — OECD index — Regular empl. Strict 1	Dismissal Strict 2	Stratification and segregation of the educational system — Number of years of comprehensive schooling	Social origin odds ratio	Retention
1	2	3	4	5	6	7	8	9	10	11	12	13	14	15	16
Group 3: Share of low-skilled persons is larger than one-third															
ISL	39			2.1		79.0	75.0						8	1.53	0
ITA	43	3	1.03	9.8	61.9	55.7	58.3	18.9	18.4	19.5	2.8	4.0	8	1.72	1.3
ESP	43	4	1.12	16.5	48.7	61.6	62.0	24.6	22.0	24.2	2.6	3.3	(10)	1.84	2.3
PRT	68	4	0.78	4.9	56.2	81.7	72.5	5.6	7.2	6.1	4.3	4.5	8	2.57	19.6

Column 1: Country.

Column 2: Proportion of 25- to 34-year-olds with less than upper secondary education (ISCED 0/1/2) (www.oecd.org/xls/Mo003000/Mo003099.xls).

Column 3: OECD classification of "upper secondary education pathways": 1 = apprenticeship system; 2 = mixed system; 3 = school-based vocational system; 4 = general education system (OECD, 2000b: 31f, 170).

Column 4: Relative unemployment risk of low-skilled person (ages 25–29) (1998) = unemployment rate of the 25- to29-year-olds with less than upper secondary education (ISCED 0/1/2) divided by unemployment rate of the 25- to 29-year-olds with upper secondary education (ISCED 3/4) (own calculations, www.oecd.org, Online database "Labour Market Statistics – Indicators").

Column 5: Unemployment rate of the 25- to 54-year-olds (1998) (www.oecd.org, Online database "Labour Market Statistics – Indicators").

Column 6: Share of regular full-time employed persons ("Normalarbeitsverhältnis") (1998) (Hoffmann & Walwei, 2000: 6ff).

Column 7: Share of employed 25- to 29-year-olds with less than upper secondary education (ISCED 0/1/2) – (1998) (www.oecd.org, Online database "Labour Market Statistics – Indicators").

Column 8: Share of employed 25- to 29-year-olds with upper secondary education (ISCED 3/4) – (1998) (www.oecd.org, Online database "Labour Market Statistics – Indicators").

Column 9: Unemployment rate of the 25- to 29-year-olds with less than upper secondary education (ISCED 0/1/2) – (1998) (www.oecd.org, Online database "Labour Market Statistics – Indicators").

Column 10: Unemployment rate of the 25- to 29-year-olds with upper secondary education (ISCED 3/4) – (1998) (www.oecd.org, Online database "Labour Market Statistics – Indicators").

Column 11: Unemployment rate of the 25- to 29-year-olds, total – (1998) (www.oecd.org, Online database "Labour Market Statistics – Indicators").

Column 12: OECD Indicator: Strictness of employment protection legislation – regular employment (at the end of the 1990s), ranging from 1 (low) to 6 (high) (www.oecd.org, Online database "Labour Market Statistics – Indicators").

Column 13: OECD Indicator: Strictness of employment protection legislation – difficulty of dismissal (at the end of the 1990s), ranging from 1 (low) to 6 (high) (www.oecd.org, Online database "Labour Market Statistics – Indicators").

Column 14: Number of years of comprehensive schooling (Lenhardt, 2002) – in parenthesis: years of compulsory schooling for the countries without segregated educational systems (Rijken, 1999: 182).

Column 15: Relative risk (odds ratio) of 15-year-olds whose parents belong to the lowest quarter of the social hierarchy (ISEI) on having only achieved competence level 1 in reading literacy – compared to the risk of 15-year-olds whose parents belong to the highest quarter of the social hierarchy (controlled for parents' education, migration, gender) (Baumert & Schümer, 2001: 400).

Column 16: Percentage of 15-year-olds who experienced delayed school entry and/or retention (proxy): if compulsory schooling starts at age 6, the proportion of students who had not reached grade 9 at the age of 15; if compulsory schooling starts at age 6 or 7 (Canada and Switzerland), half of the proportion of 15-year-olds not having reached grade 9; if compulsory schooling starts at age 7, the proxy has been fixed at zero because the derivation of the share of "deviant" school career was unpredictable (Denmark, Finland, and Sweden) (Schümer, 2001: 43).

PART THREE

INDIVIDUALS' ACQUISITION OF SKILLS AND COMPETENCIES

Learning Environments and Measurements of Skills

8 Vocational and Professional Learning

Skill Formation Between Formal and Situated Learning

Hans Gruber, Christian Harteis, and Monika Rehrl

Educational science and psychology put an emphasis on the development of individual competences and of individual performance when analyzing vocational and professional learning. Thus, intraindividual processes of skill formation are of utmost importance. Their psychological investigation mainly relies on information processing models and thus stresses cognitive components of competence. From an educational point of view, instructional models have been developed that aim at supporting the individual's acquisition of components of competence. Different opinions exist as to whether instructional support should mainly focus on reproducing systematically the to-be-learned domain knowledge, skills, and strategies, or whether instructional support should mainly focus on enabling learners to apply their knowledge in transfer situations. As a consequence, two rather different lines of instructional research can be distinguished: the one stressing formal learning processes, and the other stressing situated learning processes.

DISCUSSION ABOUT FORMAL AND SITUATED LEARNING

After the advent of the situated cognition movement, debates about formal learning and situated learning, as well as about the appropriate design of learning environments for skill acquisition, have been revitalized. The debates were grounded in the recognition of weaknesses that had been identified in so-called traditional formal learning settings. In particular, problems of knowledge application had been repeatedly observed in such learning settings: transfer from learning situations into application situations frequently failed. This was even true if the learners had proven to have mastered all learning requirements. Obviously, there is a substantial risk that knowledge that successfully was acquired remains inert (Renkl et al., 1996). It was argued that the design of learning environments had to be changed in order to overcome such difficulties.

Resnick (1987) used a contrastive approach to identify the features of promising learning environments. She suggested that four major differences could be found between learning in formal instructional settings and outside.

- *Individual cognition in formal instructional settings versus shared cognition outside*: In traditional instruction, teachers present knowledge to the learners. The main activity is introducing and explaining information (facts, ideas, theories, etc.) by the teacher. The learner's task is to individually process the information presented. Cooperation in exams is even condemned. In contrast, in professional life, cooperation is often necessary for coping with problems. Learning outside usually implies that stimuli emerge that have to be discussed with others (e.g., colleagues at the workplace). The notion of socially shared cognition is used to describe such discursive processes of collaboration and knowledge sharing.
- *Pure mentation in formal instructional settings versus tool manipulation outside*: In traditional instruction, problems are presented by the teacher and have to be solved in one's mind. Pure "thought" activities are paramount. Students should learn to perform without support of tools such as books, notes, and calculators. In exams, tools are usually forbidden. Learning outside, in contrast, usually stresses that to be competent in the use of tools is an important part of professional expertise. Thus, one is encouraged to make use of (cognitive) tools that are present in the environment.
- *Symbol manipulation in formal instructional settings versus contextualized reasoning outside*: Abstract manipulation of symbols is typical of traditional instruction. Students often fail to match symbols and symbolic processes to real-world entities and processes. This might be a consequence of the examination and selection function of instruction: students' primary goal is to pass the exam or to receive a certificate. The to-be-learned is adjusted to this purpose: for example, mathematical calculations are processed independent of the semantic context of a practical problem, but rather as a decontextualized algorithm. Learning outside, in contrast, includes reasoning processes into a set of activities that involve objects and other persons. Real-world reasoning processes are typically situated in rich situational contexts.
- *Focus on generalized learning in formal instructional settings versus focus on situation-specific competences outside*: Traditional instruction frequently uses abstract concepts and aims at teaching general, widely usable skills and theoretical principles. In professional life, in contrast, situation-specific

skills have to be acquired. Further learning is mostly aimed at competencies for specific demands in working life. Traditional instruction thus stresses the creation of general skills, knowledge, and theories, whereas learning focuses on concrete skills, knowledge, and theories in context of a specific situation.

Given that learning outside – for example, learning at the workplace – is per se applicable because learning situation and application situation are identical or at least very similar, these differences between learning in and outside are of importance for the design of learning environments. Apparently, the context in which learning takes place is of relevance. In other words, situational variables of the learning environment determine to some degree the applicability of newly acquired knowledge. Thus, learning is "situated." It is plausible that learning environments that offer affordances for situated learning processes are thus promising attempts to reduce inertness of knowledge.

In subsequent years, a number of instructional models were developed that tried to implement the characteristics of learning outside in schools, universities, and other formal learning institutions. Much attention was received in the 1980s and 1990s by anchored instruction (Cognition and Technology Group at Vanderbilt, 1992, 1997) or cognitive apprenticeship (Collins et al., 1989). Among the characteristics of learning environments that foster situated learning were authenticity, complexity, need for multiple perspectives, need for discovery of problems, conditionalization of knowledge, and discursive and cooperative learning processes.

Anderson et al. (1997) criticized that learning environments based on situated cognition concepts tend to disregard important cognitive skills that are accordingly focused in formal learning situations. Subsequently, fierce debates were conducted among "cognitivists" that argued in favor of formal learning in order to acquire proper knowledge and "constructivists" that argued in favor of situated learning in order to acquire applicable knowledge. Apparently, both positions contradict each other so that which one is adequate is an open question.

This question seems to be most important for an understanding of educational issues dealing with learning, knowledge acquisition, and skill formation in complex vocational or professional domains. Here, transfer of knowledge into vocational, occupational, or professional action is of major relevance. For more than 100 years, researchers are debating about the proper role of bringing elements of learning outside into formal learning environments (Mandl et al., 1996b). Starting from the end of the nineteenth century, the German *Reformpädagogik* criticized the traditional "book school" and instead proposed the concept of "work school" (Kerschensteiner, 1912). One instructional feature introduced in a work school was the implementation of "school garden instruction": based on authentic activities in the school garden, students learned biology, zoology, and botany, thus avoiding the gap between schoolwork and real-world activity, or – using Resnick's (1987) terminology – between learning in and outside school. A basic argument of introducing work school ideas was fostering student activities through working on complex, authentic problems that were not posed by the teacher, but rather discovered by students after a relevant problem was presented at early phases of an instructional activity. The ideas of work school prepared the ground for the development of the German vocational training system, which is widely known as the *dual system*. The dual system is a form of training tied to the place of work, with supplementary teaching in the compulsory part-time vocational school (Deutsche Forschungsgemeinschaft, 1990).

Clearly, both formal and situated learning in vocational and professional issues aim at related kinds of performance and try to foster the acquisition of expertise in complex domains. Nevertheless, it has been argued that different implications concerning the instructional design of learning environments indicate different educational goals. The respective foci have sometimes been erroneously generalized, and incongruences of both learning forms have been suggested. In formal learning, the importance of a large base of declarative knowledge organized in a systematic manner is emphasized, whereas in situated learning the notion of variable contexts is stressed, which implies that the to-be-learned depends on the actual learning situation and on the learners' interpretations of this situation. It seems as if one side favors the objective part of knowledge and skills, whereas the other side favors the subjective construction and interpretation of knowledge and skills.

We argue that a better understanding can be obtained of the role of formal and situated learning during skill formation at all stages of vocational careers, if the interplay between both forms is analyzed rather than contrasting them. In vocational and professional learning, obviously formal learning and situated learning are occurring simultaneously.

FORMAL AND SITUATED LEARNING CONCEPTS IN THEORIES OF EDUCATION

In the tradition of scientific life and apprenticeship, the distinction between academic and practical knowledge seems to be plausible and reliable. On the one hand, there is an entity of academic scientific knowledge, whereas on the other hand, there is a bulk of practical knowledge that was proven to be viable in everyday situations. Knowledge that is verified in scientific contexts does not necessarily help in solving practical problems. In theories of education, the von Humboldt idea of education since the Age of Enlightenment pleads for a strict distinction of general knowledge and vocational or application knowledge (von Humboldt, 2002; Kansanen, 2004). This idea is continuously influencing academic beliefs, even if protagonists only rarely refer to von Humboldt's writings.

As a consequence, it is not surprising that a common belief can be found that knowledge for the solution of scientific problems is to be imparted in academic life and lectures, whereas knowledge for solving practical problems has to be acquired in the field of practice. The first notion is characteristic for formal educational settings, whereas the second one characterizes settings aimed at situated learning. In the following, after a discussion of the terminology included, communalities of formal and situated learning and discrepancies are elaborated. This helps throw light on problems of polarization in academic traditions. Accordingly, an integrated model will be developed that supports a better understanding of processes of the acquisition of expertise and of professional skill formation.

Definitions of Learning

To understand disparities in learning conceptions, careful definitions of the basic concepts and their underlying characteristics are needed. From the definition of the concept of formal learning, it can be deduced which elements are constitutive. In the following, it becomes clear that formal learning is not necessarily the opposite of situated learning.

Formal learning. Situations that are deliberately generated for the purpose of learning can be described as formal learning situations. Consequently, learning is called formal learning if it occurs in such situations. When analyzing professional careers, formal learning takes place at schools, during university studies, at vocational school, during initial skill adaptation trainings, and in courses of further education. Such lists might be extended or excerpted by different subjects, but in any case they show that obviously formal learning comprises a great variety of teaching situations.

Informal learning. In contrast to formal learning, informal learning occurs in situations that are not explicitly set up or organized for learning purposes. Such situations are, for example, discussions with colleagues or supervisors, information retrieval procedures using virtual databases, trial and error learning, and reflection of mistakes or success. What seems to be apparent is that such situations frequently occur in daily work practice. Challenges of daily working life are well suited to initiate informal learning processes. There is a systematic difference between formal learning and informal learning: in formal learning situations, an explicit educational intention guided the development of the learning situation, whereas such an explicit intention is absent in the emergence of situations that foster implicit learning. (Of course, implicit learning processes can also occur in learning environments that were deliberately designed for initiating learning processes.) Informal learning, per definition, is a real antipode of formal learning.

Situated learning. The idea of situated learning emphasizes that much of content learned is specific to the situation in which it is learned (Brown et al., 1989). Without any doubt, each activity and every kind of learning is embedded in specific contexts. The idea behind attempts to develop theories of situated learning, however, is to make systematic use of including context factors in designing learning environments. Thus, theories of situated learning are to be distinguished from casual learning in action (in situ) because they comprise educational intentions (Lave & Wenger, 1991). Situated learning, therefore, does not at all mean "learning by doing anything," but rather "intentional learning by dealing with challenges and by taking situational contexts into consideration." This notion of situated learning is based on a constructivist background. From this background, it is argued that knowledge cannot be directly transferred from one situation to another because learners individually construct their knowledge on the base of their interpretation of situational affordances and constraints. If learners create knowledge in authentic real-world situations, this knowledge can be applied more easily in challenges of the real world.

The definitions of formal learning, informal learning, and situated learning presented suggest that formal learning and situated learning are not simple contradictions. However, substantial differences exist in the background of learning theories and epistemologies. When contrasting formal and situated learning, obviously the idea prevails that formal learning is related to instruction in a cognitivist view, whereas situated learning enfolds constructivist perspectives of learning. These assumptions allow the analysis of differences and commonalities of both approaches. As a consequence, it becomes evident both why the approaches frequently are seen as antagonists, and why it might be useful to investigate interactions between the approaches in order to better understand skill formation in vocational and professional domains.

Problems of Definitions and Polarization of Concepts

The definitions developed in the previous paragraph allow both the integration of components in a theoretical model of teaching and learning and their exclusion. Distinguishing between different – more or less congruent – concepts of learning helps one understand why researchers from different perspectives conceptualize learning processes differently, explain learning success differently, and organize learning environments differently. However, it is tempting to conclude that different conceptions of the same learning processes indicate incommensurate differences between the concepts in principle. In other words, the problem of different definitions is that they might falsely signalize differences and contradictions. In the discussion about learning and instruction, many researchers argue that the cognitivist and the constructivist theory of learning are opposite positions. However, they do not describe different objects, but rather the same objects and processes, and their theoretical perspectives are different. The cognitivist perspective focuses on individual information processing, storage and retrieval of information, and the structure of knowledge and memory. The constructivist perspective focuses on processes of generation of knowledge by deconstructing, interpreting, and reconstructing perception in the world. Although both perspectives focus on very different descriptions of learning processes, they are not dealing with different objects. The interpretation of both perspectives as being contradictory results from the misconstruction of different propositions about learning.

Considering Resnick's (1987) argumentation of differences between learning in traditional instructional settings and outside, the presumed contradictions can be resolved. Perceiving individual and social processes as mutually exclusive implies a narrow conception of learning processes that is mainly based on visible surface structures of interaction. The presentation of facts, ideas, and theories by teachers does not necessarily occur in an intrusive way in which learners' thinking activity is prohibited. In particular, this notion does not adequately describe learning processes in adult education. Regular seminars in vocational education usually provide reflection phases, although presentation of information frequently dominates. During reflection phases, participants have ample opportunities for exchanging ideas and thus working on socially shared cognition – even in formal learning settings. A similar objection can be made with regard to Resnick's second argument addressing pure mentation versus tool manipulation. Adults would barely accept an imposition of mental models, but rather prefer to review contents offered in instructional situations. Again, it becomes evident that it is not the context of formal learning, which in principle is responsible if "pure mentation" occurs. Typical seminars in adult education provide tools for the manipulation of the to-be-learned. As a consequence, even in formal learning situations, central aspects of situated learning are frequently met. Learners are prompted to test the consequences of one's own actions and to build up mental models. Resnick's third argument about symbol manipulation addresses a problem that is specific for formal learning. Her examples focus on how students work with mathematical formulae. Students' conceptions of formulae frequently remain abstract in nature, which is evidenced in the occurrence of inappropriate solutions for practical problems. For example, many students tend to answer "2.5" when asked how many 50-person capacity buses are needed to transport 125 persons. Such answers indicate that the phenomenon of "what you test is what you get" is a serious one in education. To give the answer "2.5" is wise if students have experienced that calculating correctly is the main operation that has to be mastered in mathematics. Requirements of this kind are what students usually experience in school instruction. In formal learning settings, students often are expected to meet test criteria rather than to increase their understanding of the subject matter. One reason is that achieving good test results and gaining certificates get increasingly important in school contexts. If instruction does not detach the connection of learning situation and test situation, it is highly probable – and wise – that learners focus on test results and do not learn to reason. However, the problem of "what you test is what you get" is also a challenge for learning environments focusing on situated learning. If students perceive that certification is the main reason for learning, they tend to resist learning environments in which teacher presentation plays a minor role. Resnick's fourth argument does not distinguish between formal and situated learning either. Whether learners develop generalized or situation-specific skills and competencies is a consequence of didactic decisions of the teacher rather than of the predominance of formal or situated learning. Situation-specific knowledge might be addressed in teacher presentations in traditional courses, and experts might focus on generalized knowledge when learning and working in specific contexts.

Taken together, the merits of distinguishing definitions consist of the allocation of a systematic perspective for analyzing processes of learning and teaching. Differences between definitions are useful for analytic purposes and, in consequence, for didactic decisions. However, the polarization of different definitions of learning is problematic if antagonisms between concepts are postulated in cases in which the concepts address different aspects of the same objects and situations. As was exemplarily shown with Resnick's argumentation, formal and situated learning are not mutually exclusive views on learning processes, but rather highlight different components. To use the words of Winn (1996), formal and situated learning "can coexist in a productive partnership" (p. 57). In the following, we argue that a better understanding of processes of skill formation in vocational and professional learning is gained if learning concepts are differentiated rather than contrasted.

Formal and Situated Learning During the Acquisition of Expertise: Components of Action Competence in Professional Domains

In educational science and in psychology, the use of the concept "competence" is closely related to the use of the concepts "performance" of even "expertise." This explains why most research takes a microperspective, focusing on how individuals process information during learning; how they perceive stimuli; how they acquire, store, retrieve, and apply knowledge; and how they solve problems within their professional field. In contrast to the notion of key qualifications that address general competences that can be used in many different situations (e.g., communication skills), professional competence is usually closely related with professional performance. It thus is domain specific in nature. The use of the concept "professional competence" in educational science and in psychology means that a discussion about learning is pointless if it contains no notion of what is being learned and what kind of behavior it enables. The focus thus is on individual cognitive functioning and development. Only recently, theories of competence have been published that extend the perspective by addressing the sociocultural development of professional practice at specific workplaces (Billett, 2001a). Most recent conceptions of expertise and professional development that emphasize expertise do not only include individual cognitive capacities but also the successful participation in a community of experts and its shared knowledge and actions, as well as the appreciation of an individual's performance by other persons (Berliner, 2001; Simons & Ruijters, 2004; Rehrl et al., 2006). Accordingly, the following model of action competence includes a component of being an acknowledged member of a community of experts.

A Model of Action Competence

During the development of vocational and professional competencies, the individual acquisition of domain-specific knowledge and problem solving on the one hand and the social embedding within communities of practice on the other hand complement each other (Mandl et al., 1996a). During vocational apprenticeship, apprentices experience vocational school and within-firm instruction in parallel and have to integrate the knowledge and skills acquired in both settings. The relation between individual and sociocultural processes is continuing over the whole span of vocational careers: employees bring their experience into formal training settings, and they transfer training contents into their work life. In both cases, knowledge has to pass examination by learners in the respective situation. Recent empirical research acknowledges the importance of such an integration of formal and situated learning (Gruber et al., 2005).

Therefore, the relationship between academic knowledge and practical knowledge is crucial because the former is transformed into the latter through professional learning. To become a professional in any occupation usually requires extensive formal learning in order to receive a certificate. Only a degree formally legitimizes working in an occupational field and, thus, allows making relevant experiences. Formal education usually alternates with a more practical phase, which takes place in occupational institutions (e.g., enterprises). In this phase, more practical skills are acquired that are relevant for the profession and that help grow into the culture of the profession (Boshuizen et al., 2004).

Research on experts' excellent performance in professional domains generated useful results about essential knowledge for vocational skill formation. However, the way of thinking about professional expertise has dramatically changed in recent years. A few decades ago, professional competence was considered to be based on the amount of specific knowledge a person had accumulated during professional life. This view has been replaced by a perspective differentiating dimensions of knowledge and action competence. It was plead to integrate both individual cognitive aspects and social and cultural dimensions of growing into a community of experts (Billett, 2001b). Individual cognitive processes such as acquisition, storage, and retrieval of knowledge in memory systems are represented by research on expertise, whereas sociocultural theories of professional development highlight processes of increasingly becoming integrated in communities of experts and acquiring practicable knowledge through directly participating in professional practice.

Accordingly, Gruber and Rehrl (2003) proposed a model for professional competence consisting of the following four elements: (1) competence for the adequate accomplishment of recurring tasks (routines), (2) competence to deal with novel situations (mental models of anticipated situations), (3) competence to acquire and recall well-founded domain-specific declarative knowledge, and (4) competence to become part of a community of practice.

Academic Knowledge: Individual Cognitive Correlates of Expertise

Traditional cognitive research on expertise defines experts as persons who, by objective standards and over time, consistently show superior performance in typical activities of a domain (e.g., medicine, physics, chess, music). Expert performance is often illuminated by comparison with individuals with limited performance, the novices. In contrast to giftedness, expertise is usually considered an acquired special skill in or knowledge of a particular subject through practical experience. De Groot's (1965) seminal work on chess masters pioneered the scientific orientation of research on expertise. The most striking difference between grandmasters and weaker players was revealed in a memory task in which subjects were presented chess positions for a few seconds and asked to immediately reconstruct them. The experts' superior recall was explained with specific perceptual structures they held in memory that were closely related to their domain-specific knowledge.

De Groot's interpretation of the findings directed the future research on expertise from the perspective of information processing theory and cognitive psychology. The focus on the analysis of cognitive correlates of expert performance (perception, memory, knowledge, problem solving) has since been maintained (Ericsson et al., 2006) and has only recently been supplemented by research on the contexts in which expert performance is situated. The main research concentrated on modeling those cognitive structures and mechanisms that characterize expert information processing, thus aiming at the description of expertise.

The most prominent empirical research method is the quasiexperimental contrastive approach (Voss et al., 1986). Experts, novices, and sometimes also subjects with an intermediate level of expertise (semiexperts) are compared. Results of contrastive comparisons show large differences between experts and novices in memory performance. These large effect sizes cannot be explained by general memory factors: no differences occur in control tasks such as digit-span. Thus, it is obvious that domain-specific practice determines the differences. To a certain degree, the cross-sectional comparison can be interpreted as a developmental model of skill formation "from novice to expert" in particular domains.

Generally, experts' superior memory performance is closely related with their knowledge. Many studies demonstrated the importance of a huge amount of academic or declarative knowledge for expert performance. At its beginning, research on expertise investigated the importance of previous knowledge in well-structured domains such as chess or physics. In particular, chess studies demonstrated the huge impact of knowledge on memory performance of shortly presented chess positions; even children with less elaborated memory abilities than adults presented better performance if they had more previous knowledge. Studies using thinking aloud protocols in the domain of physics showed positive correlations of previous knowledge and problem-solving skills (Simon & Simon, 1978).

In more practical professional fields, many expert actions are highly automatized. Field studies evidenced that academic knowledge increasingly becomes proceduralized with growing expertise. In his ACT* (Adaptive Control of Thought) model, Anderson (1982) stated that skill acquisition mainly consists of changing declarative knowledge through practice into proceduralized knowledge. This is achieved through knowledge compilation and rule tuning. Skill acquisition as a basic component of expertise can be described in three phases (declarative, compilation, tuning phase). Learners first acquire much declarative knowledge, which is later proceduralized and associated with action sequences. Then the skill is automatized and tuned through repeated practice.

According to this model, the development of specific expertise is demonstrated through several stages. In the field of medical diagnostics, Patel and Groen (1991) conceptualized four steps for expertise development: (1) beginners have declarative knowledge available, (2) intermediates have already compiled their knowledge into simple procedures; (3) generic experts command domain-specific schemata and scripts, and (4) specific experts have enriched these with case experience.

The relevance of knowledge for expert performance is so obvious that in studies on expertise, the concept of knowledge explicitly has been defined only rarely. After the "discovery" of the importance of knowledge and proclaiming the cognitive paradigm, the use of the term "knowledge" apparently became a bit careless. Research indeed showed that many different types and qualities of knowledge can be differentiated, each of them with distinguished functionality. De Jong and Ferguson-Hessler (1996) proposed a 4 × 5 matrix, in which four different kinds of knowledge (situational, conceptual, procedural, and strategic) and five different criteria of knowledge (superficial vs. deep, isolated vs. linked, explicit vs. complied, visual vs. analytic, and general vs. domain specific) are differentiated. This differentiation shows that the connotation of the concept knowledge is far from trivial. A number of the knowledge concepts described by De Jong and Ferguson-Hessler clearly indicate that acquisition, storage, retrieval, and application of knowledge are not only individual matters, but also include sociocultural components.

In sum, the research on individual cognitive components of expertise generated much evidence for the impact of knowledge on experts' perception, memory, and problem-solving skills. Results about domain specificity of expertise imply that the analysis of domain knowledge plays a major role in research on expertise.

Practical Knowledge: Sociocultural Correlates of Expertise

In contrast to traditional cognitive concepts of expertise, which focus on academic knowledge, the sociocultural approach on expertise introduces a different epistemology of knowledge, which is exclusively related to social practice.

The basic assumption of sociocultural theories is that individuals and social context cannot be analyzed as separate units (Vygotsky, 1978). Rather humans and social context are mutually interrelated because individuals are both actively constructing their cultural systems and are influenced through it. As people, from their early interactions on, develop a kind of social sense, they begin to construct their perception of the social world and selectively engage in social practices. By engaging in social practice, they in turn construct new knowledge, subjective beliefs, and experiences (Valsiner, 1991).

Thus, sociocultural theories define learning processes not as cognitive processes but rather as a personal development of increasingly becoming embedded in social interactions and increasingly shaping an identity within social systems. Similarly, the process of expertise development is described as an ongoing integration in professional communities, in which new workers are guided by more competent members and increasingly become full participants at the field of work (Lave & Wenger, 1991).

The basic idea of sociocultural research on expertise, therefore, is to stress the context dependency of knowledge and knowledge acquisition. Context is defined as historically developed culture of practice, including particular cultural artifacts and ways of interactions. Accordingly, knowledge for skill formation is bound to social activities and interactions within a particular kind of practice.

Consequently, the nature of knowledge is conceived differently in sociocultural theories than in cognitive theories. Knowledge is not considered to be an objective entity located within individuals' heads. Rather, Lave and Wenger (1991) used the concept of "knowledgeable skills" instead of declarative or procedural knowledge and thus propose a direct link between practical skills and knowledge. In their ethnographic study about midwifes, the process of knowledge and skill application is investigated through scientific observations of participation and guidance in a specific culture of professional practice.

Research on social cognition generated many linkages between mental representations and the sociocultural background in certain professional fields

(Resnick et al., 1991; Goodnow, 1996). These theories emphasize that workplaces represent a historically derived practice with unique situational factors. Expertise development is linked to the ability to learn the particular knowledgeable skill and perform effectively in a particular instance of work practice.

The most applicable research method to investigate relevant practical knowledge in different professional fields is the longitudinal ethnographic study using observations and interviews.

Results from Billett's (2003) ethnographic study in the field of hairdressing show the differences of cultural factors of workplaces (e.g., division of labor, clients, location, layout). By investigating the essential knowledge in hairdressers' activity and problem solving, conclusions of the interdependence of sociocultural practice and individual life histories could be drawn.

More recently, Rehrl and Gruber (2007) argued that a different methodology should be applied to educational fields in order to analyze sociocultural components of expertise and competence. Using the social network analysis (SNA) methodology makes it possible to analyze the position, the activity, and the power of an individual within a social community. SNA allows the investigation of processes of building professional networks as part of professional competence. The social component of professional learning is included through the analysis of social relations (e.g., trust, responsibility, knowledge exchange, teamwork) and, as a consequence, the social position of individuals within professional networks. Moreover, network analyses relate the social components of learning, which are focused in sociocultural research, with personal attributes (knowledge, memory, problem-solving capacities), which are focused in cognitive psychological research on expertise.

In sum, sociocultural research on expertise points out the practical component of knowledge in particular cultural contexts. This approach denies investigating abstract academic knowledge as essential for skillful professional performance. Because knowledge and the particular context cannot be separated, social engagement in practice is essential for expertise development. Through participating in social practice and experiencing guidance from competent workers, people learn essential knowledgeable skills.

INTEGRATION OF INDIVIDUAL AND SOCIOCULTURAL COMPONENTS OF EXPERTISE: THE ROLE OF EXPERIENCE IN SKILL FORMATION

Research on individual cognitive components of expertise generated evidence for the essential academic, declarative knowledge, whereas sociocultural research focuses on practice-related knowledge, caring little about abstract, context-free knowledge. To carry both approaches to extremes, two misleading assumptions arise, which are often discussed in instructional design debates of vocational trainings. These misconceptions reflect the misassumptions mentioned previously about incongruence of formal and situated learning.

Misconception 1: Huge amounts of academic knowledge lead to skill formation. Looking at primarily theoretical curricula for vocational training, one gets the idea that a huge amount of abstract knowledge leads to professional competence. However, recent educational studies show that providing learners with much declarative knowledge often leads to inert knowledge rather than to expert knowledge. Evidence exists in the field of commercial vocational training or of higher education that academic knowledge acquired during learning could not easily be transferred to daily life problems (Mandl et al., 1996a). Similar findings were demonstrated for the domains of teaching, medicine, and others. The impact of academic knowledge in the domain of counseling is supposed to be limited as well. After theoretical trainings in artificial environments, counselors often fall back on their subjective theories and routines (Sowarka, 1991).

Thus, despite much evidence of the huge impact of declarative knowledge for expertise development, academic knowledge seems to be a necessary component of expertise, but not a sufficient one. It is a fallacy to equate "expert knowledge" and "declarative, academic domain knowledge." As was mentioned previously, expertise comprises more than only acquisition of declarative knowledge and automatization of routine actions. Experts excel by flexibility of actions ("adaptive expertise"; Hatano & Inagaki, 1986).

Misconception 2: Huge amounts of practical knowledge lead to skill formation. The gap between theory and practice is frequently found in complex domains. Practitioners claim that workaday knowledge, common sense, and social competences are sufficient for skillful performance. It is argued that concepts of theoretical instructions are deficient. Current German discussions about leading back teacher education from university to practical professional training institutions indicate the trend to dramatically reduce theoretical and academic parts of vocational training.

However, practice without theoretical reflection does not cause deep learning processes. Declarative knowledge is essential to evaluate the quality of practice, to review problems and solutions, and to implement innovations. If it is true that practice shows unique characteristics in particular respective sociocultural contexts, then abstract knowledge is even more essential for flexibly applying given concepts for different categories of practical problems.

Like academic knowledge, practical knowledge seems to be a necessary component of expertise, but not a sufficient one. Recent theories of expertise development therefore aim at combining both aspects by introducing experience as essential knowledge. Experience is defined as episodic knowledge about how, when, and in which situation to successfully apply knowledge. In other words, such theories argue that the combination of both formal and situated learning is crucial. Expertise development does not only include accumulation of declarative and procedural knowledge, but also processes of reorganizing existing knowledge according to specific situations and to constraints set by the social community of experts in the domain. The main educational issue then is to generate experience-based knowledge structures, which show high subjective relevance and personal importance related to the experienced practice within relevant social contexts.

In sum, the "right" experience provides a basis to combine academic and practical knowledge for expertise development and skill formation. It requires the development of learning environments that foster both individual cognitive components of expertise – formal learning processes might be appropriate to foster such processes – and sociocultural assimilation and accommodation processes – preferably fostered through ideas of how to initiate situated learning. Professional experience in the previously mentioned sense increases episodic knowledge and thus contributes to the successful, flexible, and innovative use of declarative knowledge as well as to the mastery of specific practical situations.

PERSPECTIVES: INTERACTION OF FORMAL AND SITUATED LEARNING AS SILVER BULLET OF SKILL FORMATION FOR DISADVANTAGED GROUPS

In the previous section, the interaction of formal and situated learning processes was developed as a framework of how to support professional development at a high level, in particular, during the acquisition of expertise. This framework can – and should – be extended to other fields of educational activity as well.

When talking about vocational education, many agree that the purpose of learning normally is to foster humans' competence to use their knowledge in professional life. The debate about differences or commonalities of formal and situated learning thus has to be conducted within this frame as well. With reference to the idea of facilitating the acquisition of applicable knowledge, it was argued previously that an increasing role is attributed to informal learning processes, for example, in workplace learning. However, even then formal learning is still indispensable in many cases. In ordinary workplaces in which no worker excels with a high level of expertise, it is highly implausible that high-quality workplace learning can take place. That means that formal learning environments have to be provided in particular if the probability of powerful informal learning opportunities is low.

Studies conducted using instructional approaches fostering situated learning processes provided empirical evidence that under certain circumstances learning is less likely to produce inert knowledge. Explicit instructional measures were proposed that should accompany learning in learning environments that encourage situated learning (Stark et al., 1999). The common core of such attempts to relate formal and situated learning consists of few instructional principles:

- *Articulation:* Teachers and learners speak out loudly about what they think and how they perceive the contents presented.
- *Reflection:* Learners are stimulated to test their mental models. They are prompted to compare their experiences with the experiences of other learners and to explore similarities and dissimilarities.
- *Activity:* Learning activities widely comprise learners' active work on authentic problems.
- *Equality:* Every person in the learning setting has equal importance. Teachers act as coaches and do not demand a privileged position.

It is obvious that these principles can easily be integrated in formal learning. A popular approach of integrating situated learning in formal settings is cognitive apprenticeship. It describes a didactic scenario, in which problem solving occurs under varying degrees of instruction. Initially, learners observe an expert working on a problem and explicating his or her thoughts and strategies. First, learners imitate the expert strategies and discuss experiences. With growing experience, the expert withdraws and responds only on demand. At the end, learners explore themselves and develop their own strategies that should be discussed with other learners and the expert. This not only enhances the creation of applicable knowledge, but also facilitates entering a community of experts and building up a learning culture within the community. Models focusing on the growth of cognitive flexibility in learners with substantial previous knowledge propose to approach complex problems from various perspectives, in order to weaken existing, frequently oversimplified mental models and beliefs about the domain. Being able to take different perspectives in analyzing a complex problem helps recognize side effects of interventions. This ability is important for adequate acting competence in complex domains.

The integration of such didactic models into formal learning does not imply a revolution of formal learning in the field of adult education. Concepts such as learner activity, action orientation, and reflection of experience have a long history in adult education as well as in vocational and professional training (see previous paragraph about work school). However, little elaborated work has been done to integrate the ideologies of formal and situated learning. This concerns both the necessity of seriously integrating "situated aspects" in formal learning environments, for example, through the adaptation of examination systems and the necessity to integrate formal aspects in situated learning environments, because learning is arduous if the context is weak. For example, workplace learning does not automatically work smoothly but requires intensive instructional support if little expertise exists in the working team. Learning activities at workplaces, however, require time and space, and they depend on explicit rules allowing employees to follow learning activities instead of productive ones. In the respective educational and organizational research, this topic is discussed within the concept of "learning culture." Attempts to construct a learning culture in an organization require both some formal regulations and opportunities to make use of context-dependent learning processes. If both requirements are fulfilled, learning can occur even in individuals who are disadvantaged for one reason or the other and who cannot easily enter traditional formal learning environments.

For an elaboration of this argument, we put our focus in the following on vocational biographies and processes of skill formation at the workplace in order to draw a picture of professional learning. From the perspective of professional development, it becomes clear that individuals permanently change between formal and situated learning during their skill formation over the vocational life span. The probability that their skills and competencies will be developed continuously increases if formal and situated learning processes interact, if they alternate, and if they supplement each other. We underline this assumption by referring to three crucial occasions for professional learning. These occasions concern all persons in the employment system, not only advantaged ones such as experts, gifted persons, or employees on high hierarchical professional levels: career entry, adjustment to changes in the workplaces, and career advancement.

Career entry. The typical entry in a professional career is a consequence of a (first) occupational graduation in an educational institution, or, in some countries, in the dual system. Enterprises usually offer programs for vocational adjustment, during which newcomers experience both formal and informal structures and routines of the enterprise. During these processes, formal learning processes alternate with situated learning processes. In the workplace, these two types of learning frequently cannot be distinguished because they are not confined to extended time intervals that are clearly separated. Some examples show how difficult it is to distinguish the nature of formal and situated learning processes: Can official presentations of the organizational structure be interpreted as formal instruction? Do face-to-face dialogues meet the criteria of situated learning opportunities, for example when a manager introduces the rules of operational and organizational structures to new employees? It is evident that the distinction between formal and situated learning is an analytic one. It has to be noticed, however, that a didactically inspired separation makes sense if one assumes that both modalities deliver different contents. It could be imagined that an official presentation delivers information about the formal structure and routines, whereas the face-to-face dialogues deliver informal structures about usual behavior within the company. Taking this perspective, formal and situated learning are different – and their integration become all the more important because both kinds of learning are necessary for successful professional careers. However, the importance of the interplay results not only from the implication that learners inevitably access formal and informal structures, but also from the idea that it is part of their acquisition of competence to grow into the organization. Recent research supports the importance of situated learning processes for developing an understanding of the meanings of inner-firm symbols and creating a company identity (Wenger, 2003; Billett, 2006).

Adjustment to changes in the workplace. Protagonists from different disciplines and domains proclaim "change" as the only constant in the area of economy. Global markets lead to increased competition, which effect changes in the workplaces at all levels of employment. It is reasonable to assume that these changes lead to the requirement of learning for all working people: elder and younger, qualified and unqualified, managers and working staff members, white and blue collar employees – in other words, for both advantaged and disadvantaged groups. Those who stay on low qualification level receive fewer opportunities for formal education. This means that they remain in an inferior position, and that the gap between advantaged and disadvantaged persons increases. In contrast, situated learning provides more equal opportunities for learning for all employees. The importance of integrating formal and situated learning is supported from such a political perspective as much as from instructional theories and theories of learning. Situated learning opportunities prove to be particularly important for those who are embedded in the employment system but do not have sufficient access to formal learning environments.

Of course, ongoing changes in the workplace require both formal and situated learning. Contents reflecting new developments are most probably learned in formal learning environments, but have to prove substantial in professional practice. It could be argued that mutual references between formal and situated learning processes are necessary (1) in formal learning by placing contents into workplace contexts, and (2) in workplace activities by addressing lessons learned in formal education.

Career advancement. In principle, for career advancement, the same arguments apply as for the adjustment to changes in the workplaces because career advancement frequently is closely related to change of workplaces or functions. Advancement is to be understood in a wider sense and not narrowly interpreted as career development of high potentials and executives. To put it in a sarcastic way, even processes of job reduction in enterprises serve career advancement. If a global-playing industrial company reduces staff worldwide in the magnitude of several tens of thousands of workers, the remaining jobs will receive new job descriptions on a higher level of efficiency. New burdens are put on employees, and such burdens are typical characteristics of advancement.

Finally returning to the perspective of individual skill formation in a biography, it has to be stressed that those humans who show up with a high level of formal education and a high level of experience gained in situated learning contexts usually experience appreciation. Thus, the build-up of professional skills and competences at all stages of vocational careers can be understood appropriately only when analyzing the interaction of formal and situated learning rather than by contrasting them. The development of learning environments in which this plea is taken seriously is, however, only at the very beginning.

References

Anderson, J. R. (1982). Acquisition of cognitive skill. *Psychological Review*, 89, 369–406.

Anderson, J. R., Reder, L. M., & Simon, H. A. (1997). Situative versus cognitive perspectives: Form versus substances. *Educational Researcher*, 26(1), 18–21.

Berliner, D. C. (2001). Learning about and learning from expert teachers. *International Journal of Educational Research*, 35, 463–482.

Billett, S. (2001a). Knowing in practice: Re-conceptualising vocational expertise. *Learning and Instruction*, 11, 431–452.

Billett, S. (2001b). *Learning in the Workplace: Strategies for Effective Practice*. Crows Nest: Allen and Unwin.

Billett, S. (2003). Sociogeneses, activity and ontogeny. *Culture and Psychology*, 9, 133–169.

Billett, S. (2006). *Work, Workers, and Change: Learning and Identity*. Dordrecht, The Netherlands: Springer.

Boshuizen, H. P. A., Bromme, R., & Gruber, H. (2004). On the long way from novice to expert and how travelling changes the traveller. In H. P. A. Boshuizen, R. Bromme, &

H. Gruber (Eds.), *Professional Learning: Gaps and Transitions on the Way from Novice to Expert* (pp. 3–8). Dordrecht, The Netherlands: Kluwer.

Brown, J. S., Collins, A., & Duguid, P. (1989). Situated cognition and the culture of learning. *Educational Researcher*, 18(1), 34–41.

Cognition and Technology Group at Vanderbilt. (1992). The Jasper series as an example of anchored instruction: Theory, program, description, and assessment data. *Educational Psychologist*, 27, 291–315.

Cognition and Technology Group at Vanderbilt. (1997). *The Jasper Project: Lessons in Curriculum, Instruction, Assessment, and Professional Development.* Mahwah, NJ: Erlbaum.

Collins, A., Brown, J. S., & Newman, S. E. (1989). Cognitive apprenticeship: Teaching the crafts of reading, writing, and mathematics. In L. B. Resnick (Ed.), *Knowing, Learning, and Instruction: Essays in Honor of Robert Glaser* (pp. 453–494). Hillsdale, NJ: Erlbaum.

De Groot, A. D. (1965). *Thought and Choice and Chess.* The Hague, The Netherlands: Mouton.

De Jong, T., & Ferguson-Hessler, M. G. M. (1996). Types and qualities of knowledge. *Educational Psychologist*, 31, 105–113.

Deutsche Forschungsgemeinschaft. (1990). *Berufsbildungsforschung an den Hochschulen der Bundesrepublik Deutschland* [Research of vocational education in German universities]. Weinheim, Germany: VCH Acta Humaniora.

Ericsson, K. A., Charness, N., Feltovich, P. J., & Hoffman, R. R. (Eds.). (2006). *Handbook on Expertise and Expert Performance.* Cambridge, UK: Cambridge University Press.

Goodnow, J. J. (1996). Collaborative rules: How are people supposed to work with one another? In P. B. Baltes & U. M. Staudinger (Eds.), *Interactive Minds: Life-Span Perspectives on the Social Foundation of Cognition* (pp. 163–197). Cambridge, UK: Cambridge University Press.

Gruber, H., Harteis, C., Mulder, R. H., & Rehrl, M. (Eds.). (2005). *Bridging Individual, Organisational, and Cultural Perspectives on Professional Learning.* Regensburg, Germany: Roderer.

Gruber, H., & Rehrl, M. (2003). *Wege zum Können: Ansätze zur Erforschung und Förderung der Expertise von Sozialarbeitern im Umgang mit Fällen von Kindeswohlgefährdung* [Ways to competence: Researching and fostering expertise of social workers]. München, Germany: Deutsches Jugendinstitut.

Hatano, G., & Inagaki, K. (1986). Two courses of expertise. In H. W. Stevenson, H. Azuma, & K. Hakuta (Eds.), *Child Development and Education in Japan: A Series of Books in Psychology* (pp. 262–272). New York: Freeman.

Kansanen, P. (2004). The role of general education in teacher education. *Zeitschrift für Erziehungswissenschaft*, 7, 207–218.

Kerschensteiner, G. (1912). *Begriff der Arbeitsschule* [The concept of work school]. Leipzig, Germany: Teubner.

Lave, J., & Wenger, E. (1991). *Situated Learning: Legitimate Peripheral Participation.* Cambridge, UK: Cambridge University Press.

Mandl, H., Gruber, H., & Renkl, A. (1996a). Communities of practice toward expertise: Social foundation of university instruction. In P. B. Baltes & U. Staudinger (Eds.), *Interactive Minds: Life-span perspectives on the Social Foundation of Cognition* (pp. 394–411). Cambridge, UK: Cambridge University Press.

Mandl, H., Gruber, H., & Renkl, A. (1996b). Learning to apply: From "school garden instruction" to technology-based learning environments. In S. Vosniadou, E. De Corte, R. Glaser, & H. Mandl (Eds.), *International Perspectives on the Design of Technology-Supported Learning Environments* (pp. 307–321). Mahwah, NJ: Erlbaum.

Patel, V. L., & Groen, G. J. (1991). The general and specific nature of medical expertise: A critical look. In K. A. Ericsson & J. Smith (Eds.), *Toward a General Theory of Expertise: Prospects and Limits* (pp. 93–125). Cambridge, UK: Cambridge University Press.

Rehrl, M., & Gruber, H. (2007). Netzwerkanalysen in der Pädagogik – Ein Überblick über Methode und Anwendung. [Network analyses in education – An overview of methods and applications] *Zeitschrift für Pädagogik*, 53, 243–264.

Rehrl, M., Palonen, T., & Gruber, H. (2006). Expertise development in science. In H. P. A. Boshuizen (Ed.), *Lifelong Learning of Professionals: Exploring Implications of a Transitional Labour Market* (CD-ROM, Proceedings of the 3rd EARLI SIG Professional Learning and Development Conference). Heerlen: Open University of the Netherlands.

Renkl, A., Mandl, H., & Gruber, H. (1996). Inert knowledge: Analyses and remedies. *Educational Psychologist*, 31, 115–121.

Resnick, L. B. (1987). Learning in school and out. *Educational Researcher*, 16(9), 13–20.

Resnick, L. B., Levine, J. M., & Teasley, S. D. (Eds.). (1991). *Perspectives on Socially Shared Cognition*. Washington, DC: American Psychological Association.

Simon, D. P., & Simon, H. A. (1978). Individual differences in solving physics problems. In R. S. Siegler (Ed.), *Children's Thinking: What Develops?* (pp. 325–348). Hillsdale, NJ: Erlbaum.

Simons, P. R.-J., & Ruijters, M. C. P. (2004). Learning professionals: Towards an integrated model. In H. P. A. Boshuizen, R. Bromme, & H. Gruber (Eds.), *Professional Learning: Gaps and Transitions on the Way from Novice to Expert* (pp. 207–229). Dordrecht, The Netherlands: Kluwer.

Sowarka, B. (1991). *Strategien der Informationsverarbeitung im Beratungsdiskurs. Kognitionswissenschaftliche Überlegungen und empirische Analysen zur Wissensrepräsentation und subjektiven Theorie klinischer Beratungsexperten*. Weinheim, Germany: Deutscher Studien Verlag.

Stark, R., Mandl, H., Gruber, H., & Renkl, A. (1999). Instructional means to overcome transfer problems in the domain of economics: Empirical studies. *International Journal of Educational Research*, 31, 591–609.

Valsiner, J. (1991). Building theoretical bridges over a lagoon of everyday events: A review of apprenticeship in thinking: Cognitive development in social context by Barbara Rogoff. *Human Development*, 34, 307–315.

von Humboldt, W. (2002). *Werke in fünf Bänden. Band IV: Schriften zur Politik und zum Bildungswesen* (6th ed.). [Collected works. Vol. IV: About politics and the educational system] Darmstadt, Germany: Wissenschaftliche Buchgesellschaft.

Voss, J. F., Fincher-Kiefer, R. H., Green, T. R., & Post, T. A. (1986). Individual differences in performance: The contrastive approach to knowledge. In R. J. Sternberg (Ed.), *Advances in the Psychology of Human Intelligence* (Vol. 3, pp. 297–334). Hillsdale, NJ: Erlbaum.

Vygotsky, L. S. (1978). *Mind in Society: The Development of Higher Psychological Processes*. Cambridge, UK: Harvard University Press.

Wenger, E. (2003). *Communities of Practice: Learning, Meaning, and Identity* (2nd ed.). Cambridge, UK: Cambridge University Press.

Winn, W. (1996). Instructional design and situated learning: Paradox or partnership? In H. McLellan (Ed.), *Situated Learning Perspectives* (pp. 57–66). Englewood Cliffs, NJ: Educational Technology Publications.

9 How to Compare the Performance of VET Systems in Skill Formation[1]

Martin Baethge, Frank Achtenhagen, and Lena Arends

IMPACT OF INTERNATIONAL COMPARISONS IN VET

The political and economic benefits of an international large-scale assessment of vocational education and training (VET) are obvious. Due to the increasing internationalization of economic exchange relationships in goods and in labor markets, as well as to economical, political, and social standardization in Europe – under the condition of increasing knowledge intensity in working processes – educational systems have changed. In particular, vocational educational systems have gained importance for providing competences relating to occupational mobility and independent lifestyle of young people, as well as international competitiveness and innovativeness of enterprises. The European Commission (2005, p. 9) has put forward the ambitious economic and social goal of becoming "the most competitive and dynamic knowledge-based economy in the world." Therefore, improved participation in education and the labor market is playing a crucial role in reaching these goals.

The practical implications of the problems of competence measurement are reflected in the ongoing progress toward the development of a standardized European Qualifications Framework (EQF). In Europe, the ministers for VET in thirty-two countries have accepted the Maastricht Communiqué, endorsed in December 2004, consisting of an agreement for the development of an overall EQF and a European Credit Transfer System for VET (ECVET). The aim of the EQF is to provide a common set of reference levels as an integration of an ECVET and the European Credit Transfer System in higher education (Commission of the European Communities, 2005). The main objective of the EQF is to provide a metaframework for the development of a set of common descriptions for qualifications that can be applied in all educational systems in Europe.

The purpose of a comparative study of VET, modeled as a large-scale assessment along the lines of the Programme for International Student Assessment (PISA), is to figure out to what extent VET systems are able to develop occupational competences in the way outlined previously. Therefore, the aim is to assess those competences, which young people acquire during VET in their countries in an objective, reliable, and valid way, as well as to link the results to the macro- and microstructural factors. These factors, in turn, impact the development and value of competences at a later point in time in the labor market.

CONCEPT OF VET

An international comparison of VET must be based on a common understanding of the goals of VET. In accordance with the ongoing scientific discussion, there are three central goals that educational systems must address at the system level:

- The development of potentials for individual's occupational mobility, self-regulation, and autonomy
- The safeguarding of human resources in a society
- The warranty of social participation and equal opportunities

These goals function as reference points for the definition of competences, which must be developed in VET.

The first goal, *individual vocational adjustment*, denotes the ability of individuals to develop relationships with their environment and to create their educational pathways and life in society in a responsible and self-directed way. *Individual vocational adjustment* also denotes generic competences such as self-management skills, problem-solving skills, communication skills, and metacognitive skills. Individuals are considered within the context of individual aims and efforts on the one hand, and beneficial and obstructive environmental conditions on the other hand. This perception includes the goal of VET systems to provide opportunities for developing and constructing individual and occupational identities.

The second goal, *safeguarding of human resources*, subsumes every aspect of educational systems that facilitate individual abilities to act at work and in the labor market (individual economic user perspective) and helps provide workforce requirements (social demand perspective). It refers to the suitability of VET and the development of occupational systems, conceptualized in the concept of "megatrends" (e.g., Achtenhagen et al., 1995; Achtenhagen & Grubb, 2001; Baethge et al., 2003). Moreover, we can distinguish between rather quantitative and qualitative aspects: from a quantitative point of view, VET systems ought to supply occupational systems as best as possible (i.e., avoiding narrow professional qualifications or overqualifications in little demanded or seldom available domains). From a qualitative point of view, an adequate preparation for labor market requirements, which includes subject-related competences and generic skills, is the main focus. The scientific discussion labels this *specialization* versus *generalization*, which is also a focus in the context of lifelong learning and continuing education.

The third goal, *warranty of social participation and equal opportunities*, emphasizes the relationship between VET and social structures. This refers to the contribution of VET to minimize dependencies between social background and educational, life, and income opportunities, and to enhance social integration and participation of young people in processes of shaping the social and political community.

To measure and compare the performance of national VET systems regarding the three goals and be able to relate them to institutional structures and input criteria, there are at least three methodological problems: (1) How can vocational competences be measured and compared? (2) How can the relevant micro- and macrostructural conditions of VET systems in different countries be analyzed and compared? (3) With regard to the differences of job classification schemes in the participating countries, how can occupational fields and work activities be identified? The three aspects are discussed with regard to possible solutions in the subsequent paragraphs.

Following the proposal of the Organisation for Economic Co-operation and Development (OECD; 2003), we adopt three quality dimensions, *input*, *process*, and *outcome*, and add a fourth dimension, *system interdependencies*, which refers to the structure of different educational units – relating to aspects of transparency and compartmentalization. Starting from a schema such as Table 9.1, indicators for and international comparison of VET can be developed. These indicators include aspects relating to the quality of material, personal, and institutional inputs (Chapters 4 and 5), as well as material outcomes (Chapter 3). The cells in Table 9.1 contain references with regard to further operationalizations.

COMPETENCE AND MEASUREMENT TOOLS IN THE CONTEXT OF VET

Recent international comparative studies, initiated by the OECD (e.g., PISA), shifted the focus of competences to a policy context. The measurement of competences has become an instrument for benchmarking the performance

Table 9.1. Dimensions for identifying fields of indicators for an international comparison

Educational goals/individual user perspective	System dimensions			
	Input	Process	Outcome	System interdependencies
Self-regulation/ individual user perspective	1) Quality of educational offer, conditions, and determining factors of their development	2) Educational quality according to domain-specific, motivational, and participatory aspects (e.g., self-organization)	3) Competence development in different behavioral and reflective dimensions of self-regulation	4) Systematic development of competences; adjustment between subsystems
Human resources/ economic user perspective	5) Proportion of educational offers and qualitative/quantitative requirements of occupational systems	6) Quality of educational processes according to domain-specific and behavioral dimensions	7) Developable and innovative workforce, technical and behavioral skills needed in a modern economy	8) Adjustment between general, vocational, and further education according to qualitative qualification demands
Social participation equal opportunities/ social inclusion– exclusion	9) Open educational programs/target group–specific programs	10) Quality of educational processes according to aspects of social inclusion–exclusion	11) Educational careers and competence development independently from individual, social, and cultural background	12) Transparency between subsystems for every social group

of educational systems. The studies are based on the idea that institutional factors, such as student assessment, certificates, or duration of educational programs, are not sufficient criteria to compare the performance of different educational systems internationally. This is particularly important, given the heterogeneity of institutional structures in VET systems.

Competence measurement in the field of VET is more complex than in compulsory education. Whereas international large-scale assessments such as the Third International Mathematics and Science Study (TIMSS) and PISA are limited to assessing mathematics and science performance of fourth and eighth graders (TIMSS) or literacy, numeracy, science, and problem-solving performance of 15-year-olds (PISA), a PISA-VET has to take into account individuals' performances in the workplace and the labor market as well as practical aspects (motor skills, dexterity). Moreover, international student assessment programs such as TIMSS and PISA are based on well-grounded research traditions and internationally validated concepts, such as a world curriculum for mathematics. In comparison, a PISA-VET cannot draw on comparable concepts concerning the structure and development of vocational expertise in various occupational fields. The variety and heterogeneity of occupational specializations, even within a society, make it difficult to reach an international agreement concerning consistent competence standards. In addition, a variety of different competence dimensions has to be considered: vocational subject-specific competences (e.g., accounting), general subject-specific competences (e.g., literacy and numeracy), and generic competences (e.g., employability). In this regard, the objective of a feasibility study is to find possibilities without simply reducing the complexity of competence dimensions. This is of importance given that, in the context of lifelong learning, one of the interesting goals is to illuminate how the relation between general and subject-specific vocational competences changes during VET and, at a later point in time, in the labor market.

Winterton et al. (2005) presented a report with a proposal for the development of an ECVET as a basis for the development of an EQF. Using a detailed review of existing typologies in different countries, they developed a "prototype typology of knowledge, skills and competences" as common categories of all countries: *knowledge*, which is captured by cognitive competences; *skills*, which are captured by attitudes and behavior; and *behaviors and attitudes*, which are captured by social competence (interactions with others, behaviors, attitudes, motivation, metacognition). Their proposal is mainly based on managerial literature from the United States, the discussions on National Vocational Qualifications (NVQ) in the UK, and the concept of "Savoir – Savoir faire – Savoir être" from France.

Table 9.2. Structure of a European qualifications framework

Level	Cognitive competence (knowledge)	Functional competence (skills)	Social and metacompetence (behaviors and attitudes)
Level 8			
Level 7			
Level 6			
Level 5			
Level 4			
Level 3			
Level 2			
Level 1			
Level 1			

The core of the EQF is a set of common reference points within a two-dimensional matrix, which allows classification of entire training programs, as well as single modules. The vertical dimension consists of eight levels, which are described in terms of learning outcomes and expressed as competences in the horizontal dimension (Commission of the European Communities, 2005, Appendix 1).

Regarding the number of levels, an eight-level framework with general descriptors was proposed by the Qualifications and Curriculum Authority, London, which is broadly compatible with proposals by the International Standards Classification of Education (ISCED), the European Centre for the Development of Vocational Training (Cedefop), and the International Standard Classification of Occupations (ISCO). Winterton et al. (2005, p. 42) proposed a level structure of increasing complexity from level 1, covering learning normally acquired during compulsory education, to level 8, covering qualifications that recognize a leading expert in a highly specialized field with complex situations. The aim is to classify learning achievements in VET. (Table 9.2 illustrates the structure of the EQF.)

Regarding the concept of competence, Winterton et al. (2005) were facing the same problems we mentioned previously – there are multiple and varied definitions of competence in different countries, scientific disciplines, and practical domains. To use the concept of competence productively, it is necessary to use well-elaborated and theoretically well-founded concepts. Formal definitions at a very abstract level are another problem; they are often not linked to usable operationalizations.[2]

One of the central concerns with regard to an international comparison of the performance of VET is to determine suitable measurement tools. We analyzed different concepts of competence with regard to their suitability for an international comparison. The results are summarized in this chapter. The complexity of the concept of competence became apparent in our research of existing literature. In agreement with issues raised by the many authors, we come to the conclusion that there is currently neither a commonly accepted concept of competence nor an ideal framework for measurement. Referring to the term *competence* only, we detected multiple and varied synonyms in different countries, scientific disciplines, and various practical domains. For example, Oates (2004) emphasized that emerging layers of complexity in the understanding of the relation between the structures of the labor market and the content of education and training produced the following results: "an understanding of competence, and the way in which language functions to describe competence, has become increasingly difficult to obtain" (p. 56).

Often, terminological confusion arises, which is reflected in a multitude of different concepts and cultural traditions. Therefore, it is impossible to "identify a coherent theory or arrive at a definition capable of accommodating and reconciling all the different ways that the term is used" (Ellström, 1997, p. 276). In this regard, Norris (1991) pointed out: "as tacit understandings of the word [competence] have been overtaken by the need to define precisely and operationalise concepts, the practical has become shrouded in theoretical confusion and the apparently simple has become profoundly complicated" (pp. 331–332). With regard to NVQs in England, Oates (2004) recognized "one of the most significant problems in the analysis of competences for deriving outcome-based qualifications is a failure to recognize that *competence* does not exist in any simple way – it is inferred through observing how an individual performs on a number of occasions in a number of settings" (p. 60). From a Dutch perspective, Biemans et al. (2005) explained "an important reason for the popularity of the concept of competence is the expectation held by many stakeholders in the VET field that the gap between the labor market and education can (and will) be reduced through competence-based education" (p. 1). It can therefore be concluded that "the term *competence* has the function of an umbrella for divergent research strands in human capacity development and its assessment. The umbrellas themselves differ in extent and differentiation with some overlap" (Straka, 2003, p. 16). Against this background, an initial clarification of semantic differences in the usage of formally identical terms and concepts in national VET systems and the determination of a commonly acceptable working definition is essential within the context of an international comparison of VET.

In addition to the determination of a commonly accepted working definition of *competence*, the scope of application needs to be defined. Oates (2004) distinguished between "*generic* – relating to skill components that are not expressed in the form of activities specific to a particular setting"; "*occupational* – relating to descriptions at the level of an occupation"; "*task-specific but independent of specific jobs* – relating to description which give the detail of the task"; "*job-specific, enterprise-specific* – relating to descriptions of the way in which a task is undertaken in a specific work system"; and "*person-specific* – relating to the way the task/the job is undertaken by a specific individual within a specific work system" (p. 62).

With regard to the development of instruments for measuring competences, two methodological concepts can be distinguished according to the starting point for assessment: competences can be considered with regard to *individual internal conditions* as potential for application in different situations and *competent behavior in a specific situation*. Competence as a potential for behavior in different situations refers to internal conditions (e.g., knowledge, skills, motivation, values, metacognition) that are not visible to external observers, whereas competent behavior in a specific (occupational) situation is observable. Therefore, we can distinguish between two approaches for identifying and measuring occupational competences: the determination of *typical tasks/activities* in current occupational fields, and the determination of *internal conditions* characterizing expertise in a specific occupational field.

Both alternatives are discussed subsequently regarding their impact for an international comparison of VET and concerning their respective advantages and disadvantages.

Identification of Competences on the Basis of Activities

This approach is based on the idea that the presence of competence is indicated by an evaluation of performance, which requires "prototypical, typical and specific characterization of classes of performance demands, criteria and indicators of competences" (Weinert, 1999, p. 27). In the context of an international comparison of VET, internationally comparable occupational tasks for certain occupational fields would be required. One possibility might be a comparison of competence-based descriptions of intended learning outcomes of educational systems in different countries and a definition of core requirements for selected occupational fields. Nevertheless, there are problems involved (e.g., linguistic differences in formal descriptions and different conceptions of educational systems, such as dual vs. modularized systems).

Another approach, which is not primarily focused on didactical aspects of competence development, but rather on aggregated work activities, is based on an instrument, which was developed for a multidimensional occupational database in the United States (Jeanneret et al., 2002). The database was developed on the idea that work behavior is not necessarily linked to specific tasks and techniques and, therefore, can be aggregated at a higher level as generalized work activities (GWAs). In the context of higher education, Toolsema (2004) used GWAs and linked them to competences at a higher level of abstraction. He argued that competence should have a certain degree of breadth to account for flexibility in VET and, therefore, should be disconnected from the context: "competency is directly connected to behavior and not first to an intermediate layer of psychological constructs" (pp. 224–225). On the basis of a comparison of different studies, he derived six competence categories (social, participative, cognitive, physical/technical, learning, employability) and associated them with GWAs, based on the assumption that if a person performs a certain activity, he or she possesses the required competence. Activities are perceived as competence indicators at a higher level of abstraction, indicating the purpose of competences. With regard to an international comparison of VET, Toolsema's approach provides a solution for at least three problem areas: accounting for work behavior, examining differences and similarities in occupations, and defining the extent to which competences are generic. Moreover, he provides the underlying theoretical assumptions and the possibility to operationalize the relevant variables for empirical research.

Identification of Competences on the Basis of Internal Conditions

This approach requires conceptualizations comparable to international large-scale assessment (e.g., in compulsory education [PISA, TIMSS]), or in other words, internationally valid concepts (literacy, numeracy, science) of the structure and development of vocational expertise in various occupational fields. Existing national concepts need to be reviewed regarding their suitability for assessing vocational expertise. Examples for existing national concepts are the Standards for Technological Literacy developed by the International Technology Education Association, the Content Standards in Economic Education developed by the National Council on Economic Education, and the National Standards for Business Education developed by the National Business Education Association.

Considerations Regarding a Conceptualization of a Coherent Concept of Competence for an International Measurement and Comparison of VET

By distinguishing between invisible internal conditions of an individual and visible performance in a particular situation, a typology such as the one

	Competence Domains (different contextualized areas of performance)		
	Self-Competence		
	Cognitive Competence	**Functional Competence**	**Social Competence**
Individual Capacities (accessed and interpreted in different contexts)	(theoretical/analytical requirements) "applying concepts"	(technical/practical/ functional requirements) "using tools, equipments and technical resources"	(interpersonal requirements) "interacting with others"
Attitudes Values Perceptions	self-efficacy		
Incentives Motivation	effort and perservance/interest and motivation/ self-related cognition		
Metacognitive Strategies	learning strategies		
Declarative Knowledge Procedural Knowledge Strategic Knowledge	complex task for simultaneous measurement of cognitive and functional competence according to the occupational field complex task for measuring cognitive competence	complex task for measuring functional competence	questionnaire for mindful identity negotiation (consists of items for declarative, procedural and strategic knowledge in the domain for social competence)
	Competences of general education (corresponding to PISA)		

Figure 9.1. Different perspectives and dimensions of vocational competences.

depicted in Figure 9.1 can be generated to illustrate the different dimensions of vocational competence. Individual internal conditions are classified according to cognitive representations and dispositions: cognitive representations are differentiated according to *knowledge how*, as procedural knowledge, and *knowledge that*, as declarative knowledge (Anderson, 1993; Ryle, 2000). The development of strategic knowledge focuses on problem solving – using a rich and extensive declarative and procedural knowledge in order to make decisions – taking into account possible negative consequences and weighing intended main effects and unintended side effects (Achtenhagen, 2004). The impact of motivation and metacognition for the development of competences play a crucial role. For motivation, one needs a combination of items representing habitual and situational components. With regard to metacognition, concepts that are related to the contents of VET, rather than general approaches, need to be considered.

Figure 9.1 clearly illustrates that various kinds of cognitive interpretations are involved in interpersonal interactions, working with equipment and tools, and in analytic and problem-solving activities. Figure 9.1 also indicates that motivational and metacognitive structures are important factors in the development of occupational competences, according to a broad concept of VET (Chapter 2). The empty cells can be filled in at a later point in time to illustrate the kinds of capacities used for various types of competences in different occupational contexts. For example, competence in interactions (interpersonal or social competence) will require certain dispositions, as well as facility with specific procedures and metacognitive structures in the respective occupational field. For example, the type of social interactions of a nurse are very different from those of a salesperson. The learner would also need to understand the nature of interactions as a basis for choosing when and where to execute various procedures (Kanning, 2003).

Identification and Assessment of Competences

For the assessment of individual competences in general, "a model of how students represent knowledge and develop competence in the subject domain (cognition), tasks or situations that allow one to observe students' performance (observation), and an interpretation method for drawing inferences from the performance evidence thus obtained (interpretation)" is needed (Pellegrino et al., 2001, p. 2). An assessment of vocational competences on the basis of tests must include cognitive, functional, and social aspects of competence. Typical working situations and activities in the respective occupational fields need to be identified. On the basis of occupational situations, complex tasks have to be developed for the empty cells in the table. The tasks would allow the identification of existing knowledge and the ability to use it in different situations. At the same time, correlations between different aspects of competence could be assessed on the basis of motivation and metacognition. This also allows conclusions to be developed with regard to lifelong learning.

Relation Between Competences and Work/Labor Market Behavior

In PISA, the impact of self-competences on shaping one's life was implicitly presupposed within the measurement of reading, writing, and problem-solving competences. However, for competences acquired in VET, this assumption is not valid because labor markets and their contexts vary considerably with regard to occupational fields and economic conditions. Therefore, it is important to analyze whether the competences acquired in VET are necessary conditions for successfully performing working tasks in the labor market. In this regard, a PISA-VET could help illuminate interdependencies between the competences acquired in VET and the successful performance of individuals at work and in the labor market.

For measurement, a second outcome classification relating to individuals' experiences and behaviors at work and in the labor market needs to be ascertained with regard to the dimensions of success and failure. Work and labor market experiences cannot be related solely to individual competences, and aspects of economic and labor market organizational structures must also be taken into consideration. At the same time, they are related to individual competences and dispositions, shaping the daily interactions between individuals and their environments. The measurement of labor market outcomes should be based on indicators relating occupational mobility, unemployment, and position. In contrast, the measurement of working outcomes is more complex.

Typically, rather weak indicators, such as satisfaction with work or the fit between the competences acquired in VET and working tasks performed are applied. In this regard, GWAs provide an instrument for measuring subject-related competences (Jeanneret et al., 2002). The broad GWA categories could be operationalized with regard to different occupations as a basis for scaling them according to the level of complexity. This allows a more detailed measurement of work activities than measuring them on the basis of assessing the fit between the competences acquired in VET and the working tasks.

INSTITUTIONAL AND INDIVIDUAL CONDITIONS
FOR QUALITY IN VET

The measurement of competences in initial VET is important to assess the performance of skill formation in different countries. However, international educational research agrees on the relevance of institutional and individual factors for the development of individual competences. In this regard, differences in the students' competence profiles cannot be described solely with reference to individuals' learning preconditions and individuals' dispositions, the educational organization in its social, cultural, and economic context has to be taken into account (Baumert & Schümer, 2001).

Institutional and individual context factors (Figure 9.1) can help classify the competence levels of both students and occupational fields within a country. To analyze the differences in individuals' work behavior and their use of competences in work contexts, they need to be included into the research design of a PISA-VET, in addition to indicators of the labor market and its organization.

Based on these considerations, an adequate research design has to account for systematic identification and analysis of the differences in VET processes. In agreement with international education experts, we recommend a multilevel approach – an analysis of system, school, and instruction characteristics as well as their influences on the development and use of competences, taking into account interactions between individual and social factors. The framework is based on the theoretical model of the PISA survey (Scheerens, 1990; Table 1). The operationalization of influencing factors is based on the same model and is conceptualized according to input, process, and output variables at different levels of analysis (Baumert et al., 2001; Baethge et al., 2003; OECD, 2003). With regard to institutional conditions, we distinguish between systemic conditions, provided by the respective national educational system, and specific conditions of different educational institutions in the participating countries (Scheerens & Bosker, 1997).

A comparison of institutional and individual factors in comparative education statistics revealed that there is a set of indicators representing significant information about the quality in the organization of VET. Figure 9.2 and Table 9.3 illustrate the relevant context factors in a coherent framework, which at the same time reflect the objectives and the stages of activity and achievement (input, process, output), social contexts, and educational structures (context and input factors).

The need for overall information on *education and employment systems* is based on the assumption that a comparison of different initial VET programs in the context of a PISA-VET can only be explained against the background of the corresponding social, education policy-related, economic, and demographic conditions of the respective country. There are different economic, social, and political context factors impacting vocational education and training and the corresponding conditions for acting: At a macrolevel of the education and employment systems, we distinguish between systemic context factors (e.g., social, cultural, economic, and political conditions) and systemic institutional constitutions (coordinating and steering, standards and norms, and financing of VET systems). Institutional constitutions must provide the necessary conditions for steering and coordination as a basis for adjustments and arrangements of qualitative and quantitative educational offers with regard to the demand of individuals and enterprises (Lassnigg, 2000; Descy & Tessaring, 2002). Steering instruments consist, on the one hand, of

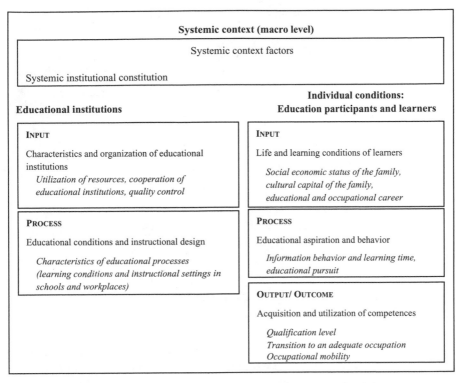

Figure 9.2. Context factors for quality in vocational education and training.

different forms for providing material resources to ensure and develop educational offers and, on the other hand, of standards and norms to condition the contents and methods of educational processes. For example, with regard to a systematic understanding of the complex and multifaceted array of VET contents, Lassnigg (2000) distinguished the following levels:

1. The way in which the various elements of qualification and contents of learning are conceptualized. The most important differentiation refers to traditional distinctions between school- and VET-related elements of qualifications (competences of general education vs. competences of vocational education). Moreover, the differentiation between general and vocational contents can be based on a decoupling model of general and vocational education or an integrated model (Lassnigg, 2000). A third differentiation refers to the relation of theoretical and practical subjects in VET. The outcomes of various weightings can be measured at an institutional level.

Table 9.3. Possibilities for operationalization and measurement of competences in VET

Internal conditions/individual abilities (person)	External performance/behavior/ action (situation)
Declarative knowledge	
Specific procedures	
General procedures	
Strategies and skills	
Values	
Attitudes	Performance
Motivation	Solving tasks in different situations
Self-efficacy	
Locus of control	
Self-control	
Anxiety	
Big Five*	
Not directly observable	Observable

* Measurement model comprising five personality dimensions: openness to experience, conscientiousness, extraversion, agreeableness, and neuroticism.

2. The structure of complex and comprehensive education and training pathways in terms of possible sequencing in flexible, modularized units.

3. The relationship between educational processes (curricula) and qualifications (certificates) and the corresponding standards, which can be aligned or separated from each other.

4. The link between vertical and horizontal educational tracks within educational systems, and their relationship to compulsory and higher education.

Particular emphasis is put on the standardization of instruction, which refers to differences in the qualification requirements of the teaching staff and continuing professional development. In this regard, it is assumed that teachers' initial and continuing professional development corresponds to their quality of instruction (OECD, 2003).

At the (meso- and micro-) level of *educational institutions*, indicators relating to the structural and organizational conditions of schools and firms play an important role. They more or less preform the learning and teaching processes (Kunter & Stanat, 2002). At the input level, this refers to the characteristics and organization of educational institutions and providers of educational services (utilization of resources, cooperation of educational service providers, quality control). At the process level, this refers to the instructional setting and the learning environment (learning conditions and instructional settings, such as self-directed learning or teamwork in schools and workplaces; learning climate).

At the level of *educational participants and learners*, one has to distinguish between individual life and learning conditions (input), attitudes and behaviors (process), and the quality of individual learning results (outcome). At the input level, we distinguish learners' life and learning conditions (socioeconomic status of the family, cultural capital of the family, educational and occupational career); at the process level, we differentiate aspects of educational aspiration and behavior (information behavior and learning time, educational aspiration); and at the output/outcome level, we refer to aspects of the acquisition and utilization of competences (qualification level, transition to an adequate job, occupational mobility).

Problems of Sampling: Vertical and Horizontal Comparability of VET

Compared to school-based comparative studies (e.g., PISA, TIMMS), a comparison of VET is different regarding institutional and content-related aspects. Despite the differences in microstructural aspects of learning, compulsory education can refer to a common curriculum of basic competences, such as literacy, numeracy, science, and comparable age groups in the classroom. In contrast, VET varies to a large extent in content, given the large diversity of occupational fields and the institutional heterogeneity within and between societies. Therefore, an international comparison of VET entails the measurement of cognitive, as well as functional, aspects of competence. The complexity of a large-scale assessment can be characterized as a twofold problem of comparison:

1. *Vertical* comparability refers to the educational level and can be determined by institution (e.g., tertiary level [academic track], secondary level) or by duration (number of years) and/or age.
2. *Horizontal* comparability refers to differences in curricula and occupational fields and to the problem of defining comparable vocational tracks.

For the purpose of linking the results of an individual competence assessment to the micro- and macrostructural context factors, both aspects of comparability are essential and have to be taken into account. From a methodological point of view, a comparison of national samples at the same educational level, incorporating the same competence requirements, involves a number of problems. Vertical comparability is problematic because it refers to national traditional backgrounds of educational systems. Horizontal comparability, in contrast, refers to national, specific, occupational profiles and the corresponding curricula within the existing structures of labor organization (Heikkinen, 2001).

Vertical Comparability

From an international point of view, the identification of comparable VET programs is based on very few and little updated data, mainly provided by the following institutions: OECD, Unesco or Eurostat/Cedefop. The most beneficial sources for identifying quantitatively relevant programs of initial VET were published by Eurostat and Cedefop – a handbook of different educational programs in different European countries – based on data from 1995 to 1996 and updated in 2000. It consists of abstracts containing information about different educational programs, the type of program (vocational preparation, general education, VET), ISCED level, and typical entrance age. Moreover, information regarding the type of labor market qualification (generic, subject specific) and the number of participants is provided. Unfortunately, the same information is not available for every country, and data on the number of beginner participants entering educational programs are entirely missing.

Based on data analysis and discussions with international experts, we come to the conclusion that ISCED is not a very suitable classification for identifying initial VET programs addressed to a medium level of proficiency because it relates to levels of general education, rather than VET. According to ISCED, the corresponding educational programs in different countries are located at levels 3 and 4 (with exceptions found on level 5). Provided that ISCED level 3 represents the lower limit for VET programs in the sample, certain vocational preparation and short-term programs[3] would be located below these categories.

Horizontal Comparability

The problem of horizontal comparability refers to identifying comparable occupational field and educational tracks in different countries. An initial identification could be based on the following broad occupational fields:

- Industrial/technical occupations in industry and trade
- Commercial and commercial/administrative occupations in commerce and other services

• Health care occupations in the field of personal services, and information and communication technology in the field of information/technical
services

However, there are still problems remaining. First, there is neither an
internationally consistent competence-based concept of the structure and
classification of initial VET programs/occupational fields nor a report to rely
on (Lisbon-to-Copenhagen-to-Maastrich Consortium Partners, 2004). This
does not imply that classification systems are completely missing, but what is
needed are basic data in a usable format. At an international level alongside
ISCO 88 (for occupational fields), an occupational classification of discrete
fields of training has been developed on behalf of Cedefop (Andersson &
Olsson, 1999). However, neither classification has been accepted as part of
the ongoing reporting at the European level.

With regard to the previously mentioned problems of international sampling, we can conclude that they are resolvable, however, not within a single
homogenous sample and not without tradeoffs in weighing comparison criteria. National differences of institutional interrelations between education
and employment systems, on the one hand, and the impact of nonstandardized vocational biographies, on the other hand, requires considering the
following aspects.

Incorporating nonstandardized vocational biographies is only feasible on
the basis of retrospective measurement of educational experiences within
a cross-sectional study. The sample should be based on employed population with criteria, including age and occupational tasks according to level
and breadth to reconstruct vocational biographies. Representativeness in this
approach is limited due to institutional aspects of education; for example, the
"fuzziness" of retrospective measurements of level and content of different
VET programs.

Provided that VET programs, levels, and institutions highly correlate with
occupational fields and levels (e.g., in Germany based on the *Berufsprinzip*),
and at the same time, cover most occupational tasks at a medium level,
vertical (based on occupational tasks) or horizontal (based on VET programs)
sampling does not seem to make a big difference to the outcome. However,
even in Germany, this correlation does not apply in every occupational field,
and in Anglo-Saxon countries, there are few segments of this type. With
regard to a panel study starting from educational institutions, a sampling
based on the structure of occupational tasks is recommended. Nevertheless,
for pragmatic reasons, a sample based on the structure of VET programs has
to be taken into consideration. The differences between the two options are

Table 9.4. Selected occupational tasks, ISCO codes, and employment rates in different occupational fields at the age of 15–25 years

Segment	Occupational field	ISCO code of specific occupational tasks	Employment rate in different occupational fields (15–25 Years) (in %)
Industrial/technical occupations (industry and trade)	Metal and electrical work	72	15.0
Commercial/ administrative occupations	Commercial and office work	522, 523, 3416, 3419, 411, 343	9.7 11.9
Social, education, and health care occupations	Nursing	322, 323	8.8
Information technology occupations	Skilled data processing workers	312	1.0

due to the remaining efforts in preparing the sampling and evaluating the weight of each sample in different segments. Both options are connected to the construction of vocational subsamples.

First Option: Broad Sample Based on Occupational Tasks

This method is based on occupational tasks to be performed at a particular age (e.g., 24 years). The sample is defined on the basis of the "European Labour Force Survey." The ISCO 88 classification provides a basis for approaching a comparable sample in the most important occupational fields (industrial and technical; commercial and administrative; social, education, and health care; information and technology). ISCO 88 has been implemented within the "European Labour Force Survey" and indicates not only the level, but also the contents of occupational tasks. In this way, aggregates of homogeneous occupational contents and levels, which are representative (at least in Germany) of a considerable number of individuals in the same age, could be identified. (Table 9.4): with the exception of skilled data processing workers (constituting a proportion of 1% of information technology occupations), the sample represents the most important occupational field of employees, comprising 47% of young adults in this age. The information value of ISCO data can be considered a solid basis for the level and content of occupational tasks, even though occupational fields are not always explicitly distinguishable. Thus, an adjustment procedure for the purpose of a representative identification of bundles of tasks must be conducted.

The adjustment procedure is based on an analysis of work requirements according to the main functions – production, distribution, and personal services – and focus of contents. The job profiles could be used as a basis in an iterative procedure for sampling in which they provide reference points for identifying national tasks corresponding to the respective profiles. This allows adequate classification of the tasks that are related to adjoined levels or different bundles of tasks according to ISCO 88. Problems of classification help identify clearly distinguishable occupational profiles at an international level as a basis for developing measurement tools.

The bundles of tasks could be combined with national data on educational background variables derived from national labor force surveys, to identify the (quantitatively) most relevant VET programs and levels in the corresponding occupational field. The identified VET programs are the foundation for institution-based sampling. However, this method is particularly problematic with regard to Anglo-Saxon countries because broad sampling includes a variety of institutional arrangements that must be accounted for. A stratified sample would have to account for different institutions and regional differences, as well as for the identification of homogeneous age groups.

Second Option: Narrow Sample Based on Widespread and Well-Defined VET Programs

This method is based on VET programs with comparable curriculum contents, preparing young people between 16 and 20 years of age to enter the labor market. This method consists of two steps: (1) the development of two schemata – one consisting of a preselection of designated VET programs (Table 9.4) and another based on Eurostat/Cedefop data, supplemented by information on relevant VET programs[4] from non-European countries; and (2) based on this extract, a proposal for sampling, incorporating the main occupational fields while also providing a basis for comparing level and age, should be developed (Table 9.5).

The field of trade is represented by the European occupational profile of Car Mechatronics, of which a similarly structured profile can be found in the United States and Australia. The field of industrial metal occupations is represented by electricians and mechanics (industry), although the latter may be replaced by tool makers at some point. Contrary to Germany, vocational

Table 9.5. VET program, corresponding ISCED levels, and age range at entrance

Occupational field	VET program	ISCED levels (Internationally)	Age range at entrance
Metal and electrical occupations	Car Mechatronic	3	16–20
	Mechanic (industry)	3	16–20
	Electrician (industry)	3	16–20
Commercial/ administrative occupations	Banker	3–5	17–20
Health care occupations	Nurse	4–5	18–20
Information and communication technology occupations	Skilled computer scientist	3–5	17–20

qualifications of bankers, skilled computer scientists, and nurses are formally located at a higher proficiency level in most other countries. However, with regard to the contents of curricula, they appear comparable.

The sampling option outlined does not provide a solution for every problem. However, aspects with regard to comparing levels (e.g., nursing) could be solved relatively easily on the basis of discussions with international experts and statistic centers.

Despite the remaining uncertainties regarding an appropriate age range for entering a VET program, there are possibilities for identifying an age homogeneous overall sample. The relevant age would be 18 to 19 years – a measuring point at the beginning of VET in this age cohort (e.g., 18-year-old beginners). Due to the specific starting points of each method (broad occupational tasks vs. single VET program curricula for comparatively adjusted employment), the probability of identifying additional relevant VET programs, covering the same occupational tasks, is relatively low. Therefore, the selection method of the second option needs to be checked on the basis of a task analysis of educational backgrounds.

OUTLOOK: HOW TO MEASURE PERFORMANCE
OF SKILL FORMATION WITHIN VET-PISA

This chapter explores and highlights the problems, possibilities, and corresponding work steps toward a realization of an international comparison of VET.

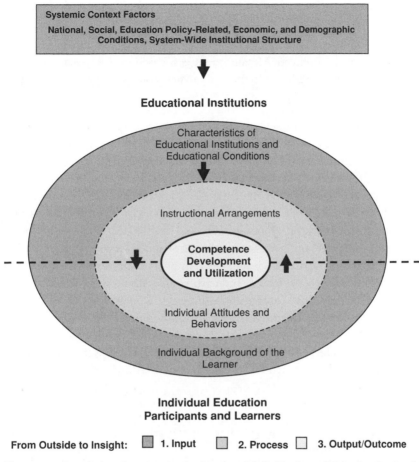

Figure 9.3. Correlations between institutional and individual conditions for the development and utilization of competences.

Taking into consideration the goal of comparing competences and their development in VET in different countries and at the same time measuring the effects (outcomes) of these competences after entering the labor market, a longitudinal design with three panel waves is recommended:

- The first wave should take place shortly after entering a VET program to measure the initial competence level of students.
- The second wave should take place shortly before completing a VET program and after approximately 2.5 years (provided the study is of a 3-year duration) to measure competence development during VET.

- The third wave should take place 3 years after completing a VET program and after the transition into the labor market to evaluate whether the individual is working in a job, enrolled in a program of continuing education, or unemployed. Measurement is focused on the sustainability of competences, in addition to their expansion and usability in the domains of work and everyday life.

Measurement of competences will refer to generic, cross-occupational, and subject-related vocational dimensions (Figure 9.1), taking into consideration institutional and individual contexts of learning (Figure 9.3). Intending to involve the entire variance of vocational competences requirements, institutional and biographical arrangements, and so on into the research design would not be realistic because the entire variety of occupational fields cannot be incorporated. From a pragmatic and methodological research point of view, a stratified sample is therefore recommended. A sample construction is needed that comprises a relevant (e.g., important employability segments and institutional arrangements) and comparable extract (e.g., "middle" level of competences, similar content-related focus of knowledge and skills, same age) of initial vocational education consisting of young people between compulsory education and work. Measurement will have to be conducted in quantitatively relevant occupational fields in order to assess the major tracks of competence development.

Notes

1. Contrary to the measurement of competences in general education, which is based on large-scale assessments initiated by the OECD, there is no comparable international study to measure the performance of VET systems. Therefore, this chapter focuses on a draft report for a feasibility study on the quality of VET, which was developed in cooperation with a team of international experts on behalf of the federal government of Germany.
2. The EQF consists of eight levels for classifying vocational competences individuals develop throughout their lives. To classify the levels of qualification and compare them internationally, a comparative assessment consisting of three competency clusters (Chapter 3) is needed in every country.
3. Germany: basic vocational education (Berufsgrundbildungsjahr, einjährige Berufsfachschule); Denmark: basic vocational education; Switzerland: "Anlehre"; Hungary: secondary VET schools; United States: vocational high schools; UK: NVQ level 1 or 2.
4. Program refers to separable institutional fields of VET determined by their affiliation with a particular subsystem of VET (e.g., dual system), characteristics of possible qualifications, and curricula.

References

Achtenhagen, F. (2004). Curriculum development as modelling of complex reality. In N. M. Seel & S. Dijkstra (Eds.), *Curriculum, Plans, and Processes in Instructional Design* (pp. 193–210). Mahwah, NJ: Erlbaum.

Achtenhagen, F., & Grubb, W. N. (2001). Vocational and occupational education: Pedagogical complexity, institutional diversity. In V. Richardson (Ed.), *Handbook of Research on Teaching* (4th ed., pp. 604–639). Washington, DC: American Educational Research Association.

Achtenhagen, F., in cooperation with J. W. Nijhof & D. Raffe. (1995). *Feasibility Study: Research Scope for Vocational Education in the Framework of COST Social Sciences.* European Commission, Directorate-General Science, Research and Development, COST Technical Committee Social Sciences, Vol. 3. Brussels: ECSC-EC-EAEC.

Anderson, J. R. (1993). Problem solving and learning. *American Psychologist*, 48, 35–44.

Andersson, R., & Olsson, A.-K. (1999). *Fields of Education and Training.* Brussels: Eurostat. Appendix A3: Commission of the European Communities, pp. 18–20.

Baethge, M., Buss, K. P., & Lanfer, C. (2003). *Konzeptionelle Grundlagen für einen Nationalen Bildungsbericht – Berufliche Bildung und Weiterbildung/Lebenslanges Lernen.* Bonn, Germany: Bundesministerium für Bildung und Forschung.

Baumert, J., Klieme, E., Neubrand, M., Prenzel, M., Schiefele, U., Schneider, W. Stanat, P., Tillmann, K.-J. & Weiß, M. (2001). *PISA 2000: Basiskompetenzen von Schülerinnen und Schülern im internationalen Vergleich.* Opladen, Germany: Leske & Budrich.

Baumert, J., & Schümer, G. (2001). Familiäre Lebensverhältnisse, Bildungsbeteiligung und Kompetenzwettbewerb im internationalen Vergleich. In J. Baumert, C. Artelt, E. Klieme, M. Neubrand, M. Prenzel, U. Schiefele, W. Schneider; K.J. Tillmann & M. Weiß (Eds.), *PISA 2000: Die Länder der Bundesrepublik Deutschland im Vergleich* (pp. 159–202). Opladen, Germany: Leske & Budrich.

Biemans, H., Nieuwenhuis, L., Poell, R., Mulder, R., & Wesselink, R. (2005, April). Competence-based VET in the Netherlands: Background and pitfalls. bw@ (online journal), (7), 1–14. Available at: www.bwpat.de/7eu/biemans_eqf_en.pdf.

Commission of the European Communities. (2005). *Commission Staff Working Document: Towards a European Qualifications Framework for Lifelong Learning.* Available at: http://europa.eu.int/comm/education/policies/2010/doc/consultation_eqf_en.pdf.

Descy, P., & Tessaring, M. (2002). *Kompetenz für die Zukunft – Ausbildung und Lernen in Europa: Zweiter Bericht zur Berufsbildungsforschung in Europa: Synthesebericht.* Reihe Cedefop reference series. Bd. 5 Luxemburg: Amt für Veröffentlichungen der Europäischen Union.

Ellström, P.-E. (1997). The many meanings of occupational competence and qualification. In W. J. Nijhof & J. N. Streumer (Eds.), *Key Qualifications in Work and Education* (pp. 39–50). Dordrecht, The Netherlands: Kluwer.

European Commission. (2005). *Auf dem Weg zu einem Europäischen Qualifikationsrahmen für Lebenslanges Lernen.* Brussels: Kommission der Europäischen Gemeinschaften.

Heikkinen, A. (2001). Ist eine stärkere Berücksichtigung der historischen und kulturellen Dimension in der Vergleichenden Berufsbildungsforschung erforderlich? In Cedefop/DIPF (Eds.), *Vergleichende Berufsbildungsforschung in Europa. Ansätze, Politikbezüge und Innovationstransfer* (pp. 118–134). Thessaloniki: CEDEFOP/DIPF.

Jeanneret, P. R., Borman, W. C., Kubisiak, U. C., & Hanson, M. A. (2002). Generalized work activities. In N. G. Peterson, M. D. Mumford, W. C. Borman, P. R. Jeanneret, & E. A. Fleishman (Eds.), *An Occupational Information System for the 21st Century: The Development of O* NET* (pp. 105–125). Washington, DC: American Psychological Association.

Kanning, U. P. (2003). *Diagnostik sozialer Kompetenzen.* Göttingen, Germany: Hogrefe.

Kunter, M., & Stanat, P. (2002). *PISA 2000 – Dokumentation der Erhebungsinstrumente.* Berlin: Max-Planck-Institut für Bildungsforschung. Available at: www.kmk.org/ schul/pisa/Datensaetze/Gesamt-Druckversion.pdf.

Lassnigg, L. (2000). *Steuerung, Vernetzung und Professionalisierung in der Berufsausbildung.* Wien, Germany: Institut für Höhere Studien. Available at: www.lebenslangeslernen.at/downloads/IHS_SteuerungBerufsausbildung_1100.pdf.

Lisbon-to-Copenhagen-to-Maastrich Consortium Partners. (2004). *Achieving the Lisbon Goal: The Contribution of VET – Final Report to the European Commission.* Available at: http://europa.eu.int/comm/ education/policies/2010/studies/maastricht_en. pdf.

Norris, N. (1991). The trouble with competence. *Cambridge Journal of Education,* 21, 1–11.

Oates, T. (2004). The role of outcome-based national qualifications in the development of an effective vocational education and training system: The case of England and Wales. *Policy Futures in Education,* 2, 56–58.

Organisation for Economic Co-operation and Development (OECD). (2003). *Education at a Glance.* Paris: Author.

Pellegrino, J. W., Chudowsky, N., & Glaser, R. (2001). *Knowing What Students Know: The Science and Design of Educational Assessment.* Washington, DC: National Academy Press.

Ryle, G. (2000). *The Concept of Mind.* London: Penguin Books.

Scheerens, J. (1990). School effectiveness research and the development of process indicators of school functioning. *School Effectiveness and School Improvement,* 1, 61–80.

Scheerens, J., & Bosker, R. J. (1997). *The Foundations of Educational Effectiveness.* Oxford, UK: Pergamon Press.

Straka, G. A. (2003). *Zertifizierung non-formell und informell erworbener beruflicher Kompetenzen.* Münster, Germany: Waxmann.

Toolsema, B. (2004). *Werken met competenties: Naar een instrument voor de identificatie van competenties.* Enschede, The Netherlands: Universiteit Twente.

Weinert, F. E. (1999). *Concepts of Competence.* München, Germany: Max Plank Institut. Available at: www.statsitik.admin.ch/stat_ch/ber15/deseco/weinert_report.pdf.

Winterton, J., Delamare-Le Deist, F., & Stringfellow, E. (2005). *Typology of Knowledge, Skills and Competences: Clarification of the Concept Prototype.* Thessaloniki, Greece: Cedefop.

Index